CHINESE MEXICANS

CHInese mexicans

Transpacific Migration

and the

Search for a Homeland,

1910–1960

Julia María Schiavone Camacho

Published in Association with

The William P. Clements Center for Southwest Studies,

Southern Methodist University,

by The University of North Carolina Press, Chapel Hill

The paper in this book meets the guidelines for permanence and
durability of the Committee on Production Guidelines for Book Longevity of
the Council on Library Resources. The University of North Carolina Press
has been a member of the Green Press Initiative since 2003.

Library of Congress Cataloging-in-Publication Data
Schiavone Camacho, Julia María, 1974–
Chinese Mexicans : transpacific migration and the search for a homeland, 1910–1960 /
Julia María Schiavone Camacho.
p. cm.
Includes bibliographical references and index.
ISBN 978-0-8078-3540-1 (cloth : alk. paper)
1. Chinese—Mexico—History—20th century. 2. Chinese—Cultural assimilation—
Mexico—History—20th century. 3. Race discrimination—Mexico—History—20th century.
4. Mexico—Emigration and immigration—History—20th century. 5. Mexico—
Emigration and immigration—Government policy. 6. Mexico—Race
relations—History—20th century. I. Title.
F1392.C45S44 2012
304.8089′51072—dc23
2011045261

A portion of this book appeared, in somewhat different form, as
"Crossing Boundaries, Claiming a Homeland: The Mexican Chinese
Transpacific Journey to Becoming Mexican, 1930s–1960s."
Pacific Historical Review 78 (2009): 545–77. Used by permission.

16 15 14 13 12   5 4 3 2 1

Para los expulsados y sus descendientes

For the expelled and their descendants

Contents

Illustrations, Maps, and Tables

Note on Names and Terms

I use "Chinese Mexican" throughout the book to denote new cultural formations and to emphasize the Mexicanness of the expelled, who "became Mexican" in China. Retaining the original spellings from Spanish-language sources, I use the names Chinese men adopted in Mexico to integrate into local society; when available, I also give their Chinese names as they appeared in the sources. As a result of the legacy of Spanish colonialism, Mexican women have historically kept their paternal surnames and added their husbands' paternal surnames to the end of their names; at times, the patriarchal "de" (of or belonging to), signaling the tradition of coverture, is used between the two surnames. Children's surnames are commonly given in reverse order to privilege that of the father. For example, the wife of Chinese migrant to Mexico Felipe Chan is known as Rosa Murillo de Chan, and their eldest child's name is Ramón Felipe Chan Murillo. Upon widowhood, some women have traditionally added "viuda de" (widow of) to their names to indicate their new status.

When discussing the crisis of "Chinese refugees from Mexico" in the United States, I refer to the U.S. Immigration and Naturalization Service (INS). The Bureau of Immigration and the Bureau of Naturalization fused in 1932 and became the INS. The agency was under the Department of Labor during the 1930s.

I use the common pinyin transliterations of proper Chinese names in the book; pinyin is the romanization system adopted by the People's Republic of China. There are, however, a few instances in which I have kept nonstandard usages as they appeared in Spanish-language archival material. I use "Chee Kung Tong," for example, and indicate the standard "Zhi Gong Tang" spelling in parentheses. I have used the original spelling, along with the standard, to acknowledge the importance of that organization to Chinese migrants in Mexico, who were mainly from southern provinces. In other instances, I use the names for villages in China given by Mexican women in their letters to consuls when the exact origins of these places were difficult to locate. Conversely, I have used the standard, updated spellings for places such as "Chungsan" (Zhongshan), "Kongmoon" (Jiangmen), and "Nanking" (Nanjing). In the past, "Canton" referred both to the city known today as Guangzhou and to the southern province of Guangdong. While I have used the standard spellings of these places, I have kept the commonly used adjective "Cantonese."

Acknowledgments

Many people in the United States, Mexico, Macau, and Hong Kong have helped make this project possible. I am especially indebted to the Chinese Mexicans who kindly shared their stories with me: Gabriela Strand Bruce, Alfonso Wong Campoy, María de Los Angeles Leyva Cervón, Sergio Chin-Ley, Ignacio Fonseca Chon, Antonia Wong Enríquez de López, María del Carmen Irma Wong Campoy Maher Conceição, Bertha Lourdes Amador Gil, Marta Elia Lau de Salazar, Guillermo Chan López, Fernando Ma, José de Jesús Tapia Martens, Elena Morris, Paul Tsang, Luisa María Valdez, Luis Chan Valenzuela, and Cristóbal Chua Wong.

In Sonora, where I began the research, archivists, historians, chroniclers, professors, and students provided invaluable assistance. I thank in particular Carlos Lucero Aja, David Allen, Rafael Martínez Álvarez, Gastón Cano Avila, Alicia Barrios, Ignacio Almada Bay, Juan Ramírez Cisneros, Pamela del Carmen Corella Romero, Jesús Verdugo Escoboza, Juan Manuel Romero Gil, Servando Ortoll, Cynthia Radding, Raquel Padilla Ramos, Manuel Hernández Salomón, and Leo Sandoval. Clara Guadalupe Peña Becerra, Julieta Gastelum, Julieta López Griego, Eva Nohemí Orozco García, Victor Manuel Osuna, Marcela Preciado, María del Carmen Tonella, and Ana Luz Ramírez Zavala provided crucial companionship and laughter during my research trips. Special thanks go to my uncle Jorge Sosa Salazar and family friend Delfino "Pino" Robles for helping me find Alfonso Wong Campoy.

In Macau and Hong Kong, I owe a profound debt of gratitude to Victor Aguilar, José Angel Castellanos, Coralia Castro, Belisa Hurtado Cheng, César Guillén-Nuñez, Vincent W. K. Ho, Adriana Ing, Lau Mian, Marta Lei, Ricardo Sánchez Leong, Victor Mejía, Isabel Maria da Costa Morais, Karen Ivone Abud Rivera, Lancelot M. Rodrigues, Catalina Carmen Sánchez, Tereza Sena, Sara Fereira da Silva, Beatriz Mariño Tancock, Luz Lucrecia Chang Un, Cristal Vásquez, Elena Chang de Wu, Xi Yan, and Peter Thomas Zabielskis. I extend special thanks to the Asociación de Mujeres de Habla

Hispana de Hong Kong, and Ngai Mei Cheong, Chan Prado Ka Wai, and Zhang Xin at the Macao Association for the Promotion of Exchange between Asia-Pacific and Latin America (MAPEAL). I am highly grateful to the Macao Foundation for a research grant that allowed me to conduct further research in the former colony.

I express my deepest thanks to the following people, who read and offered comments on drafts of the manuscript: Meredith Abarca, Jason Oliver Chang, John R. Chávez, Stephanie Cole, Grace Peña Delgado, Crista J. DeLuzio, George T. Díaz, Daniel Herman, Evelyn Hu-DeHart, Benjamin H. Johnson, Erika Lee, Yolanda Chávez Leyva, Cheryl E. Martin, Alexis McCrossen, Sandra McGee Deutsch, Jacqueline M. Moore, María Cristina Morales, Mae M. Ngai, Gina Nuñez, Emma Pérez, Lok Siu, Sherry Smith, Joshua M. Price, and K. Scott Wong. The generous support of the William P. Clements Center for Southwest Studies at Southern Methodist University helped bring the work to fruition; the provocative manuscript workshop led by the center was invaluable. I am indebted to Andrea Boardman and Ruth Ann Elmore for their tireless support and advocacy both during the year I had the fellowship and ever since. The Gaius Charles Bolin Dissertation Fellowship at Williams College, the Immigration and Ethnic History Society's George E. Pozzetta Award, and a Mexico-North Research Network Transnationalism Fellowship as well as a University Research Institute Grant, a Francis Harper Research Award, a Krutelik Graduate Scholarship, and the Graduate Excellence Award from the University of Texas at El Paso helped me complete the original research.

Editors Carl Abbott, David A. Johnson, and Susan Wladaver-Morgan as well as anonymous readers at the *Pacific Historical Review* provided invaluable feedback that continued to help me enormously as I worked on the book. The journal's Louis Knott Koontz Memorial Award allowed me to further the research in Macau.

I also thank many friends, colleagues, and former professors: Constance An, Kif Augustine-Adams, Bert Barickman, Michelle Berry, May-lei Blackwell, Stephania Boswell, Scarlet Bowen, Laura Briggs, Maritza Broce, Erika Castaño, Verónica Castillo-Muñoz, Guadalupe Castillo, Ondine Chavoya, Kenton Clymer, Dong Jingsheng, Nicole Etcheson, Maureen Fitzgerald, Josie Gin Morgan, Fredy González, Gayatri Gopinath, Kiana M. Green, Judith Halberstam, Miranda Joseph, Keng We Koh, Regina G. Kunzel, Julian Lim, George C. S. Lin, Monica Lizaóla, Kathleen López, Leisa D. Meyer, Isabelle Lausent-Herrera, Alfonso Morales, José Muñoz, Lydia Otero, Clark Aidan Pomerleau, Isabela Seong-Leong Quintana, Raúl A. Ramos, Chandan Reddy, Gerardo Rénique, Robert Chao Romero, Raquel Rubio-Goldsmith, Jessica Santascoy, Nayan Shah, Laura Shelton, Chris Sopithakul, Rachel Soto, Sandra K. Soto, Paul Spickard, Raquel Torres, Armando Vargas, Deborah R. Vargas, Diane Wai, and Marsha Weisiger.

I learned a lot from people at the Escuela Popular Norteña in Valdez, New Mexico. Mildred Beltré, Geoff Bryce, Aurelia Flores, Sarah Hoagland, Cricket Keating, Laura DuMond Kerr, María Lugones, Rafael Mutis, and Joshua M. Price taught me to appreciate resistance to oppression in its interlocked forms. Since then Joshua M. Price has been a sweet friend and a staunch advocate.

I have benefited tremendously from discussions about writing and research with my colleagues and friends in the history department at the University of Texas at El Paso. I thank Chuck Ambler, Adam Arenson, Michelle Armstrong-Partida, Sam Brunk, Brad Cartright, Ernesto Chávez, Maceo C. Dailey, Paul Edison, Keith Erekson, Joshua Fan, David Hackett, Carl Jackson, Yasuhide Kawashima, Charles Martin, Manuel Ramírez, Jeffrey P. Shepherd, Michael M. Topp, and Ron Weber. I have learned a tremendous amount from doctoral, master's, and undergraduate students at UTEP over the years when I was a student and since I joined the faculty. I thank in particular Dennis J. Aguirre, Nancy Aguirre, Susannah E. Aquilina, Michael K. Bess, Cristóbal Borges, Joanna Camacho-Escobar, Hector Carbajal, Selfa A. Chew, Scott Comar, Jill Constantin, Pat Cross, Michael de la Garza, Winifred Dowling, Sandra Enríquez, José Sebastian Estrada, Anna Fahy, Ann Gabbert, Eva Nohemí Orozco García, Nancy González, Richard Gutiérrez, Cullen Haskins, Marjorie Ingle, Miguel Juarez, Gary Kieffner, Ceci Gándara Ley-Alarcón, Karim Ley-Alarcón, Antonio Reyes López, Denise Loya, Jeff Lucas, Aaron Margolis, Alejandro Rodríguez Mayoral, Violeta Mena, Monét Muñoz, Lina M. Murillo, Nancy Nemeth-Jesurún, John Paul Nuño, Stephanie Parham, Nicol Partida, Gloria Paxson, Adrian Pérez, Alex Prado, Michael Reese, Cynthia Rentería, Laura Rodríguez, Melanie Rodríguez, David D. Romo, Fernanda Ruiz, Jaime R. Ruiz, Heather Sinclair, James Starling, Christopher Tarango, and Mario Villa. For the past decade, Will Guzmán has been a great friend and confidante; I am lucky to know him. I owe special thanks to Alma Ileana Acosta-Valles, Gaby Araiza, Iliana Rosales, and especially Edith Yañez for all of the work they have done and their support over the years.

Cheryl E. Martin was an amazing adviser who asked me provocative questions about my work at exactly the right times. With ease and grace, she helped me make the transition from student to colleague. Our many discussions since have helped me tremendously with the book. I treasure my many conversations with Sandra McGee Deutsch about research, writing, and teaching. Her thoughtfulness and attention have guided me through the process of completing the book. I have deeply appreciated Emma Pérez's unyielding support and encouragement over the past decade. Her strength inspires me. For nearly two decades, Yolanda Chávez Leyva has been a solid friend and a stalwart scholar-activist from whom I have learned a great deal. I am amazed by her dedication to the community and constant struggle to build connections between intellectual pursuits and community activism. Her unrelenting friendship sustains me; her fervor never ceases to amaze me and give me hope for the future.

I have learned and benefited from my colleagues and friends beyond the history department: Carlos M. Chang Albitres, Anne Allis, Gloria Ambler, Shelley Armitage, Cynthia Bejarano, Dennis Bixler-Marquez, Howard Campbell, Yvonne Carranza, Chyi Shinping, Irasema Coronado, Howard Daudistel, Matt Desing, Bill Durrer, Aileen El-Kadi, Ruben Espinoza, John Fahey, Sandra Garabano, Fernando García Núñez, Josiah Heyman, Laura Hollingsed, Maryse Jayasuriya, Cindy Juarez, Lin Yu-Cheng, Antonio López, Yvonne López, Lowry Martin, Lucía Martínez, Oscar J. Martínez, Kristine Navarro, Kirsten Nigro, Jonathan F. Nogueira, Pedro Pérez del Solar, Richard Pineda, Brenda Risch, Claudia Rivers, Marion Rohrleitner, Juan A. Sandoval, Tom Schmid, Arvind Singhal, Stacey Sowards, Kathy Staudt, Tom Stover, Socorro Tabuenca, Gita Upreti, Alfredo Urzúa, Abbie Weiser, Brian Yothers, and Zhou Liye. I also thank Ken Hammond and Elvira Hammond at the Confucius Institute at New Mexico State University for their tremendous generosity. The friendship of Virginia Navarro, Fred Perea, Elia Pérez, Angel Pineda, Pam Stover, Albert Wong, and Yang Jing has brought me great happiness. I have felt accompanied by them, and for this I extend my heartfelt thanks.

At the University of North Carolina Press, Chuck Grench believed in the project from the beginning. I deeply appreciate his vast insight, support, and guidance throughout the process. I also thank Dino Battista, Paul R. Betz, Kim Bryant, Sara Jo Cohen, Sydney Dupre, Susan R. Garrett, Beth Lassiter, Rachel Berry Surles, and the other staff whose work and expertise have made the book possible. I thank as well Ellen D. Goldlust-Gingrich for aiding me in polishing the final version of the manuscript. As external readers, Madeline Y. Hsu and Elliott Young helped sharpen my thinking and pushed me in ways I found deeply stimulating and productive. I am profoundly indebted to them for sharing their remarkable insight. I am deeply grateful to Monica Perales for her advice, support, and kindness. Her willingness to share her experiences helped ease me through the process.

I give my deepest thanks to my family. First, I honor the memory of those who have departed. My dear cousin Wyatt James Hoskinson; grandfather Mario "Otto" Schivone; and grandmother Yolanda Tramonte Schivone, provided love and support I always deeply appreciated. For teaching me about the beauty of Sonora and history, I thank my great-grandmother Guadalupe Corral Salazar and great-aunts María Luisa Salazar Corral Navarro, Armida Salazar López, Guadalupe Salazar Félix, Adelina Salazar Robles, and Irma Salazar Sosa. My tata (grandfather), José María Camacho, and nana (grandmother), María Julia Salazar Camacho, brought incredible love, warmth, and joy to my life. My nana was a second mother whose fervent, unconditional love for me as well as my mother was the bedrock of the first part of my life. I thank them for taking me to Sonora and teaching me to love history. My father, Ralph Nicholas Schivone, was always proud of me; I can still feel his love even though he is no longer here. I deeply cherish our talks about history and our time together.

In Sonora and Tucson, my extended family has provided support, love, and laughter while I worked on the book. My stepfather, Kevin Kattner, has become an integral part of the family, and I thank him for all of his love, kindness, and friendship. My great-aunt Carmella Schivone and the extended Schivone family have been wonderful. My aunts and uncle Ann Johnson, Linda Schivone, Tina Schivone, and Michael Schivone are some of my best friends. I deeply value the time we spend together and am thankful that they are a part of my life. I am equally grateful to have in my life my nino (godfather), José María Camacho; tía (aunt), María Beatrice Medina Camacho; and sweet cousins Emilio Camacho and Elení Camacho. Berenice Barreras Ayala has been my friend and family over the years. She has always been there for me, and for this I am deeply grateful. It is a joy to have in my life my adopted brother and beloved friend Daniel Luera Sierra and my dear friends Ariany Hendrata, Jacqueline Larriva, and Norma Navarro. I treasure deeply the love and companionship of my brother Andrew M. Schivone and my sister Monica E. Schivone. It is a blessing to have such a beautiful, caring, and amazing sister. My youngest sibling, Gabriel M. Schivone, always understands me, and his smile and wit have brought me much delight and laughter. I am in awe of him for his work, passion, and commitment to struggle and all that he has taught me over the years about justice and perseverance. Having him in my life is a gift. It is next to impossible to fully express my love for my mother, María Jesus Kattner. She is always there for me, and her love has been a pillar of my life. I adore her with all of my being. I am eminently thankful to be a part of her life and that of my stepfather.

Liu Xiaolong 刘小龙 has in a short time brought immense sweetness into my life. I am utterly happy now that he is in it, finally. Every day I feel his love and support, and I know that I am truly fortunate.

CHINESE MEXICANS

Introduction

"Mexico delights me. Navojoa delights me," said Alfonso Wong Campoy, the eldest son of a Chinese father and a Mexican mother, with a warm smile. As I sat in his living room in Navojoa, Sonora, in 2004, he described the hardship and tragedy as well as the joy that characterized his family's experiences. Local hatred for his mixed-race family drove the Wong Campoys out of northern Mexico in 1933, when Alfonso was four years old. Nearly thirty years would pass before he saw Navojoa and Mexico again. He would ultimately resettle in the same town from which regional authorities expelled his family when he was a boy, and he has subsequently remained there.[1] Wong Campoy's strong sense of love for his town, Navojoa, and his nation, Mexico, became palpable to me during our conversation. I left wondering how someone who had been through all that he had could love Mexico the way he does. Since then, I have thought about that question, and it has driven this project. Having left at a young age, Wong Campoy learned about Navojoa and Mexico from his mother and father and the community they forged abroad. With his Chinese Mexican compatriots, he yearned for Mexico and struggled for years to return. He became Mexican in China. The expulsion of his family and three decades across the Pacific did not break his ties to his homeland. On the contrary, those experiences fostered his sense of self as a Mexican. Although he and others genuinely loved Mexico, the Chinese Mexican community claimed Mexicanness strategically to leave China during a time of intense social and political turmoil; in turn, that community helped to shape postrevolutionary Mexican citizenship and Cold War politics.

This book is a journey that follows the paths of the Wong Campoys and other Chinese Mexican families. Along the way, it traces the emergence of a Chinese Mexican identity rooted in an imagined Mexican homeland and the memory of that history. Chinese Mexicans pushed the boundaries of what it meant to be Mexican: The expulsion from Mexico and stages of repatriation ensured that these families would forge strong transpacific

1

Alfonso Wong Campoy at his fruit stand in the Navojoa Central Market. Photograph by author.

ties and become profoundly cosmopolitan people: The national identity they developed had a transnational foundation. The book explores the tensions therein and studies what the history of Chinese Mexicans can teach us about nations, borders, and belonging. It examines how the story of Chinese Mexicans has both informed and been erased from the history of Mexico and the Mexican-U.S. borderlands.

Scholars of transnational migration and diasporas assert that people develop stronger national identities outside the nation's borders as they experience a sense of longing for the homeland. Chinese Mexicans became Mexican only after authorities deported them to China. By tracing the transpacific journeys and national identity formation of Chinese Mexicans, this book adds to and complicates the literature in borderlands, Mexican, Latin American, and U.S. history as well as that of transnational migration and diasporas and of overseas Chinese, Asian American, and gender studies. The book explores the complex intersections of identity, citizenship, racialization, gender ideology, and class in Mexico, the United States, and China in a single narrative frame. Treating transnationalism trilaterally, the book views the construction of borders and the politics of belonging in three countries in light of each other; it studies the tripartite foreign relations that emerged with the Chinese Mexican expulsion from northern Mexico. Contesting the public/private split, it rethinks the implicitly public focus of diaspora studies by centering on the family and interpersonal relations as key to identity. Adding to a growing body of scholarship that challenges nationalist studies of Mexico as sealed off from other nations, the book works against assumptions of ethnic homogeneity and questions notions of *mestizaje*—the ideology of the nation's heritage of racial and cultural mixture—that recognize only Spanish and indigenous ethnic and cultural influence in Mexico.

The complex ties Mexicans and Chinese formed in northern Mexico during the late nineteenth and early twentieth centuries and the integration of Chinese men into local communities led to racial and cultural fusion and over time to the formation of a new cultural identity—*Chinese Mexican*. Racially and culturally hybrid families straddled the boundaries of identity and nation. They made alternating claims on Chineseness and Mexicanness during their quest to belong somewhere, especially as social and political uproar erupted in Mexico, the United States, and China.

During the tumult of the Mexican Revolution of 1910, a group of working- and middle-class Sonorans began organizing against the Chinese and those Mexicans with whom they had formed bonds. In particular, they scorned as race traitors the Mexican women who had established romantic unions with Chinese men. A wide gulf between anti-Chinese activists and Mexicans who maintained relationships with the Chinese soon became perceptible in Sonora. Mexicans and Chinese drew on myriad resources to continue with their lives in spite of the movement. But in time, anti-Chinese crusaders infiltrated Mexican local, state, and eventually national politics, using Chinese people as scapegoats for a myriad of social problems. The return of Mexican workers from the United States during the Great Depression brought the movement to its peak, as these Mexicans needed jobs; within two decades of the start of the anti-Chinese campaigns, activists achieved their long-term goal of mass expulsion. Chinese men fled or were driven out of Sonora as well as its southern neighbor, Sinaloa, where the maniacal hatred had spread. Keeping families intact, Mexican women and Chinese Mexican children accompanied their men, whether by choice or by force.

Chinese Mexicans took a number of routes after local and state government officials began mass expulsions from northern Mexico. Some of the persecuted remained in their communities by hiding with the help of complicit family members and friends. Officials allowed a few Chinese with certain skills to remain but nonetheless confiscated their assets. Sonoran and Sinaloan Chinese moved to areas of Mexico less infected by virulent anti-Chinese campaigns. Some entered the United States and stayed there. Others traveled to China, either via the United States as refugees or directly from Mexico. Settling in communities in Guangdong Province or in Portuguese Macau or British Hong Kong, some became part of those societies and never left. Others moved to Portugal or the United States, eventually taking on Portuguese or American identities. Still others developed Mexican senses of self during their years abroad and ultimately returned to Mexico. The book explores these distinct paths but pays particular attention to people who pursued the final course—that is, interracial families who traveled from northern Mexico to southeastern China and finally back to Mexico, some after decades of effort to gain permission to return. Mapping out this geographic and symbolic journey, the project focuses on the politics and history of repatriation and Mexican national identity formation in a transpacific context. The voyages of Chinese Mexicans and the process of becoming Mexican abroad, which encompassed diasporic longing and heartfelt love for Mexico as well as political exigency, helped shape modern Mexico.

Yet the nation has failed to recognize Asians' importance in its cultural history and the national imaginary. Such key early-twentieth-century Mexican thinkers as José Vasconcelos (1881–1959) and Manuel Gamio (1883–1960), among others, theorized new visions of *mestizaje* and the nation that emphasized the European and indigenous elements of Mexican racial and cultural synthesis. They reclaimed Mexico's indigenous spirit while arguing that all Mexican citizens could and should assimilate to forge a unified population. Nationalist ideology during and after the Mexican Revolution cast the Chinese and other unwanted foreigners as outsiders or denigrated them as threatening to the body politic. Vasconcelos, for example, believed that the failure to Christianize and the long history of isolationism had set the Asian races on a downward spiral. As Alan Knight and Gerardo Rénique have shown, anti-Chinese racism was the logical consequence of *indigenismo* and new notions of Mexican *mestizaje*. *Antichinismo* served as a crucial bridge between the state of Sonora and the Mexican nation. Moreover, anti-Chinese ideology and policy offered a much-needed form of political coherence in the postrevolutionary era.[2]

Indeed, anti-Chinese activists in Sonora elaborated their ideology of hate and the movement intensified as new theories of race and *mestizaje* took hold in Mexico in the 1920s. Sonoran public intellectual José Angel Espinoza and his contemporaries fomented racial panic by drawing on the ideas of Vasconcelos and others. This published propaganda engendered paranoid and delusional fears of the demise of the Mexican race as a consequence of unions between Chinese men and Mexican women and the general presence of Chinese. *Antichinistas* created highly racialized and gendered caricatures not only of the Chinese but also of *chineras* and *chineros* (Chinese-friendly Mexicans) who maintained ties with Chinese persons in spite of the movement's vitriolic efforts.[3] Reaching its height during the Great Depression, the anti-Chinese movement set Chinese Mexicans on a fundamentally new course. They would experience the transnational reverberations of expulsion for decades to come.

Local and Regional versus National Identity

Prior to the expulsions, Chinese Mexican families had been wedded less to the Mexican nation than to local and regional areas.[4] After migrating to Mexico, Chinese men came to regard their towns as second homes, especially after living there for long periods, as many did. These men met and formed unions with women who were also tied to those places. Anchored to local communities and regions, Chinese Mexicans were unconcerned on a daily basis with being part of the Mexican nation until local and state authorities excluded these immigrants, compelling them to contend with U.S. immigration agents and ultimately to face a new life in China. Disrupting local and regional identities, the expulsion eventually led to new connections with the Mexican nation. National affinity grew as people appealed to national authorities in Mexico for assistance and articulated their senses of the "homeland" while they were abroad. Ramón Lay Mazo, a Chinese Mexican man who had left Sinaloa with his family as a small child during the expulsion era, became a key figure in the movement to repatriate to Mexico after World War II, when he moved from Taishan County in Guangdong Province to Macau and began working for the Catholic Church.

Yet even as people imagined Mexico, Mexican local and regional identities remained alive. Notions of the places they had left behind and visions of the Mexican nation became entwined as families from diverse local areas of Mexico met and forged a community in southeastern China. That community's deep connections with Mexico and people's persistent longing to return to the homeland in time transformed them into a diasporic enclave—a community of people whose identities were deeply tied with a nation they had left and for which they yearned from afar. To survive in a land that was foreign to them, Mexican women formed networks, congregating in particular areas of Guangdong Province and later Macau and Hong Kong, and wrote to Mexican consuls and federal officials seeking permission to repatriate. As they formed relationships that bridged their differing local and regional origins, Chinese Mexican families from

Sonora, Sinaloa, and elsewhere began to find that being Mexican went beyond their associations with particular communities or regions. After all, authorities in their local areas had expelled them, complicating their relationships with those places. Chinese Mexican families who met in China created a romantic and nostalgic concept of the Mexican homeland that rested on both the memory of local communities before the anti-Chinese movement had made it impossible to remain openly and the profound sense of longing they felt for Mexico after leaving.

Having lived on the cultural and geographic fringes of the nation, these Chinese Mexicans became Mexican only after they struggled from abroad with federal authorities; they sought tenaciously the official legitimization of their racially mixed families as Mexican. In the process, the Mexican identities they formed were both heartfelt and strategic, born in the context of conflict in mid-twentieth-century China. Confronting political and economic hardship, Chinese Mexicans claimed Mexico as their homeland and argued that their families belonged there because they wanted to leave China. Political constraints fueled these desires. Mexico became increasingly attractive as they stacked their memories of it against their daily lives in China. The concept of a Mexican homeland became ever more salient as China experienced invasion by Japan, the Sino-Japanese War, World War II, the communist revolution, and the Cold War. Over the years, Chinese Mexicans romanticized Mexico and developed a sense of national loyalty from afar—a diasporic Mexican citizenship. Although they sincerely wanted to return to Mexico, Cold War politics framed the intense nationalistic rhetoric and ideology they elaborated. When they finally repatriated, some became disillusioned. They had long believed that their lives would be better in Mexico. Reality, however, was far different.

Treating Mexican national identity formation among racially and culturally mixed citizens, the book complicates the literature on postrevolutionary and postwar Mexico by placing the nation in a larger transpacific frame. It follows Chinese Mexican families across borders and oceans as they left northern Mexico, developed a Mexican national identity, and eventually repatriated. Adding to scholarship on gender, it addresses the ways Mexican women challenged dominant notions of citizenship in Mexico that had stripped them of their nationality for marrying Chinese men. After persuading the nation to reincorporate them, the women combated local prejudices and fought for jobs and other resources for their mixed-race children. In making a case for the Mexicanness of their families, Chinese Mexicans pressed the concept of *mestizaje* to include them.

This history sheds light on the formation of the Mexican nation and the ways it sought international legitimacy in the postrevolutionary era. By reincorporating previously excluded citizens, Lázaro Cárdenas attempted to demonstrate Mexico's concern for its citizens abroad and standing in the world during the Sino-Japanese conflict. Occurring alongside the admittance of Republican refugees during the Spanish Civil War, the repatriation of Mexican women and Chinese Mexican children helped Mexico fashion itself as a modern, independent nation. But the federal government exerted strict control over who could claim Mexicanness through a rigid repatriation policy that barred even those Chinese who prior to the expulsions had lived in Mexico for years, become naturalized, established local families, and adopted Mexican customs. While Mexico admitted thousands of Spanish citizens—one of the only nations to lend Spanish Republicans its full support—Cárdenas refused entry to the small numbers of Chinese men who had remained with their Mexican-origin families in China and wanted to repatriate to Mexico in the late 1930s. Even though he repudiated the policies of his anti-Chinese predecessors, Cárdenas fell short of fully renouncing their hatred and inhumanity. Preventing Chinese men from returning brought intense suffering to some families. This policy was especially heartrending for those Chinese men who had in their own way become Mexican and wanted to stay with their families but were simply unable to make ends meet in China. Widower Roberto M. Fu's family, for example, carried a special burden after being split apart. In the end, Cárdenas's exclusionary repatriation fell in line with dominant revolutionary and postrevolutionary notions of race and *mestizaje* that excluded Asians.[5]

The Chinese Mexican saga also illuminates Mexican Cold War politics and the ways the nation attempted to gain further international recognition. Chinese Mexicans astutely drew on anticommunist notions as they called on the Mexican government to "rescue" them from communism after the creation of the People's Republic of China in 1949. Even though Macau and Hong Kong remained refuges throughout this period, Mexicans in China argued that the two foreign colonies were liable to fall into communist hands at any moment. The people who wanted to repatriate were well aware of what Mexican officials wanted to hear, exploiting fears of communism in pleading to return. Arguing that Chinese men—who had become culturally Mexicanized, formed unions and families with Mexican women, and contributed to Mexico's growth—were also part of the nation, some families pushed the Mexican government to allow Chinese husbands and fathers to return. Supporters in Mexico also recognized the economic and cultural contributions of Chinese and urged officials to welcome them back. Expressing its concern for the nation's global status, the Lions Club in Mexico used Cold War ideology to call on the government to repatriate its citizens who lived abroad in misery; adding insult to injury, they were in the shadow of communism and gave Mexico a bad reputation in the world. In 1960, as a result of the Lions Club campaign and the work of Chinese Mexicans in China, Adolfo López Mateos sponsored a second official repatriation that included Chinese men who wanted to return to Mexico with their families. In repatriating its citizens and including Chinese, the nation took a strategic political stance as world allegiances repeatedly shifted.

The book also contributes to scholarship on borderlands history, moving beyond the U.S. Southwest and focusing instead on northern Mexico. It was no coincidence that Chinese concentrated in the Mexican north and that anti-Chinese campaigns were most successful on the northern border. Moreover, the expulsion of Chinese from Sonora and Sinaloa (1931–34) partially coincided with the massive forced repatriation of Mexicans from the U.S. Southwest (1929–late 1930s, with the majority of deportations occurring in the early years) and the epoch of Chinese exclusion from the United States (1882–1943), which played out dramatically on the Mexican-U.S. border. In northern Mexico, the return of Mexican workers, whom Americans had blamed for depression-era economic instability in local areas of the U.S. Southwest, added great momentum to the anti-Chinese movement. These interconnected migratory and exclusionary processes in the borderlands finally brought to fruition the anti-Chinese activists' most lofty mission—the widespread removal of Chinese residents. When Sonoran authorities forced Chinese men and Chinese Mexican families across the northern border, they became refugees in the United States, ultimately facing deportation to China under the policy of Chinese exclusion as well as gendered notions of citizenship and the ideology of coverture. Mexican-U.S. regional and national competition and a shared racialization of the Chinese as an inassimilable menace framed the Chinese expulsions/deportations. Mexican officials literally pushed Chinese Mexicans across the boundary in a resentful display of regional and national power as well as a pragmatic ploy to force the nation to the north to use its greater resources to deport the unwanted arrivals. In their own small way, Sonoran local authorities contested the humiliation of the massive forced repatriations of Mexicans from the United States. This chapter was but one episode in a much longer story of Mexican-U.S. contentions, which have often reached their boiling points on the geopolitical division.

The Mexican-U.S. border region has been linked with the rest of the Pacific Rim not only by migration but also by the transpacific ties and complex, hybrid, and diasporic identities that Chinese Mexican individuals and families created over time. Developing a diasporic citizenship in China, Chinese Mexicans became imbued with a strong sense of Mexican nationalism and a profound yearning for the homeland, which they cultivated across three decades. The notion of diasporic citizenship has helped to highlight the interstitial status of Chinese Mexicans in China and their deep devotion to Mexico during their time abroad.[6]

In distinct ways, Chinese men, Mexican women, and Chinese Mexican children became diasporic citizens. By creating multiple connections between their homeland and places of residence, Chinese men were already diasporic in Mexico. They had established links with fellow countrymen overseas and upheld bonds with the villages or regions from which they emigrated, bringing with them social and economic institutions from home and adapting them in new contexts.[7] Their families in Mexico often became part of larger transpacific familial and other migrant networks. For example, Chinese men sent Mexican-born sons to China to live with relatives, including at times the same men's Chinese wives, to learn Cantonese and Taishanese languages and customs and work in local communities.[8] These sons were later reunited with their fathers, mothers, and other siblings when they arrived during the expulsion period. Mexican women and Chinese Mexican children became diasporic citizens after leaving Mexico with expelled Chinese husbands, companions, and fathers. In China, Chinese Mexican families developed distinct relationships and became part of their new settings while working for repatriation to Mexico.

Theirs was a history of combating rejection. The struggle to be included in Mexico would not be easy and would in some cases take decades. Nevertheless, Chinese Mexicans held onto the dream of returning to Mexico. Like other peoples relegated to the fringes of nation-states by virtue of race, gender, class, language, culture, or affiliative ties, they fought for a place. Their story underscores how people on the periphery of the nation can tell us about the center. A strong diasporic inclination and a passionate national identification emerged following forcible removal, loss, pain, and longing for the homeland. This book helps reclaim the rightful place of Chinese Mexicans in the Mexican nation as well as in Mexican and borderlands history. It also further illuminates and complicates Mexican *mesti-*

zaje by showing how mixed-race families claimed Mexico and persistently argued that they were part of the nation and deserved the same treatment as all other citizens. In this way, Chinese Mexicans pressed Mexico to uphold its obligation to protect the civil rights of its complex citizenry.

Migration and the Politics of Exclusion in the Mexican-U.S. Borderlands

For centuries, the Chinese emigrated predominantly from Guangdong Province, Fujian Province, and other coastal areas in search of new economic opportunities. Even though departing China was illegal until 1893, they created overseas communities in Southeast Asia, Australia, Europe, Africa, North America, Latin America, and elsewhere, becoming part of a global Chinese diaspora. A predominantly male phenomenon, the diaspora's most significant patterns included trade, labor, sojourning, and return migration. Chinese experiences varied widely, and emigrants fulfilled myriad economic and social roles overseas. In Peru, Cuba, and the United States, for example, the Chinese were indentured laborers. In addition to laborers, Chinese shopkeepers and peddlers became a "middleman minority" group in northern Mexico, as in Southeast Asia, where there were far more migrants. The economic niches filled by the Chinese in Mexico earned them enormous visibility, ultimately feeding the potent anti-Chinese crusade. In each place they settled, Chinese established not only families but also institutions such as mutual aid organizations, churches, newspapers, and business associations. The connections represented by these groups helped Chinese contest the hatred and discrimination they encountered. While in some places Chinese integrated partially by forming families, elsewhere they lived largely in bachelor communities with the intent of returning eventually to their families in China; in locales geographically closer to China, emigrants were more likely to return home within a short time. Many Chinese overseas migrants practiced polygyny, maintaining multiple homes if they had the means to do so and sending remittances to their Chinese families. But some men lacked the resources to send money home or establish families in China and continue their lineage. Chinese men of varying economic standing in Southeast Asia, Latin America, and elsewhere forged unions with local women. These relationships at times resulted in the Chinese men's conversion to Islam, Catholicism, or other religions.[9]

Although Chinese migrants arrived in America as early as the sixteenth century, the pace of such immigration expanded greatly in the mid-nineteenth century. These arrivals came largely from the city of Guangzhou and surrounding areas in Guangdong Province not only because of population growth, economic transformation, political unrest, religious persecution, and natural disaster but also as a consequence of the region's key role in Chinese history, especially its relationship with the external world. In particular, Chinese emigrated from Taishan County, an important *qiaoxiang* (place with a tradition of a high emigration rate).[10] Chinese as well as other immigrants flocked to California after the discovery of gold in 1848.[11] A decade later, white workers there began organizing anti-Chinese campaigns. Racializing the Chinese as outsiders who took resources that rightfully belonged to the white working class, the movement became crucial in the formation of the state's class politics.[12] Local and state laws throughout the southwestern United States eventually embraced anti-Chinese sentiment, which ultimately spread to the national level.[13] In the late nineteenth century, U.S. discourse increasingly portrayed Chinese immigrants as threatening the national polity. Federal law came to define Chinese in particular racial and gender terms. The 1875 Page Law was the first to set Chinese apart from other immigrants. It barred the entry of Chinese prostitutes, classifying these women as moral pollutants; although it targeted prostitutes, it shut out Chinese women immigrants in general. In 1882, the federal Chinese Exclusion Act forbade "Chinese laborers," broadly defined, from entering the United States. The measure was renewed several times and remained in force until the World War II era.[14] This legislation had a tremendous impact on Chinese migration as well as broader immigration law in the United States during and beyond the exclusion era. As Chinese increasingly traveled elsewhere, U.S. policy influenced migration patterns in other parts of the Americas.[15]

The hemispheric turn in Chinese diaspora studies has shown that people not only arrived directly from China but also moved within the Americas in dynamic circular and serial migrations in the nineteenth and twentieth centuries.[16] Formal exclusion from the United States sparked some of this migration, as Chinese often traveled to Canada and Mexico with the intent of surreptitiously crossing the northern and southern borders.[17] Indeed, illegal immigration across land borders became a successful business enterprise by the turn of the twentieth century, and an estimated 17,300 Chinese crossed the northern and southern borders into the United States between 1882 and 1920 alone.[18] While many arrived in northern Mexico hoping to enter the United States, others found opportunities and remained. Chinese increasingly arrived in Mexico as the United States effectively closed its border with Canada to them in the early twentieth century.[19]

Mexico welcomed the Chinese at the same time that the United States began to exclude them; later, however, northern Mexico would remove the Chinese as the United States broadened its expulsion efforts to include not only Chinese but also Mexicans. In the late nineteenth century, Mexican dictator Porfirio Díaz (1876–1911) at first attempted to recruit southern and eastern European immigrants to help whiten and modernize Mexico. When this endeavor failed, Porfiristas encouraged Chinese to immigrate. In the eyes of the *científicos*—Díaz's inner circle of positivist, technocratic advisers—the lighter skin of the Chinese, even though it fell short of being white, could help dilute Mexico's indigenous and mestizo population.[20]

Chinese settlement patterns in the United States and Mexico diverged markedly. Social and commercial openings in Mexican society allowed Chinese men to integrate in ways that were impossible in the United States, where, during the exclusion era, they could neither become citizens nor legally wed American women. While American and Chinese gender customs differed starkly, Mexican and Chinese norms overlapped in significant ways. These distinctions and the relatively low number of Chinese enabled them to become part of local Mexican communities, while segregation in Chinatowns was the model in the United States, where higher numbers allowed the establishment of separate ethnic enclaves.

Mexicans had moved back and forth across the Mexican-U.S. border since officials first began drawing the international boundary in the midnineteenth century; for decades, the line was blurry. In the 1880s, Mexican immigration to the United States grew as laborers found opportunities to work on rail lines and in other sectors in the Southwest. People sought refuge north of the border during the Mexican Revolution of 1910. Mexican men traveled to the United States to work under the first Bracero Program, implemented during World War I. Big business advocates won the extension of the labor agreement beyond the war. By 1930, the line between white American and Mexican became fixed, and the border became less porous. During the Great Depression, U.S. officials rounded up and forcibly "repatriated" at least a million Mexicans, including U.S. citizens, in the Southwest. The United States embraced Mexicans once more during World War II, beginning the second Bracero Program in 1942. After white American servicemen returned from the war and needed jobs, Operation Wetback again removed Mexicans en masse. Such was the revolving door that controlled Mexican work and migration patterns in the twentieth century. The United States welcomed Mexicans in boom times when it wanted their labor and excluded them in moments of crisis.[21]

Migratory movements and nativist campaigns against both Chinese and Mexicans in the border region have been deeply intertwined as people elaborated local scapegoat politics and anti-Chinese notions circulated in North America. Crusaders constructed an intricate set of vicious stereotypes of Chinese as miserly, lying, cheating, diseased, moral contaminants who were abusive toward women. Ideas originating in California decades earlier made their way to northern Mexico, where people refined the concepts as the Chinese population grew. While some Chinese intended to cross the border illegally, others found economic opportunities in the developing border economy of northern Mexico.[22] The U.S. repatriation of a million Mexicans gave Sonoran and Sinaloan anti-Chinese crusaders increased ammunition. The majority arrived in Mexico between 1931 and 1933, precisely the years when Sonora and Sinaloa evicted most of their Chinese residents. Mirroring the treatment Mexicans received north of the border, anti-Chinese crusaders blamed the Chinese for northern Mexico's social and economic woes.[23]

Although they were interconnected and shared some similarities, anti-Chinese movements in the borderlands also differed. In the United States, white workers justified violence against Chinese and their ultimate exclusion by arguing that the Chinese "coolie" labor force hampered the "free" labor market. In northern Mexico, where Chinese were both laborers and shopkeepers, anti-Chinese activists focused on businesses, contending that they took jobs, resources, and women that rightfully belonged to Mexican men, a decidedly gendered racialization of the Chinese as dangerous to the Mexican body politic.

This project is part of a larger conversation about Chinese in the borderlands as well as the broader Chinese diaspora. Evelyn Hu-DeHart has conducted important and pioneering work on the Chinese in Mexico and Latin America, transforming the study of overseas Chinese and opening up this field in the Americas. Yong Chen, Grace Delgado, Madeline Hsu, Erika Lee, Kathleen López, Adam McKeown, Robert Chao Romero, Lok Siu, Elliott Young, and others have mapped the complex and divergent transnational orbits of Chinese migrants in the Americas. Kif Augustine-Adams, Verónica Castillo-Muñoz, Jason Chang, Fredy González, Julian Lim, Isabela Seong-Leong Quintana, Gerardo Rénique, and others have taken the study of Chinese in Mexico and the Mexican-U.S. borderlands in exciting new directions. My work is part of a dialogue with all of these scholars.

This book also speaks to a wider group of scholars working on transnational movement and identity formation and gender and the family. It is the first monograph to inquire into what became of the mixed-race families that Chinese migrants established in Mexico. No one has studied the Chinese who became so entrenched that they stayed in Sonora either secretly or with special permission. This book is the first to follow the families who passed through the United States as "refugees" and ultimately arrived in China to begin new lives and face fresh challenges. No one has studied the process of Chinese Mexican diasporic identity formation or the official repatriations to Mexico during the mid-twentieth century. Tracing the transnational geography of Chinese Mexicans, the book charts their migrations, ruptures, identities, and complex searches for home. It shows how they operated within the confines imposed by three nations and eventually worked out their personal and legal stakes in national belonging in Mexico.

Sources and Methodology

The book tracks movement in and between the Mexican-U.S. borderlands and southeastern China. Using a borderlands migration framework, it views with one lens Chinese exclusion, the deportation of Mexicans from the United States, Chinese expulsion from northern Mexico, and Chinese Mexican repatriation. It approaches the history of Chinese Mexicans via human relationships and identity formation. While the stories of other families are crucial and also fill the pages of this book, the Wong Campoy family in particular exemplifies both the hardship and the resolve embedded in the journeys of Chinese Mexicans. The narrative uses their story to provide an intimate window into a larger tale.

The book relies on diverse Spanish- and English-language archival and oral material collected in Mexico, the United States, Macau, and Hong Kong. The court testimony of Mexicans and Chinese in Sonora provides rich insight into the intricacies of their relationships and the texture of daily life. Although fundamentally skewed and racist, anti-Chinese papers offer clues about these liaisons insofar as activists attempted to curtail and ultimately eradicate them. This book is the first to use U.S. Immigration and Naturalization Service (INS) records of the refugee crisis. Chinese testimony before U.S. immigration agents vividly describes the expulsion and the pain and hardship it caused Chinese men and their families. INS lists document the passage through the U.S. Southwest of Chinese men and their Mexican-origin families as "refugees" from Mexico. Shedding light on international relations, communications between these agents show that U.S. authorities negotiated with Chinese officials for the repayment of deportation costs and believed that the Mexican government took advantage of its northern neighbor by forcing Chinese to cross the border illegally. Another new set of documents, Chinese Mexican letters and consular reports in China, illuminates the transpacific paths Chinese men's Mexican-origin families traversed. Mexican women's letters to consular officials in East Asia and government authorities in Mexico during the 1930s illustrate the changes their families underwent after the expulsion and the networks, diasporic community, and identities they forged abroad. Communications from Chinese Mexicans who sought to repatriate to Mexico between the 1930s and 1960s as well as letters of support from individuals and organizations in Mexico and elsewhere shed light on the scope of the enclave, the social and religious institutions on which people relied to survive, and their profound, unwavering, yet tactical desire to return to the "Mexican homeland."

Oral history interviews in northern Mexico, the U.S. Southwest, Macau, and Hong Kong both corroborate and augment the documentary evidence of the journeys of Chinese Mexicans. Some of the people I interviewed whose families encountered anti-Chinese hatred in Mexico also appeared in the archival sources. Their memories are central to this work. Oral histories not only enrich the record but also speak to the importance of remembering the Chinese and Chinese Mexicans. People whose oral testimonies I took have fashioned dynamic, hybrid identities and honored their ancestors and their struggles in striking ways. By doing so, they have refused to forget Mexico's anti-Chinese past and in turn have worked against the erasure of Chinese from the national imaginary.

I use the term "Chinese Mexican" throughout the text to highlight the hybridity of these families while emphasizing their Mexicanness. The core of the book explores what happened to the families Chinese migrants established in Mexico, with a focus on the experiences of Mexican women and mixed-race children who followed the men across the Pacific. This story contains relatively few voices of Chinese husbands and fathers. While glimpses of the men's stories are present in certain sources, such as the testimonies before INS agents, the book centers on the people who ultimately became Mexican. Although widower Roberto M. Fu and other

Chinese men took this path, too, the story is mainly about Mexican women and Chinese Mexican children who ultimately repatriated to Mexico without their husbands and fathers.

Chapter Organization

The chapters in the book sketch the transnational paths of Chinese Mexicans. The first four chapters take place in northern Mexico and the Mexican-U.S. borderlands. Chapter 1 explores Chinese emigration, traveling with Chinese men from Guangdong Province to the border region. Describing their settlement, it paints a picture of everyday life in local communities in Sonora and the broad range of ties Chinese created with Mexicans throughout the state. It examines the formation of Chinese-Mexican relationships and families to show how Chinese became integral to local society by the early twentieth century.

The second chapter turns to the emergence of campaigns against Chinese and the Mexicans with whom they were linked during the Mexican Revolution of 1910. Describing the available options and diverse resources on which Chinese Mexicans drew to challenge anti-Chinese campaigns, it addresses the split that came to exist in Sonora as some Mexicans maintained their ties with Chinese while others vehemently organized against the new immigrants. Chapter 3 treats the culmination of the movement in the depression era. Although authorities allowed some Chinese to remain and others stayed by hiding, officials or angry and crazed mobs forced the vast majority of Chinese out of Sonora as well as its southern neighbor, Sinaloa.

Several thousand expelled Chinese and some of their Mexican-origin families entered the United States illegally in the early 1930s. They quickly created a refugee crisis for that nation, and that crisis is the subject of chapter 4. INS officials held Chinese men and their families in immigration jails before deporting them to China. Owing to the dominant gender ideology of coverture, or the "feme covert," in both the United States and Mexico, U.S. immigration officials applied Chinese exclusion to Mexican women—even those in free associations with rather than legal marriages to Chinese men—and sent them to China rather than back to Mexico.

Chapter 5 crosses the Pacific with the U.S. deportees as well as the people whom authorities expelled directly from Mexico. Focusing on the challenges Chinese Mexican families faced in Chinese men's communities in Guangdong Province, where some of the men already had wives, the chapter shows how Mexican women in China helped reshape post-revolutionary citizenship policy as they appealed to Mexican federal authorities for their return.[24] Chapter 6 examines Lázaro Cárdenas's Mexico and follows the first Mexican women and Chinese Mexican children to repatriate to Mexico in 1937–38. Prohibiting Chinese men, the first official repatriation tore some families apart, while others decided to stay unified in China, where they would remain for years as a consequence of war and revolution there and a lack of attention to them in Mexico. Tracing the formation of a coherent Chinese Mexican community in cosmopolitan Portuguese Macau and nearby British Hong Kong, chapter 7 studies national Mexican identity formation against a diasporic backdrop and explores the three-decade-long struggle to repatriate to Mexico. Over time, numerous individuals and organizations in Mexico and East Asia became involved in the plight of Chinese Mexicans.

The final chapter circles back to Mexico to track repatriation in the postwar era. Allowing Chinese husbands and fathers into the nation, the Mexican government orchestrated a second and more inclusive repatriation in 1960. Small groups also returned outside the official movement through the mid- to late twentieth century. Examining how Chinese Mexicans continued to claim a place in the nation, chapter 8 explores the repatriates' experiences as they readjusted to Mexican society after decades abroad. Acting as brokers, Mexican women persistently argued that their mixed-race children and families belonged in the nation and deserved the same treatment as other citizens. The conclusion explores the memory of Chinese Mexicans in northern Mexico and southeastern China. Reflecting on the process of becoming Mexican in China, it considers how these families can teach us about national identity and belonging.

PART ONE

Chinese Settlement in

Northwestern Mexico and

Local Responses

CHAPTER ONE

Creating Chinese-Mexican Ties and Families in Sonora, 1910s–Early 1930s

This story begins in southeastern China in the mid-nineteenth century, when Chinese men increasingly departed their villages and towns and formed diasporic overseas communities around the world, becoming *huaqiao*, "Chinese sojourners."[1] Among the emigrants from Guangdong Province several decades later was Wong Fang, Alfonso Wong Campoy's father. Around the turn of the twentieth century, when he was a very young man, Wong Fang traveled to San Francisco with his uncle, who became a businessman there. Wong Fang continued his journey to Sonora and settled in Pueblo Viejo, a community adjacent to the small town of Navojoa, a semitropical area in the valley of the Río Mayo near the state's southern border with Sinaloa. He went to school, learned Spanish, and worked in the community; he later moved to Navojoa proper.[2]

Adapting to local society, Wong Fang became "Alfonso Wong Fang," adding a common Mexican given name and using his Chinese names as surnames, a regular practice among Chinese in Latin America.[3] With his uncle remaining in San Francisco, he benefited from cross-border ties among Chinese men in northern Mexico and the southwestern United States, eventually becoming an associate of an important Navojoa enterprise, Ching Chong y Compañía, which sold a wide variety of goods. As a

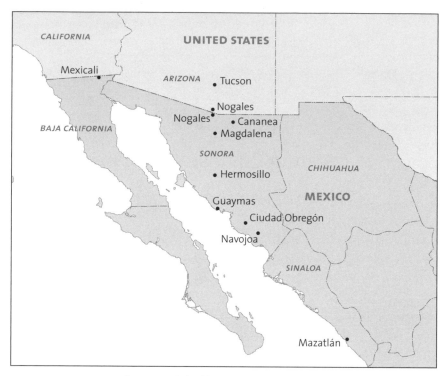

Sonora and the Mexican-U.S. Borderlands

businessman, he traveled to other towns in Sonora and Sinaloa, but his primary home was in Navojoa. Wong Fang also ran a shop that sold candy and ice cream and employed a woman named Dolores Campoy Rivera. Campoy Rivera's family was from Navojoa; her father worked in the local post office. In time, Dolores and Alfonso married and started a family. Their first child was born in Navojoa on 12 October 1928, and in keeping with Mexican custom, the parents named their first-born son after his father and used the father's family name as the first surname, followed by the mother's paternal surname: Alfonso Wong Campoy. Business dealings caused the young family to travel often over the next few years; as a result, the couple's second child, María del Carmen Irma Wong Campoy, was born in Hermosillo, Sonora's capital, and the third, Héctor Manuel Wong Campoy, was born in Culiacán, Sinaloa.[4] By forging culturally hybrid Chinese Mexican families and adopting local social norms such as naming practices while maintaining a sense of Cantonese or Taishanese identity and passing it on to their children, Chinese men became part of Sonoran society.

Chinese in Sonora

In the late nineteenth and early twentieth centuries, Alfonso Wong Fang and other Chinese men settled in a fluid, culturally diverse, and ethnically and class stratified Mexican society.[5] Situated on the border with the United States, Sonora drew influence from both central Mexico and its northern neighbor and in time became a hybrid "contact zone."[6] The marginalized indigenous groups residing in Sonora included the Yaqui, Tohono O'odham, Seri, Apache, and Mayo. The export economy had attracted foreigners interested in taking part in mining enterprises and trade throughout the nineteenth century. French, British, German, and American immigrants had married into wealthy Mexican families. As its border economy took shape between 1860 and 1900, the state gained more newcomers from the United States, Europe, the Middle East, and Asia. Mexicans from elsewhere in the nation also migrated north during this time in search of work in mines, on haciendas, and in nascent border towns. Isolation from markets in central Mexico increased Sonoran economic dependence on the United States, and foreign investment came to dominate the economy by the turn of the twentieth century. As Mexicans and Americans came into increased contact, they engaged in cultural exchange as well as conflict. The new border towns eventually led to a complicated Mexican-U.S. economic interdependence, but vast inequality characterized the burgeoning relationship. As a consequence of the Spanish colonial past and the persistent presence of foreigners since Mexican independence in 1821, people in Sonora often viewed themselves as ethnically distinct from other Mexicans, and Sonorans' notions of race explicitly privileged the lighter skinned.[7]

The Chinese increasingly migrated to Sonora after the passage of the Chinese Exclusion Act in the United States in 1882: Mexico offered points of illegal entry into the nation to the north as well as opportunities in the developing border economy.[8] The presence of Chinese added to Sonora's complexity. As a consequence of Chinese gender norms and exclusionary policies in the Americas, Chinese migration to Sonora was overwhelmingly male.[9] By the early twentieth century, the Chinese were the largest foreign colony in the state, which housed one of Mexico's biggest Chinese populations. Nonetheless, the Chinese comprised only 1–2 percent of Sonora's overall population between 1910 and 1930. Concentrating in particular towns and communities, however, they eventually gained disproportionate attention.[10]

TABLE 1. The Chinese Population in Mexico, Sonora, and Sinaloa

	Mexico	Sonora	Sinaloa
1895	907	301	190
1900	2,319	850	233
1910	13,203	4,486	667
1921	14,498	3,639	1,040
1927	24,218	3,758	2,019
1930	17,865	3,571	2,123
1940	4,856	92	165

Source: José Jorge Gómez Izquierdo, *El movimiento antichino en México (1871–1934): problemas del racismo y del nacionalismo durante la Revolución Mexicana* (Mexico City: Instituto Nacional de Antropología e Historia, 1991), 77, 78, 109, 127, 150.

Robert Chao Romero has shown that the Chinese in Mexico were part of two broad socioeconomic categories. Agricultural laborers and unskilled employees, on the one hand, exhibited lower rates of assimilation. Skilled artisans and merchants (including sole proprietors and high-class, mid-level, and small businessmen), on the other hand, had more wealth and tended toward greater assimilation. As elsewhere in Mexico, the Chinese were crucial in Sonora, filling a number of roles in local communities. They participated in the traditional rural economy by becoming landowners or laboring on the haciendas, on the ranchos, and in the fields of Mexican as well as Chinese landowners. But the Chinese also helped Sonora modernize by becoming the first petit bourgeois class. Fulfilling a variety of needs, Chinese brought merchandise and services to towns across Sonora. They established businesses either individually or in conjunction with their countrymen, selling inexpensive household goods and food, establishing laundries, and providing key domestic services. Because Chinese businessmen generated revenue and provided necessities, they at first enjoyed the protection of municipal authorities. Although some were large-scale operations, most Chinese enterprises were small and local. Chinese had more businesses but less overall capital than other groups in Sonora. Rather than displacing Mexicans or other foreigners, they found new commercial openings. For example, Chinese commonly set up businesses in mining centers, selling inexpensive merchandise to Mexican and indigenous workers. Offering items on credit further attracted mine workers and upset larger Mexican, American, and European business owners. Chinese drew on transnational economic networks in a way that local residents could not, receiving capital and inexpensive goods from China and other parts of the Americas that enabled these Chinese businessmen eventually to establish a monopoly on low-end consumer goods. The Chinese ultimately created the state's first economic infrastructure. As in other areas where Chinese settled, they took the role of peddler and merchant in Sonora because the local population was tied up in the traditional rural social hierarchy, in which some Chinese also participated. As the growing border economy pushed northern Mexico toward the commercial and the modern, and in the absence of a native petite bourgeoisie, the Chinese found an important economic and social niche.[11]

Among the many kinds of small enterprises Chinese created, street peddling earned them enormous visibility in local communities. Selling vegetables and other goods from house to house, Chinese peddlers formed relationships with their clientele. North American and European immigrants—many of whom were businessmen who possessed far larger sums of capital than their Chinese counterparts—were simply absent from Sonoran working people's day-to-day lives. Chinese peddlers as well as laborers and small shopkeepers, however, were in view on a daily basis.[12]

Chinese in Sonora became diasporic citizens by maintaining connections with the Cantonese and Taishanese towns and villages from which they had emigrated, forming voluntary associations and transnational ties with Chinese elsewhere in the diaspora. These networks included cross-border ties with compatriots in the United States that helped provide opportunities and sustain economic enterprises in the borderlands.[13] By the early twentieth century, Chinese immigrants in Sonora formed the Fraternal Order of Chinese, a crucial organization that fostered community and helped protect Chinese in the state.[14] In particular, it assisted new arrivals in surviving in an unfamiliar land.

Chinese politics played out in Sonora in a number of ways. For example, in January 1912, Chinese in Hermosillo staged a parade to celebrate the overthrow of the Qing Dynasty and the establishment of the Republic of China.[15] In the 1920s, political affiliation and ideology among overseas Chinese took a violent turn when rival factions—the Kuomintang, associated with the local Fraternal Union, and the more conservative Chee Kung Tong (Zhi Gong Tang)—battled in Sonora's Chinese establishments and on the city's streets. These "tong wars" would spark anti-Chinese organizing.[16] But many local Chinese had little or nothing to do with the tong wars.

Chinese maintained diasporic overseas connections and forged bonds among themselves while integrating into Sonoran society. Like Chinese elsewhere in Latin America, emigrants in Sonora often learned Spanish and became naturalized citizens.[17] As Sonorans accepted Chinese into existing social and economic networks and the migrants created new such networks, they became deeply incorporated into local communities. While the businesses they started became critical to Sonora's modernization, the relationships they established with Mexicans grew to be culturally important in the state, with a new Chinese Mexican identity taking shape. Chinese made local communities their second homes, and many immigrants died before returning to their places of origin. Chinese cemeteries in towns throughout Sonora house the grave sites of men who contributed to Sonora's growth.

Although it had begun a process of modernization, Sonoran society still featured cultural and racial holdovers from the colonial period. For example, people continued to use the Spanish title "Don" for male heads of households of good social standing. Sonorans still went to court over *abuso de confianza* (abuse of trust), another idea dating from the colonial period. As they became part of Sonora, the Chinese internalized key cultural concepts such as *confianza*, the notion of sharing with someone a bond that involved mutual trust and understanding.

Chinese Mexican Ties

Chinese were able to integrate into Sonoran society because the Mexican government allowed them to immigrate, naturalize, and marry local women, at least at first. The Porfiriato (the reign of Porfirio Díaz, 1876–1911) encouraged Chinese immigration during the late nineteenth century. Unlike in the United States, the Chinese could become naturalized citizens and legally marry Mexican women. In addition to providing companionship and love, marriages to Mexican women helped Chinese men become part of local societies and drew Mexican clientele to Chinese-operated businesses. Unions with Chinese men offered Mexican women and their families economic stability and prestige. Chinese men were known for being frugal, for being good providers, and for saving for their children's futures.[18] Along with the romantic feelings and love they felt for their partners, these were attractive qualities for poor and working-class Mexican women.

Overlapping cultural norms and the relatively small numbers of Chinese in Sonora also facilitated their relationships with Mexicans and integration into local society. While segregation in Chinatowns became the norm in the United States, northern Mexico's Chinese population was too small to re-create Chinese ethnic communities. Rather, the Chinese became incorporated into local society. While American and Chinese gender customs diverged significantly, Mexican and Chinese norms had some common threads. Ideas of family, marriage, honor, and death and the interconnections among these concepts coincided. Extended families were key to social organization, and people honored the dead in homes and public spaces, often with food. But perhaps the most striking parallels were in marriage practices. Even though bigamy was officially illegal, it was widely accepted that Mexican men could have multiple households if they could afford to maintain them. Historically, men of greater means kept such households, and the families knew about each other, a practice that bore some resemblance to the long history of concubinage among China's wealthy. A key difference, however, was that in Mexico, these households were generally not in the same vicinity, unlike in China, where concubines were part of one larger household. Still, Chinese men adapted with ease to culturally understandable gender customs in northern Mexico. Marta Elia Lau de Salazar knew well, as she recounted to her niece, Berenice Barreras Ayala, that her father, Concepción Lau Wong, had had other children with Mexican women in the Sinaloan town of Mazatlán and in Sonora's Huatabampo and Hermosillo. He ultimately settled with Lau de Salazar's mother, Preciliana Yocupicio, staying with her until his death.[19]

The intersections among Mexican and Chinese cultural norms and the small Chinese population enabled the men to form an array of everyday neighborly, social, romantic, and economic relationships with Mexicans in Sonora. The class positions of Chinese enabled them to establish bonds primarily with working- and middle-class Mexicans. Interactions evidenced in court records, newspapers, and oral histories paint a vivid picture of how Chinese became integral to Sonoran communities. Chinese hired Mexican lawyers and used the court system to assert rights. Chinese endeavors frequently relied on existing local structures and contributed to the economic welfare of Mexican people and communities.

Chinese and Mexicans labored together as domestic service workers and formed working-class bonds. In 1921, Raúl Lim lived and worked as a cook, and Luisa Padilla was an ironer in the Guaymas home of wealthy American immigrant J. A. Macpherson. After the robbery of a number of personal items from his room, Lim used his close connection with Padilla to go to local authorities to help recover what he had lost. Padilla knew intimately Lim's daily routine and confirmed to Guaymas police that a suitcase confiscated from a local soldier containing clothing and other articles, including a personal object that he had routinely kept under his pillow, was Lim's property.[20]

Mexican neighbors, friends, and authorities helped Chinese protect their businesses in towns throughout Sonora during a time when robberies and assaults were commonplace and indiscriminate.[21] A number of townspeople in northwestern Caborca assisted in finding the perpetrators of a robbery of Juaquín Chan and Company in 1921. The business was located in the home of Guadalupe Viuda de García ("viuda de" indicates that she was the widow of a man with the surname García);[22] she had rented it to the proprietor, Alejandro Chan. Signaling the Chan enterprise's importance in the town, Miguel Palafox, Caborca's *presidente municipal* (akin to mayor), personally accompanied authorities to the scene of the crime and provided the local police force with soldiers and arms to search for the stolen merchandise and the perpetrators.[23] In another case, Luis Chan told court officials that his closest neighbor, María Paco, was someone "con quien tiene confianza" (with whom he enjoyed a bond of trust and understanding). As a result of their close ties, Chan asked Paco to keep an eye on his business in El Ranchito, a small community outside Hermosillo, in 1927, while he was away. During that time, Paco witnessed a robbery and helped her neighbor take the matter to court.[24]

Ordinary Mexican citizens and local leaders alike incorporated Chinese into the local body politic by aiding them in keeping their businesses secure and upholding justice. After the robbery and brutal murder of businessman Rafael Yee, Mexicans in Masiaca, a small town near Sonora's southern border, denounced the act and called for punishment of the criminals. A self-described group of upstanding, honorable local citizens and "padres de familia" (family men) wrote to the governor of Sonora on 3 October 1925 with a long list of men suspected as having been involved in the crimes against Yee, providing details of other crimes these individuals had likely committed and the sources of the information. After Yee's death, local authorities paid various men salaries for several weeks to guard his store, pointing to its significance in Masiaca.[25]

Gastón Cano Ávila, who was born in Hermosillo in 1926, remembered visiting Chinese stores as a young boy and the bonds his parents had formed with the owners and workers. During my interview with him, Cano Ávila presented me with a copy of a 1930–31 commercial directory that listed thirty-one Chinese businesses in Hermosillo. He then took me on a walking tour of the capital's commercial center and pointed to the former locations of large and small Chinese businesses he had visited with his father and mother. The Chinese treated him kindly, and certain shopkeepers gave him sweet treats while his parents shopped and visited.[26] Born in the capital in 1925, Jesús Verdugo Escoboza remembered seeing numerous Chinese peddlers selling vegetables and other items from street carts when he was a young boy.[27] María Luisa Salazar Corral Navarro remembered a time when Chinese businesses lined the streets of Navojoa. Born in the small southeastern mining village of Las Minitas in 1924, Navarro moved with her family to the nearby and larger town of Navojoa when she was very young. She accompanied her father to a variety of Chinese businesses but particularly recalled his connections with the Chinese owners of Ching Chong y Compañía, where Alfonso Wong Fang was an associate.[28]

Local memory of the notion of "el pilón" (the tip of a cone of *piloncillo*, or brown sugar in a crystallized form) has reflected the importance of Chinese businesses in Sonora's history. Because of the Chinese presence, "el pilón" became a metaphor for something over and above the expected— "un detalle" (a little extra), in the words of some Sonorans. Chinese business owners regularly gave their customers some sort of "pilón," or small gift with a purchase. Chinese businessmen were quite apt at attracting and keeping their Mexican clientele. Some Sonorans believed that this practice marked the difference between Mexican and Chinese business owners and explained the latter's greater success. In some instances, Chinese shopkeepers simply gave customers a little more of what they were already buying or pieces of candy. At other times, "el pilón" was a special gift. At Christmas, Ignacio Fonseca Chon's grandfather gave patrons Chinese plants and flowers he had ordered from compatriots in San Francisco or coins wrapped in paper, which he described as customary Chinese gifts.[29]

People bought food items every day during the late nineteenth and early twentieth centuries, in large part because they had no way to refrigerate. They frequently sent children to buy groceries from local shops. Knowing that Chinese stores often gave candy with a purchase, children chose Chinese stores over others. Many people remember siblings fighting for their turn to buy groceries so they could claim their "pilón." Lau de Salazar remembered kids demanding "!Danos pilón! [Give us pilón!]" when the practice waned after the expulsion of Chinese. Similarly, Leo Sandoval's 1990 novel, *La Casa de Abelardo*, a story about Abelardo Juanz, a prominent Chinese restaurateur in Sonora, describes children screaming, "¡Quiero mi pilón! [I want my pilón!]" after the official shuttering of Chinese businesses.[30]

Certain Chinese businessmen became renowned in local communities. Fermín Ley, who lived in Hermosillo for more than thirty years, owned La Mariposa (later La Abeja). When he died in early 1927, local newspapers celebrated the "well-esteemed Chinese" man's life. His property was by then in the possession of two local Mexican women, Emilia Félix and Josefa Félix.[31]

Conflicts also ensued in business settings, and Chinese used the legal system to claim rights in local areas. In 1911, Enríque Lay, a Chinese resident of Hermosillo and a worker at a compatriot's store, lent Carmen Esparza an expensive ring that belonged to his Chinese boss, Federico León Qui, in *confianza*. When she failed to return the ring, Lay took Esparza to court for *abuso de confianza*, or taking advantage of his trust and their amiable relationship. He had believed that Esparza knew someone who wanted to buy a high-quality ring and that she would bring it back if she failed to sell it. But after a week of unsuccessful attempts to resolve the matter informally, he took her to court.[32] In another conflict, María del Valle and Tiburcia Rodríguez accused washer Manuel Yec of robbing del Valle of ten pesos at a Chinese laundry in Nogales, Sonora (across from Nogales, Arizona), in 1919. The worker upheld his position as an honorable member of the community, and the court dismissed the case for lack of evidence.[33]

Chinese also often formed ties with marginalized indigenous peoples. The Mayo, who have historically lived in the Río Mayo Valley in southern Sonora, frequented Chinese stores in Navojoa and the surrounding area. Alfonso Wong Fang came into contact with Mayos in his everyday life as well as during business dealings at Ching Chong y Compañía. The Yaqui, whose ancestral home was central and northern Sonora and southern Arizona, shopped at Chinese businesses in towns such as the port of Guaymas. As local historian Juan Ramírez Cisneros has noted, in the first part of the twentieth century, it was typical, especially on weekends, to see many Yaquis—particularly women—shopping at Fu Pau Hermanos, one of the most important businesses in Guaymas, among other Chinese stores. Yaquis, he wrote, "preferred that business for the simple reason that its owners, Agustín and Pablo, two gentlemanly Chinese who were impeccably dressed in suits, attended [to the Yaquis] personally, speaking to them in their own language, which [Agustín and Pablo] commanded as perfectly as they did Spanish, so much so that, as someone who knew them once remarked, they spoke in a highly educated manner."[34] Marta Elia Lau de Salazar's father, Concepción Lau Wong, also formed economic and social bonds with Yaquis in the small southern community of Bacobampo, located on the Río Mayo, near Navojoa. Lau Wong had migrated to Sonora from Guangdong Province and married Preciliana Yocupicio. Born in 1935, the couple's first child, Marta Elia, recalled that her father got along well with Yaquis, learned to speak their language, and hired them as laborers in his agricultural fields.[35] Chinese in Sonora not only became skilled businessmen who knew well how to draw on Yaquis both as customers and workers but also developed a hybrid sensibility. They formed new cultural and linguistic practices as they learned Spanish, Yaqui, and other indigenous languages to interact with their neighbors.

Marriages and Unions

Chinese men and Mexican women in Sonora formed an array of relationships between the 1910s and early 1930s. Mexican women married working-class as well as middle-class Chinese men who owned businesses.[36] These relationships began in a number of ways. Men and women met simply by going about their daily lives, as women shopped or worked in Chinese businesses. In some cases, women's families disapproved of such relationships, and they were conducted in secret. In other instances, families negotiated unions between their daughters and Chinese men, with both parties seeking social and/or economic stability.[37]

Marriages to Mexican women helped Chinese men claim a place in Sonoran society. Manuel Foo was married to Celia Gil de Foo in Santa Ana, a north-central town, when authorities arrested him for producing and selling opium in his home in 1924. They initially detained Celia but soon released her. She resided at the Hotel Reforma in nearby Magdalena while she cared for a health matter during the time of the case. The Foos portrayed the head of the household as a good, upstanding, law-abiding family man: Foo worked to support his family and had never trafficked in drugs. Gil de Foo registered with authorities her utter disbelief that her husband had done anything contrary to the law. The couple proved their innocence, and the court ultimately fined another Chinese man, José Juan, who had lived with the Foos during the previous year, 150 pesos. Juan's countrymen took up a collection to pay his fine, an example of the mutual aid networks and social organizations that Chinese men had established in Sonora.[38]

Chinese agricultural growers and their workers arranged marriages for social and economic security and so that the children would eventually work on the land. Luis Chan Valenzuela was born in Hermosillo in 1933 to a Chinese man, José Chan, and a Yaqui woman, Dolores Valenzuela Romero. Her father worked on Chan's agricultural lands near Hermosillo, where he had settled after migrating to Sonora from Guangdong Province. Although the marriage had been arranged, Valenzuela Chan told her son, Luis Chan Valenzuela, that she and her husband were happy together.[39] The union of Candelaria Wilson, a Mexican woman with some American ancestry, and Manuel Loyetoía, a Chinese immigrant who had naturalized as a Mexican citizen, was probably also arranged. Wilson was fifteen years old and Loyetoía, an agricultural grower in southeastern Sonora, was thirty-four. Her father, Epigmenio Wilson, and Loyetoía appealed to local judge Ramón T. Mendivil, who performed the civil ceremony on 21 June 1930, at Rancho del Sombrerito, a community near the small southeastern Spanish colonial town of Alamos.[40] In this way, Chinese men integrated into rural society and took part in the long-standing tradition of arranged marriages in the countryside.[41]

While some Sonoran families went to great lengths to guarantee that their daughters married Chinese men, others forbade such romantic ties. Delfina Siqueiros maintained a clandestine relationship with Roberto Chong in the northeastern town of Nacozari de García. In 1924, Siqueiros's father, Don Agustín Siqueiros, accused Chong of breaking and entering into his home. Delfina's brother, Jesús Siqueiros, had perceived Chong as an intruder and attacked him. Authorities arrested Chong, who spent two weeks in jail before Frank Fong of the local business operation Frank Fong and Brothers put up his home, worth seven thousand pesos, for his compatriot's release. Chong had failed to obtain the head of the household's permission to enter the residence. Describing his *confianza* with Delfina, Chong said that he had visited on previous occasions because his girlfriend had invited him. To maintain her honor and obey her parents, Delfina Siqueiros denied both that she was his girlfriend and that she had invited him into the home.[42]

Chong soon produced a photograph of himself with Delfina, a small black-and-white image showing a smiling man standing side by side with a smiling, lighter-skinned woman who looked coyly away. The new evidence led authorities to call her back to court, but her family had moved her to Douglas, Arizona, across the border from Agua Prieta, Sonora. Chong's defense attorney, José C. Arvisu, nonetheless argued that the photograph was irrefutable evidence that his client and Delfina Siqueiros had been involved in an amorous relationship. The image revealed that Chong and Siqueiros had enjoyed "an idyllic love," as they appeared to be "in perfect oneness." Their relationship had developed while she worked in his *dulcería* (candy shop). Arvisu further contended that Don Siqueiros, under outside influences, had accused Chong to divert attention from the damage that Jesús Siqueiros had inflicted on the Chinese man. The court sentenced Chong to four months in prison and a fine of fifty pesos, finding that his entrance into the house through a side door was unacceptable, regardless of Delfina Siqueiros's invitation. Chong appealed, however, and was ultimately declared not guilty.[43] The photograph and Siqueiros's disappearance were enough to convince authorities that Chong's actions fell within the bounds of Mexican law. In the end, the court upheld a woman's right to form a union with a Chinese man, even if it defied patriarchal authority in her home—another sign of modernization.[44]

Antonia Wong Enríquez de López's parents also had a secret relationship in Sonora. Her father, Felipe Wong Ley, had migrated to the state from Guangdong Province and worked as a medic in the central town of Baviácora, where he met the much younger Ester Enríquez Andrade. Disapproving of their daughter's relationship with an older Chinese man, Enríquez Andrade's family moved to Nogales. But the love between Wong Ley and Enríquez Andrade, abetted by the girl's younger sister, kept them together. In 1927, the couple headed south to marry in Mocorito, Sinaloa. Shortly thereafter, Wong Ley and Enríquez Andrade moved back to Sonora and their first daughter, Antonia, was born in Baviácora in 1928. Enríquez Andrade's family ultimately accepted the marriage.[45]

Like all human relationships, Chinese Mexican ties were complicated and could be fraught with hostility. Chinese men and Mexican women at times went to court over domestic disputes. José Tang, a Chinese man who had naturalized as a Mexican citizen, and his lover, Clemencia Martínez, were living together in Magdalena in 1929 when a fourteen-year-old, Sofía Alvarez, accused the couple of kidnapping her infant son. The baby had been born out of wedlock and bore a surname different from hers, she said, because Tang and Martínez had taken advantage of her state of poverty and inexperience. "Tang," the surname listed on her son's birth certificate, Alvarez decried, "far from belongs to him." While working as a domestic servant in the Tang-Martínez home, Alvarez had mentioned to the couple that she planned to take her unregistered child to the civil registry. Instead, Tang and Martínez seized the opportunity to do so themselves. Furthermore, they had forced her out of their house and kept her son behind locked doors.[46]

Tang argued that Alvarez had lived in his house as a guest rather than a *criada* (servant), after having asked to reside there because she lacked the resources to care for her young child. Tang had never told Alvarez to leave; on the contrary, she had abandoned her son to travel to Nogales, Sonora. He denied keeping the child away from his mother, nor had Alvarez tried to retrieve her son; if she had, however, he would have refused to save the child from suffering as a consequence of his mother's "poco decoroso" (indecent) way of life. Tang had subsequently perceived himself as being obligated to care for Alvarez's son but insisted that he would return the boy if authorities ordered him to do so. The court dismissed the case, noting that officials were unable to formulate a reasonable accusation against Tang.[47]

Prostitution

Chinese men and Mexican female sex workers also formed complex and diverse relationships in Sonora. Mexican authorities had created *zonas de tolerancia*, well-defined and limited areas that tolerated prostitution (red-light districts) in an effort to contain vice during the revolutionary era. In Sonora, the government of Francisco S. Elías regulated the zones in 1922, and subsequent administrations attempted to control sex work until Lázaro Cárdenas abolished regulations on prostitution in 1940.[48] The zones bred romantic and economic ties and conflicts during the early twentieth century.

Violence and tragedy were sometimes inescapable for people on the margins of society whose lives were tied up with vice. Enríque Ley Ton's relationship with Mercedes Juárez ended sadly in 1930 when she died of gunshot wounds in the hotel room in Magdalena where she had lived and worked as a prostitute. Ley Ton, her lover and the Chinese owner of the Hotel Reforma, became a suspect in her murder. Relying mainly on the testimony of female sex workers in the hotel, the prosecution held him to the same social-sexual obligations required of all men in Mexico, arguing that he had "failed to uphold the consideration he owed the deceased given her sex and because, as his lover, she should have been under his protection." In his defense, Ley Ton said that he and Juárez had had a disagreement when she took out a gun and threatened him. Fearing for his life, he had fled to a nearby casino, where he soon heard a shot. When he returned to the hotel and saw her lying on her bed, her clothes stained in blood, a deep sense of anguish enveloped him. He wept uncontrollably at her side. He had always loved and would never have harmed her.[49]

The couple had lived together for more than a year. Juárez's mother, believing that Ley Ton was innocent, said that he had been very good to her daughter. She had witnessed firsthand his love for her child, especially while the couple had stayed with her. The mother also knew that her daughter had had a violent, jealous, and highly anxious nature. She had once become so severely ill after an angry fit, a "boiling of the blood," that she was bedridden for five days. By the end of the episode, the white part of Juárez's eyes and her hands and nails had yellowed. The court ultimately found that she had taken her own life and dismissed the case against Ley Ton.[50]

Chinese Mexican Cultural Formation

Over time, and through the myriad relationships they forged, Chinese and Mexicans created a new cultural category—Chinese Mexican. As they built relationships and hybrid families, distinct cultural, linguistic, and culinary mixtures emerged that have persisted in modern Sonora. Lau de Salazar described the special ear for linguistic fusion that her family acquired because of her father and their culturally fluid household. Speaking Cantonese, Spanish, and English in addition to Yaqui, Lau Wong blended sounds and words from the different languages. As a result, the family developed particular skills for understanding unconventional linguistic forms. For example, Lau de Salazar had a "gringo" uncle (a gringo being an American or Mexican person living in the United States, or an Americanized Mexican) who could be understood by no one in the extended family or community other than Lau de Salazar and her sisters. Since their father also spoke *mocho* (broken Spanish), they easily understood their uncle. Chinese Mexican families such as Lau Wong's developed creative approaches to language and helped establish Sonora's hybrid culture and society. The family also produced new culinary traditions. Except for the time when Lau Wong lived in Sonora secretly during the expulsion period, he did most of the household's cooking, and many of his dishes included rice and beets, staples in the meals of his upbringing. His wife, Yocupicio, in turn, developed an exceptional Chinese Mexican cooking style while her husband was in hiding and after he died. As a consequence of the beets she adopted from his cooking, her local dishes, such as *chilorio* and *chicharrones*, often came out dark red and were distinct from other native varieties. She formed a new cuisine by combining aspects of Cantonese and southern Sonoran as well as Sinaloan culinary practices.[51]

Chinese Mexican families and enterprises in modern Sonora underscore the importance of the Chinese and the relationships they established with Mexicans in the late nineteenth and early twentieth centuries. The numerous well-liked Chinese Mexican restaurants in contemporary Sonora are a tribute to this history. Well-respected and known by many in the society, restaurateurs enjoy a certain status in local communities. Fernando Ma's popular restaurant, Jo Wah, has operated in Hermosillo for almost fifty years. Although his family had wanted him to stay in Mexicali, where they resettled after repatriating following World War II, he moved to Sonora to open the restaurant in the 1960s. He visited Mexico City and met his wife, who had come to Mexico from Hong Kong, during the 1968 Olympics. They married in the Mexican capital and traveled together to Hermosillo, where they later had a son and a daughter. When asked how he conceived of his identity, he discussed the many Chinese associations that have historically existed throughout Mexico and most prominently in Mexicali. Chinese ambassadors and private citizens tied to these organizations have often visited him at his restaurant. Calling himself both Mexican and Chinese Mexican, he noted that while he enjoyed their visits, they were unimportant to his identity: He had no need for them. Moreover, the Cantonese-speaking Ma had difficulty communicating with the Mandarin-speaking visitors. In his view, Chinese Mexicans, whom he calls "café con leche" (coffee with cream), have easily learned Spanish and blended into Mexican society because they have "Mexican blood in their veins." Born in Mexico, Ma came of age in China and returned to Mexico when he was around twenty; he claims Mexico as his primary homeland.[52]

Felipe Wong Enríquez's restaurant, Hong Kong, and Cristóbal Chua Wong's establishment, Chao's Garden, have likewise become renowned in the Sonoran capital. Both restaurateurs are well respected among Sonorans. Numerous people I met at local archives, universities, museums, and associations told me about the two men and suggested that I visit their businesses and meet them. Chua Wong's notions of identity and the connections he draws between Chinese and Mexican cultural norms are indicative of his complex sense of belonging. Expressing a strong Chinese Mexican pride, he first pointed out that his ancestors underwent great hardship when they were expelled before saying that he has nonetheless felt at home in Sonora. Concepts of the family and the corresponding notions of unity and obligation, as well as ideas of luck and death, have bridged the two sets of cultural tradition for Chua Wong. For example, he recounted, in Mexico and China alike, people customarily honor the dead both in homes and public spaces, and these rituals often include food. Chua Wong has found it important to teach his children about their cross-cultural heritage. His wife is Mexican, and since their children grew up in Sonora and are "only 25 percent Chinese," he has been especially committed to imparting Chinese culture and taking them to visit China; the family had recently traveled to Beijing.[53]

Establishing a novel enterprise that underscores the importance of Chinese immigrants in Sonoran history and culture, José de Jesús Tapia Martens and Jorge Tapia Martens's family developed a distinctive Chinese Mexican culinary tradition that younger generations have carried on. Following in their grandfather's and father's footsteps as businessmen, the brothers have for years prepared and sold their family's special Lau Ket Chorizo Chino in Hermosillo and the surrounding areas; operating by word of mouth, they sell the product out of their homes or by special order. As local archivist Carlos Lucero Aja and I sat at his kitchen table in the Sonoran capital, José de Jesús Tapia Martens prepared the delicious *chorizo chino* while describing the family's history. The dish's emergence framed the story, helping Tapia Martens weave the narrative of his family history. The food was named for their grandfather, Lau Ket, who arrived in Sonora via San Francisco as a young boy and later became a businessman. On a commercial trip to San Miguel de Horcasitas, a small town near Hermosillo, he met Ernestina Carranza Campillo, and the couple later married. They eventually had several children, one of whom was Tapia Martens's father, Francisco Lau Tapia. An older Chinese man, a comrade of the grandfather who became a good friend to his children, passed on the recipe to the siblings. Continuing the family tradition, the brothers eventually learned it from their uncles and aunts. José de Jesús Tapia Martens remembered the older man as a fun-loving person who enjoyed smoking and gambling. He maintained strong kinship bonds with three generations of the family.[54]

Prepared with liquor, honey, soy sauce, and other ingredients, *chorizo chino* is a pork sausage dish known by different names in Sonora and other places where Chinese have settled. But Lau Ket Chorizo Chino has a unique, secret recipe that has evolved over the years. The Tapia Martens siblings grew up eating it over rice, and, since it was one of their favorite foods, they thought others would also enjoy it. They attribute their success in selling it to Sonorans' love of Chinese Mexican food and more specifically of Sonoran Cantonese mixtures of flavors and spices. Selling the dish has also offered the Tapia Martenses a way to honor their grandfather and father while earning a living. Participating in cross-border commercial enterprises like their grandfather and father, the Tapia Martens brothers are third-generation Sonoran businessmen. Making, selling, and continuing to enjoy the family's special *chorizo chino* has been an expression of pride in their Chinese ancestry. It has kept alive the memory of their grandfather and father as well as the history of their close friends and compatriots.[55] Lau Ket Chorizo Chino has become a living document, a testament to the cultural and economic importance of Chinese in the history of Sonora.

Chinese men settled in Sonora around the turn of the twentieth century, either as a consequence of opportunities in the rising border economy or because they were prohibited from entering the United States after Chinese exclusion in 1882. They became crucial in the state's economic development and modernization. By creating myriad and complex ties with local Mexicans, they became part of Sonoran and Mexican society. Marriages and unions with Mexican women helped Chinese men become integrated into local communities and contributed to the success of their businesses. While some Mexican families frowned on romantic associations with Chinese, others sought out these men as partners for their daughters to ensure economic stability for their families and the next generation. New hybrid Chinese Mexican cultural practices that survive to the present began to take shape as Chinese formed mixed-race families. While some Mexicans developed bonds with Chinese, others from the same social and economic classes organized against them. Sonorans would soon become deeply split along these lines. As the anti-Chinese movement emerged in Sonora, Mexicans and Chinese—and Chinese Mexican families—drew on the available resources to confront the movement's inherently vicious racism.

CHAPTER TWO

Chinos, Antichinistas, Chineras, and *Chineros*

The Anti-Chinese Movement in Sonora and Chinese Mexican
Responses, 1910s–Early 1930s

In 1917, Juan R. Mexía wrote to José María Arana, the founder of the first organized anti-Chinese campaign in Sonora and, by extension, in Mexico to urge the leader of the movement to visit Mexía's unnamed community. Mexía had heard Arana speak in Nogales, Sonora, and believed that one of his speeches would be advantageous in Mexía's town, where "contented Asians are united by indissoluble bonds of friendship and caring with some Mexicans who have forgotten their true roles."[1] He hoped that Arana's charismatic anti-Chinese rhetoric would inspire local Chinese-friendly Mexicans, whom anti-Chinese crusaders derided as *chineras* and *chineros* (Chinese-loving individuals), to break their bonds with Chinese.

Destroying the strong Chinese-Mexican ties that had developed in Sonora over the previous decades became a central anti-Chinese goal. Mexicans and Chinese nonetheless sustained their relationships during the era of anti-Chinese organizing in Sonora, which lasted from the Mexican Revolution through the Great Depression. *Antichinistas* failed to recruit all Mexicans to their cause. Rather, a chasm opened in local communities and the larger state. Groups of Mexican campaigners worked against the small but highly visible Chinese population, paying special attention to Chinese-Mexican liaisons. Other Mexicans, by contrast, used

39

their local cultural, economic, and organizational resources to maintain their connections with Chinese, often with the support of local authorities and communities. Attesting to the strength of their relationships, Chinese Mexicans carried on with their lives in spite of severe and increasing hatred and persecution.

When Mexican workers began to return from the United States during the depression, some Mexicans scorned the Chinese as undesirable foreigners who took jobs and resources from "real" Mexicans—an ironic mirror of the sentiment against Mexicans in the United States. Since the Chinese had established businesses and become a visible petit bourgeois class, they were an easy scapegoat for the economic troubles that beset Sonoran communities.

The Mexican Revolution of 1910 and the Anti-Chinese Movement

The Chinese had experienced prejudice since they first arrived in Sonora in the late nineteenth century. Negative attitudes and jokes abounded, and for more than fifteen years, an anti-Chinese newspaper circulated.[2] Some Mexicans perceived Chinese as different and foreign. North American and European immigrants were insulated from this pattern by the legacy of Spanish colonialism and by Sonoran notions of ethnic distinctiveness that privileged lighter-skinned foreigners. Even so, anti-Chinese sentiment was neither widespread nor organized in Sonora until the revolutionary era.[3]

The revolution set into motion vast social change, however. Among the transformations it brought were challenges to traditional gender norms. Social revolutions have often allowed people to question sexual mores. As all members of the society—men, women, and children—mobilize in support of the struggle, people become freer to forge new types of relationships. After the violent phase of a revolution ends, people engage in more "personal" conflicts over social norms.[4] In this way, the Mexican Revolution made it ever more possible for Mexican women and Chinese men, as well as Mexicans and Chinese more generally, to form new connections, angering some Sonorans.

The fighting and chaos of the Mexican Revolution did not forestall Chinese immigration to Mexico.[5] In Sonora, the revolution allowed Chinese businesses to flourish because most Mexican men were active in civil conflicts and had no opportunity to establish enterprises to compete with Chinese shops. As towns as well as mining and railroad communities continued to need goods and services, revolutionaries of all factions relied on the provisions Chinese supplied. As foreigners, the Chinese maintained a neutral position and thus could cater to all of the revolutionary splinter groups without much difficulty. Further strengthening their position, Chinese establishments replaced German, French, and Spanish entrepreneurs who left Mexico as traditional trade connections with Europe diminished during World War I, which overlapped with the revolution.[6]

The Mexican Revolution and Mexican outmigration, partially as a consequence of U.S. labor shortages during World War I, set notions of race, citizenship, and *mestizaje* in flux. Revolutionaries repudiated the Porfirian tradition of privileging foreigners and fair-skinned Mexicans. Some Sonorans began increasingly to resent Chinese and their purportedly undeserved economic success. In 1916, about twenty people founded the Commercial Association of Businessmen in the small northern mining town of Magdalena.[7] Led by Arana, the group proposed to defend "Mexican" merchants and rid Sonora of Chinese business owners. This action signaled the beginning of an organized anti-Chinese movement in Mexico. It is significant that the campaigns started in Sonora, and more specifically Magdalena, a town very near the Mexican-U.S. border. Mexican men had left Magdalena to fight in the revolution or work in the United States.[8] Some local people grumbled that Chinese men had filled the void, "stealing" both capital and women that rightfully belonged to Mexican men. Anxiety over the sex imbalance among Mexicans fueled anti-Chinese sentiment. Spreading quickly, anti-Chinese campaigns in Sonora, like those in California during the 1860s and 1870s, portrayed the Chinese as dangerous outsiders who had infringed on rightful citizens' domain.[9]

These campaigns were organized by working- and middle-class Mexicans, members of the same social and economic groups that had formed bonds with Chinese. *Antichinistas* focused on Chinese-Mexican relationships, arguing that romantic unions and marriages in particular threatened the integrity of the Mexican race and nation. Anti-Chinese activists labeled Mexicans who maintained ties with or were kind to Chinese *chineras* and *chineros*, terms that appeared in Arana's speeches and communications and in his newspaper, *Pro-Patria*, as early as 1917.[10] Spending enormous time and resources on their struggle, anti-Chinese proponents recruited people, organized protests and boycotts, and published stunning amounts of *antichinista* propaganda. One drawing depicted a gigantic dragon emerging from Asia and stretching across the Pacific, with one

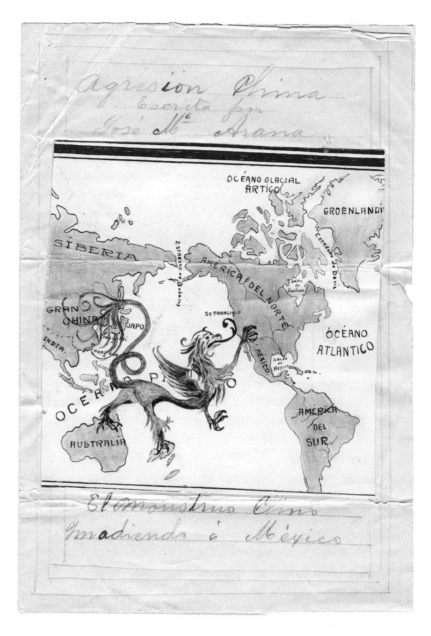

Anti-Chinese Dragon Map. From 1917 Folder, Papers of José María Arana,
Special Collections, University of Arizona. Used with permission.

......y quienes no oyeren mis palabras, mañana llorarán la agonía de la Patria que fuimos incapaces de defender.

José María Arana.

Anti-Chinese Drawing. "Mexicano." The banner in front of the gesturing speaker says, "Mexican man: Of every peso you spend buying from a Chinaman, fifty cents go to Shanghai and the other fifty keep you in chains and prostitute the women of your race!!!" The caption below the picture says, ". . . and those who do not hear my words will lament tomorrow the agony of the Motherland we failed to defend." From José Angel Espinoza, *El ejemplo de Sonora* (Mexico City: n.p., 1932).

of its arms reaching menacingly toward Mexico. Another illustration portrayed Arana appealing to his followers to boycott Chinese businesses because they benefited China instead of Mexico, limited Mexican men's economic opportunities, and financed the abuse of Mexican women. *Antichinistas* bred hatred through a highly racialized and gendered polemics that played on people's fears by invoking images of invasion and domination by a dangerous and alien force.[11]

The anti-Chinese movement gained vigor along with the revolution. Mexico's long and complex history of colonialism and a racial hierarchy that favored lighter-skinned people and denigrated darker-skinned indigenous peoples and mestizos meant that the ground was fertile for the exclusion of Chinese and other unwanted foreigners, as activists imagined

La noche de bodas.....

y cinco años después

Anti-Chinese Drawing. "The wedding night . . . and five years later." From José Angel Espinoza, *El ejemplo de Sonora* (Mexico City: n.p., 1932).

and worked to reclaim an indigenous and mestizo Mexico.[12] Revolutionaries developed the ideology of *indigenismo*—the belief that the nation needed to honor and embrace its indigenous as well as mestizo character—as they renounced the Díaz regime. In spite of such rhetoric, however, Mexico continued to marginalize indigenous peoples during the revolutionary and postrevolutionary eras. But this ongoing practice required a dramatic shift in the dominant rhetoric as a result of broader changes in the thinking about the Mexican nation, race, and citizenry. Since elites developed the notion, "the Indians themselves were the objects, not the authors, of *indigenismo*." This ideology became incorporated into the new regime's official philosophy. Drawing on *indigenismo*, the discourse of *mestizaje*—the concept of Mexico's heritage of racial and cultural mixture—emphasized the nation's indigenous spirit.[13] *Mestizaje* crystallized during the revolution and has since been the centerpiece of modern Mexican nationalism.

Mexican nationalist Manuel Gamio (1883–1960) theorized a new vision of the nation to unify its incongruent citizens during the revolutionary era; a tract advocating cultural assimilation, *Forjando patria* (1916), and other works helped establish him as a key theorist of Mexican nationhood. In time, revolutionary ideology gave rise to a view of the mestizo as neither Indian nor European but Mexican in essence. Celebrating the ways that

¡Ah infeliz!. . . . Creíste disfrutar de una vida barata al entregarte a un chino y eres
una esclava y el fruto de tu error es un escupitajo de la naturaleza . . . .

Anti-Chinese Drawing. "¡Ah Infeliz!" The caption printed with the picture says, "Oh
wretched one! You thought you would enjoy an easy life upon surrendering yourself
to a Chinaman, and now you are a slave and the fruit of your error is a freak of nature."
From José Angel Espinoza, *El ejemplo de Sonora* (Mexico City: n.p., 1932).

the European and indigenous past had enriched the Mexican people, these
nascent ideas of Mexicanness ignored or disparaged Chinese and other
Asians as well as Africans.[14]

One of Mexico's most important thinkers of the early twentieth century,
José Vasconcelos (1881–1959), theorized Mexican *mestizaje* in the postrevolutionary era. In *La raza cósmica* (1925), Vasconcelos explored the question of whether unlimited and inevitable racial mingling had positive or
deleterious effects not just on the nation but on the world. He compared
historical periods of relative racial homogeneity with those of more inten-
sive racial mixture. The Egyptians, for example, built a second and more
advanced and impressive empire after a period of racial amalgamation.
Moreover, the history of Europe, which Vasconcelos saw as the fount of
modern culture, had involved significant racial fusion. After treating a

MUJER MEXICANA:—Si la locura o la ignorancia te hace esposa o manceba de un chino y éste te quiere llevar a su patria, antes que resolverte a seguirlo apura una dósis de veneno o clávate un puñal en el corazón......

Anti-Chinese Drawing. "Mujer Mexicana." A dire warning underscores the image: "Mexican woman: If madness or ignorance makes you the wife or concubine of a Chinaman and he wants to take you to his homeland, before resolving to follow him take a dose of poison or thrust a dagger into your heart." From José Angel Espinoza, *El ejemplo de Sonora* (Mexico City: n.p., 1932).

number of historical cases, Vasconcelos determined that the mingling of similar lineages had positive effects. When dissimilar races fused, the impact could also be beneficial, but a new and productive race would take longer to form in such cases. Even contradictory or counterintuitive mixtures had the potential to become positive, especially if aided by spiritual uplift. Indeed, the Asian races were in decline, he diagnosed, as a result of isolationism and the failure to Christianize. Conversely, Christianity had helped indigenous societies advance "from cannibalism to relative civilization" in a few centuries. Nonetheless, the Americas had become home to four races—white, red, black, and yellow—and needed them all. A "fifth race," enriched by the "treasures of all of the previous ones," had come into being in the Americas—"the last race, the cosmic race." Still, Vasconcelos privileged European elements. Mexico, Peru, and Columbia, he contended, were centers of civilization during the colonial period. After independence, Mexico descended into chaos, from which he believed it had not fully escaped at the time of his writing. Argentina, however, had flourished after independence as a consequence of its sturdy European foundation, making it the strongest and most beautiful country in Latin America.

TABLE 2. Sonora's Population and Sex Ratio by Sex and Working Age, 1910 and 1921

1910: TOTAL POPULATION (ALL AGES): 265,383

Age	Men	Women	Difference
15–19	13,306	15,131	1,825 more women
20–24	13,880	12,456	1,424 more men
25–29	13,741	12,762	979 more men
30–34	8,984	6,905	2,079 more men
35–39	9,829	8,199	1,630 more men
40–44	5,058	3,867	1,191 more men

1921: TOTAL POPULATION (ALL AGES): 270,707

Age	Men	Women	Difference
15–19	13,638	15,915	2,277 more women
20–24	13,343	14,046	703 more women
25–29	10,944	11,368	424 more women
30–34	8,908	8,725	183 more men
35–39	8,835	7,897	938 more men
40–44	7,076	6,731	345 more men

Source: Departamento de la Estadística Nacional, Censo General de Habitantes, 30 November 1921, State of Sonora.

Note: Anyone over the age of fifteen could be considered working age. Changes in the sex ratio of people in their twenties between 1910 and 1921 reflected the departure of younger Mexican men as a consequence of the Mexican Revolution and World War I, which caused labor shortages in the United States and thus drew Mexicans there.

As Alan Knight and Gerardo Rénique have shown, anti-Chinese ideology followed naturally from *indigenismo* and celebratory *mestizaje* and helped tie Sonora to the nation during the formative postrevolutionary era.[15]

As they elaborated their ideology of hate in the same period, Sonoran public intellectuals such as José Angel Espinoza helped create a racial panic by taking the ideas of Vasconcelos and others to their logical, if frightening, conclusions. Espinoza and others imagined Mexico as facing the serious threat of an undesirable and inassimilable Chinese "race." They took deeply to heart Vasconcelos's notion that the "Asian races" were in declension but ignored his idea that even "undesirable" mixtures could become "productive" races in time. It made no matter to them that some Chinese men had become deeply Mexicanized—marrying local women, learning Spanish, becoming naturalized, and even adopting Catholicism to varying extents. A handful of leaders and the intelligentsia of the anti-Chinese campaigns cultivated an unequivocal and unrelenting hatred for all Chinese and the Mexicans with whom they had forged connections.

Anti-Chinese Policy

Although its power would never be total, the anti-Chinese movement's tentacles stretched further and further over time as it infiltrated state and national politics. Plutarco Elías Calles, the governor of Sonora from 1915 to 1919, became an avowed anti-Chinese ideologue (although Calles's ethnic background included Middle Eastern heritage), and Arana praised Calles's support of the anti-Chinese movement. Arana served as *presidente municipal* (mayor) of Magdalena from 1918 until his death by poisoning two years later. In 1919, Adolfo de la Huerta, backed by Calles, became governor and publicly endorsed anti-Chinese politics. Huerta, like Calles, supported the publication of Arana's *Pro-Patria* and the formation of additional anti-Chinese committees. Anti-Chinese leaders Espinoza and Alejandro C. Villaseñor became elected officials during the next decade. In 1925, the Anti-Chinese Convention in Hermosillo created the Liga Nacionalista Pro-Raza (Pro-Race Nationalist League), an umbrella organization for the country's anti-Chinese committees. Sonoran, Sinaloan, and Baja Californian representatives in Congress, with the help of the Liga, became an anti-Chinese voting bloc. As a congressional representative, Espinoza established the Steering Committee of the Anti-Chinese Campaign to function as a branch of the Partido Nacional Revolucionario (National Revolutionary Party).[16]

As Sonoran anti-Chinese politicians expanded their base, the "Sonora Dynasty" carried *antichinismo* to the national stage. Calles served as Mexico's president between 1924 and 1928 and then became the *jefe máximo* (supreme chief) of the Mexican Revolution for six years, the period known as the "Maximato." Although other men were officially the national leaders, Calles's role as *jefe máximo* accorded him great power over the presidencies of Emilio Portes Gil (1928–30), Pascual Ortiz Rubio (1930–32), and Abelardo Rodríguez (1932–34).[17] During Ortiz Rubio's administration, someone chalked on the gate of the president's castle, "The president lives here. The man in charge lives across the way," referring to the Calles home in Chapultepec.[18]

Members of Calles's family, who shared his anti-Chinese hatred, also controlled Sonora. Calles's uncle, Francisco S. Elías, served as governor from 1929 to 1931, and his successor, Calles's son, Rodolfo Elías Calles, held the post from 1931 to 1934, during which time he enacted the massive expulsion of Chinese.[19] Thus, anti-Chinese politicians exerted enormous influence both in Sonora and at the national level during the 1920s and early 1930s. Anti-Chinese activity nonetheless was most significant at the local and regional levels rather than in the national arena.[20]

Indeed, the extremity of anti-Chinese dogma was most palpable in Sonora when it became subsumed into state legislation. In 1919, Governor de la Huerta oversaw passage of a labor law that included among its provisions the requirement that enterprises owned by foreigners employ 80 percent Mexicans (defined by race and citizenship, since many Chinese had naturalized as Mexican citizens). A few years later, Villaseñor introduced two anti-Chinese proposals in the state legislature, and both passed unanimously in December 1923: Law 27 set out to create Chinatowns (although they never materialized), and Law 31 banned marriages and unions, which *antichinistas* called "illicit friendships," between Chinese men and Mexican women.[21] The law explicitly applied to Chinese men who had naturalized as citizens, a common practice.[22] Municipal officials were responsible for enforcing the ban and had the authority to fine violators between one hundred and five hundred pesos. While authorities never enforced Law 27, they punished people who violated Law 31, albeit in an uneven manner. In the spring of 1924, Mexican federal officials communicated to the state government their objections to the two Sonoran anti-Chinese laws.[23]

Racialized and Gendered Stereotypes of Chinese

In the context of changing views of Mexican identity and who did and did not fit, anti-Chinese activists developed a number of stereotypes about the economic, racial, and sexual threat that the Chinese posed to the Mexican people and nation. *Antichinistas* argued that Chinese were greedy and dishonest businessmen. Associating them with filth and vice, anti-Chinese crusaders believed that Chinese endangered public health and drugged and poisoned people with toxic, alien substances. Portraying Chinese men as brutal and unfeeling, *antichinistas* declared that they habitually abused their Mexican wives, lovers, and children, both physically and sexually, and prostituted girls and women. The children of Chinese-Mexican unions were depicted as diseased and degenerate mongrels.

Although Chinese in Sonora used local economic networks and their enterprises benefited Mexicans, anti-Chinese activists exaggerated the Chinese economic success and created a caricature of the Chinese grabber. They feared that working-class Mexicans had become economically dependent on the Chinese. In 1919, Reynaldo Villalobos lamented to Arana that "the Chinese man's immense capital has been dispersed among *chineros* who . . . are determined to defend them because those wretched unpatriotic souls do not have any other way to earn a living."[24]

Anti-Chinese activists often cast *chineros* as more threatening than the Chinese themselves. Using nationalist rhetoric, activists argued that these Mexicans had sold out both themselves and their fellow Mexicans. A propaganda poster depicting "The Chineros in Action" warned that *chineros* were "allied with Chinese" and therefore the "eternal enemies" of Mexicans. Circulating in Nogales, Sonora, in February 1924, the poster denounced a pro-Chinese piece that had attacked Congressman Villaseñor. *Antichinistas* maintained that Chinese had compensated pro-Chinese Mexicans to reproduce and pass out the propaganda against Villaseñor, whom they lauded as working for the good of the race and nation.[25]

Notions of class, race, and gender were inseparable in anti-Chinese ideology. The belief that Chinese men had taken capital and women that belonged to Mexican men remained a central theme throughout the anti-Chinese activism. Arana had been concerned with the *chinización* of working-class Mexican women and positioned them as what one scholar describes as "the vehicle for the penetration and contamination of the national organism." *Antichinistas* persistently represented women who formed bonds with Chinese as agents in the deterioration of the race and traitors to the nation.[26]

Anti-Chinese crusader Ramón García's propaganda piece, "Contact between Chinese Men and Mexican Women Is Dangerous," underscored the rampant sense of racial panic that plagued him and his brethren. It told the tale of local Chinese resident Pancho Jin and the Chinese men and Mexican women who worked at his cigar factory. This everyday contact vexed García: "The conniving Chinese, taking advantage of the absence of fathers and brothers, or their failure to notice, have made advances at women despite their gestures of rejection." While visiting the factory, he painfully observed "the familiarity with which women workers and the yellow-skinned treat each other." He left "indignant at hearing Chinese and Mexicans joking with each other as if they were equals!" Having learned that a female worker was involved in an "illicit friendship" with one of the "Mongols" and that their union was a secret from her family, he warned, "If we continue to tolerate the perilous daily contact between Mexican women and the hateful Asian microbe," such hidden relationships would continue unchecked and "our race will take rapid, giant steps toward ruin and degeneration." Before long, "children with slanted eyes and sickly constructions [will] emerge from the factory."[27] Anti-Chinese doctrine constructed a dual image of Mexican women: On one side lay those who were dangerously vulnerable to Chinese men; on the other were the women who were disturbingly comfortable with those men. At the same time, *antichinistas* disparaged Chinese Mexican children.

Espinoza, a key Sonoran anti-Chinese public intellectual and congressional representative, believed that Chinese men also jeopardized Mexican women's well-being by encroaching on the domestic sphere. In his view, Chinese men not only robbed Mexican men of jobs, compelling them to go to the United States in search of work, but also took employment opportunities from Mexican women. Chinese men thus upset the traditional gender system by performing duties—such as laundry service—that had been women's domain. Moreover, he argued, by establishing monopolies on domestic services, Chinese men had forced Mexican women to turn to prostitution to earn a living.[28]

Similarly concerned with prostitution, Alfredo G. Echeverría, a leading *antichinista* in Hermosillo, traveled to Mexicali, Baja California, to speak in 1927. Sonoran anti-Chinese activists had developed a special relationship with their counterparts in territorial Baja California, where the movement had spread by this time. Echeverría called for a moralizing campaign to rescue Mexican women from exploitation by foreigners—that is, the Chinese—in the corrupt social environment of the *zonas de tolerancia* (red-light districts). A local governmental edict had confined prostitution to certain areas and consequently put Mexican women at the service of Chinese men, whom he believed to have brought Mexico so many ills. Recent suppression of the *zona de tolerancia* in Mexicali, however, had pushed women to Chinese hotels, doubly subjecting them to exploitation by Chinese and expanding the area in which prostitution took place, according to Echeverría. (Mexican travelers, he added, often had no place to stay because Chinese hotel owners denied them rooms.) He contended that Mexican women's self-worth and patriotism had crumbled because they routinely became "infected by the false treatment and great quantities they receive from these men." Appealing to his fellow citizens to help save Mexican women's "dignity and love for what is national," he argued that Mexican men bore responsibility for shielding Mexican women from the Chinese manipulators and for preventing foreigners from profiting from vice in Mexico.[29]

Women's Campaigns

Some Sonoran women became powerful anti-Chinese proponents. In 1917, Professor María de Jesús Valdez told men, women, and girls in Magdalena that "the sacrosanct call of patriotism also burns in women's hearts." She ended her talk with a chant: "Down with the Chinese!!" She and other women would become crucial to the campaigns.[30]

By the mid-1920s, the anti-Chinese movement organized women into separate "female subcommittees" in the towns of Nogales, Cananea, Hermosillo, and elsewhere. The subcommittees sought to promote nationalism among women to dissuade them from entering into unions with Chinese men. In 1924, *antichinistas* met at a Nogales dance hall to recruit women. Drawing on female moral power to educate their sex, organizers believed that the propaganda developed by women offered one of the most "practical" means to achieve success for the campaigns. Advertisements invited "all the wives" of the "abnegated working classes" to a gathering that would feature anti-Chinese speeches on important themes, which "the good daughters of our national ground" were sure to find pertinent in their lives. By the following year, activists in Nogales had recruited sufficient women to the campaigns to hold an inauguration of the female subcommittees. They called on the public to attend the celebration, enjoy its speeches and musical pieces, and witness the enthusiasm with which "a group of Mexicans works for a nationalist cause." Anti-Chinese crusaders were anxious about those women who had formed romantic ties with Chinese men. They considered it a great boon to have on their side other women who could work more efficiently than male activists to prevent future Chinese-Mexican unions.[31]

Within a few years, female campaigns had also emerged in Mexicali, where local women enlisted the support of Sonorans during the depression years. In 1932, members of the Cooperativa Mexicana de Lavandería Antiasiática (Anti-Asian Mexican Laundry Cooperative) wrote to Mexican government employees and society at large to offer their "honest" laundry services. The women, declaring themselves Mexicans by birth, pled with fellow citizens to help them through the difficult times: "In the name of our sacred nationality, as a means of sustaining our families and at the same time cooperating with the government toward a solution to this problem, we speak to the hearts of all good Mexicans to safeguard us by giving us clothes to wash" instead of taking them to Chinese laundries. By providing key services to Mexicans at low prices, local Chinese had inhibited women's economic security and hindered "our national richness as well as our interests and pride as citizens." The women bewailed that so many families suffered because Mexicans had failed to help each other during the trying economic times and instead patronized Chinese businesses: "Who will dare believe that our children can learn in school when they suffer from malnutrition?" They signed their entreaty, "For the sons of Mexicali." Drawing on gender rights and obligations, they invoked family, children, food, and education to stir men's sympathies. Echeverría, who had founded an anti-Chinese organization in Baja California the same year, wrote to congratulate the women and inquire about the names and addresses of the members of the cooperative, adding that the Hermosillo campaign would use their laundry services at the first opportunity. He also informed them that his comrades hoped to follow their lead and open a similar business in their city that would employ only Mexican women.[32]

Insults

Anti-Chinese activists used long-standing notions of sexual propriety and deviance to malign Chinese men and the Mexican women with whom they formed bonds. Spanish colonizers had introduced the intertwined concepts of honor and shame to the northern borderlands of New Spain, and these ideas, embedded in the legal system, retained their purchase in modern northern Mexican society. Women's morality and sexual purity were important indicators of social position not only for a woman but also for her family and above all its male members.[33]

In the midst of Sonora's growing anti-Chinese climate, *chinera* became a formidable insult to a woman's honor by the 1920s. Conflicts arising from the use of the insult propelled people to go to court. For some people who had internalized anti-Chinese logic, the label connoted immorality, and they used the legal system to try to curtail its potential damage to their reputations. Those who brought suits argued that the public nature of the insults caused them undue humiliation. Women used *chinera* and related verbal assaults against other women who were romantically involved with Chinese men, but these offenses also became generalized insults. The courts tried, fined, and jailed women for leveling such insults at other women. While some women denied having had ties with Chinese, others admitted to them in court but nonetheless defended their honor. In so doing, they went against the grain of anti-Chinese logic.

In 1926, Rafaela A. Viuda de Ochoa was accused by her neighbor in Nogales, Josefina Sánchez de Sam Lee, the wife of a prominent Chinese businessman, of insulting her morality. Manuel Sam Lee owned the Manuel Sam Lee Produce Company, a vital enterprise in the border economy that sold large quantities of tomatoes and other vegetables wholesale to Mexicans and Americans. His wife told the court that A. Viuda de Ochoa had incessantly directed repugnant and injurious words at her and her younger sister, Carolina Sánchez, who also lived in the home, in a loud voice. Most recently, A. Viuda de Ochoa had called Sánchez de Sam Lee the *madrota* (madam) of a brothel that "receives Chinese, Japanese, American, and Mexican clients," had labeled the sisters rotten "hijas de la chingada" (daughters of the fucked woman), and had described Sam Lee as "a pimp who has to step aside so that other men can come and sleep" with his wife and her sister. Another neighbor, Elena Anaya, had heard A. Viuda de Ochoa yell numerous insults at Sánchez de Sam Lee, including calling her a "*chinera*, slut, who has a brothel that accepts Chinese." The diatribes had offended the sisters' honor, and they hoped the suit would bring an end to their undeserved public degradation.[34]

Unimpressed with anti-Chinese ideology that disparaged Chinese-Mexican marriages such as her own, Sánchez de Sam Lee defended her honor. The case occurred at the same time that anti-Chinese female subcommittees in her town tried to recruit local women to the cause and prevent further Chinese-Mexican unions; local *antichinistas* had just inaugurated the subcommittees in Nogales during the previous year. This and similar cases illustrated the deepening divide between *antichinistas* on one side and *chineras* and *chineros* on the other. Chinese-Mexican relationships continued even as anti-Chinese organizing grew more and more egregious throughout the 1920s.

As *chinera* retained its negative connotation, some women went to court when other women dredged up past relationships or simply insinuated that they were open to forming unions with Chinese men. Josefa Araiza accused her Magdalena neighbor, Argelia Barreras, of defamation along these lines in 1927. Barreras had insulted Araiza's honor by telling people that Barreras remembered when Araiza had lived with a Chinese man. Araiza appealed to the court to punish the offense because it had caused her dishonor and discredit.[35]

Other cases show that *chinera* became a generalized insult that had little if anything to do with women's relationships with Chinese men. Trinidad Valverde Viuda de Salazar charged her neighbor in Hermosillo, Josefina Bustillo de Woolfolk, with insults and defamation in 1929. When the two women left their homes simultaneously one day, Bustillo de Woolfolk loosed a barrage of crude expressions at Valverde Viuda de Salazar, only some of which she could bring herself to repeat in court: "public woman, *chinera* who wants to steal my husband," and "your mother is the madam" of a brothel. Valverde Viuda de Salazar testified that although she was intensely embarrassed at going before the court to defend her honor and dignity, her social position had obligated her to do so. Moreover, because the verbal assault had taken place in public, Bustillo de Woolfolk had exposed Valverde Viuda de Salazar to the disdain of all those who listened. Local residents José S. Palomares and Jesus Esquer testified that Bustillo de Woolfolk had called Valverde Viuda de Salazar a wretched, shameless *chinera* and "quitamaridos" (one who takes away other women's husbands), claimed that she was ignorant of her father's identity, and accused her mother of being a "madam." According to the two witnesses, Valverde Viuda de Salazar had refused to engage her hateful neighbor and made no response. Although Bustillo de Woolfolk denied the allegations, the court sentenced her to eight months in prison and a fine of three hundred pesos, which she appealed.[36]

In some cases growing anti-Chinese sentiment also influenced men who became involved in gendered insult cases. In 1927, Antonio Chan accused Pedro Mestas of insults, threats, and fraud in Nogales. Chan was Mexican by naturalization, a photographer who lived at his shop, Fotografía Moderna. Mestas, also a photographer, was from the southern town Navojoa and frequented Chan's store when he traveled north. Their business dealings soon developed into a friendship, and Chan loaned money to Mestas. The relationship soured, and the men exchanged letters airing their grievances, and with both ultimately feeling themselves injured. Chan had doubted that Mestas possessed the resources of which he boasted, since he had for so long failed to repay the small amount he owed the shop owner. Mestas replied that he should have expected such insults from a Chinese man, since his people were "a social plague" and "the biggest impediment we have in the nation." Mestas threatened to travel to Nogales to dare Chan to say to his face the insults in his letters and vowed to prove that he was "more honorable and more of a man" than his former friend. Mestas then confronted Chan on the street in Nogales, adding to his earlier invective and threats a description of Chan and his business as "mierda" (shit). Chan subsequently took the matter to court, where he argued that the Chinese were "laborious workers, and we try to comply to the fullest with the laws of this country that we have adopted as a second homeland." Relaying to officials Mestas's hotel and room number, he begged the court to take action before his nemesis returned to Navojoa that night.[37] Chan's defense claimed a place for himself in Sonoran society. In this case as in many others, the anti-Chinese movement tested relationships.

Public Debate and the Split between *Antichinistas* and *Chineras/Chineros*

Although anti-Chinese activists went to great lengths to recruit their fellow citizens to the cause, some Mexicans defied the anti-Chinese logic. *Antichinistas* learned early on that connections between Chinese and Mexicans were difficult to destroy, leading to the vehement campaigns against *chineras* and *chineros*. Some Mexicans publicly defended Chinese and denounced anti-Chinese activists. Mexican lawyers represented Chinese in discrimination and other kinds of cases. In addition, local officials treated Chinese as lawful residents of Sonora throughout the period.

Antichinistas pressured local authorities to adopt their ideology and deny equal treatment to the Chinese. When they refused, officials faced efforts to remove them from power. Crusaders wrote to Arana complaining about "public employees who fail to uphold their duties to keep the Chinese contented" and vowing to bring down such *chineros*.[38]

Anti-Chinese activists stirred local tensions and complicated authorities' jobs. In October 1917, Pilares de Nacozari businessman Francisco Ibáñez wrote to inform Arana that local Chinese "riffraff," assisted by a lawyer, Professor Diego Serrato, "cursed be he," and a judge named Fuentes, had arranged to have a young boy arrested for taking down Luis Quintero's Chinese flag, which had been displayed higher than the Mexican flag on 16 September, Mexican Independence Day. The boy had been among several angry citizens who protested the Chinese flag's presence, which they had perceived as a disgrace. Quintero was Chinese but had "regrettably" naturalized as a Mexican citizen. *Antichinistas* persistently tried to define the Chinese as outsiders and pressured public officials to deal with them as such.[39]

Officials and private citizens challenged or ignored *antichinista* ideology. Using the legal system, Chinese and their Mexican supporters took anti-Chinese leaders to court. As Robert Chao Romero has shown, the wealthy Chinese proprietor Juan Lung Tain brought a defamation case against Arana in October 1916, just after he and others organized the first anti-Chinese campaign. Arguing that the anti-Chinese leader had slandered him in a recent newspaper article, Lung Tain sought to bar Arana from running in the mayoral election that year. Local judge Jesús Gallo issued an arrest warrant, and state law disqualified Arana from running in the election until the case was decided. Nevertheless, Arana won by an overwhelming majority. After a protracted series of political dealings, Arana failed to assume the post (although he did win election again two years later). According to Romero, Chinese appeared to have negotiated with politicians behind the scenes to block Arana from political office in 1916. Nonetheless, some of his supporters secured him a seat as secretary of the town council. But the anti-Chinese leader was arrested and jailed, along with some of his followers, for inciting serious crimes against Chinese. After being transferred to a prison in Hermosillo, Arana later appeared before General Calles, who reprimanded him, pressured him to relinquish his political position, and set him and his colleagues free.[40]

Additional legal cases emerged as Chinese and Mexicans alike continued to try to limit the power of *antichinistas* in the state. In 1917, Francisco del Rincón accused Arana of insults and defamation. Del Rincón charged that Arana and *Pro-Patria* had not only dishonored and discredited him but also interfered with his duties as Magdalena's *administrador subalterno del timbre*, a fiscal position. Arana had portrayed del Rincón as a "staunch defender" of the Chinese, thereby subjecting him to the scorn of anti-Chinese Mexicans. Arana argued that such an important office should be in someone else's hands and accused del Rincón of favoring the Chinese, who had been "grateful" to him since he accepted the position; his assumption of office, furthermore, had caused "general alarm" and discontent among members of the public, especially Mexican businessmen.[41]

Also in 1917 in Magdalena, Santiago López Alvarado, a lawyer who resided in Guaymas, accused Francisco Monroy and Marcos Palomino of insulting him. López Alvarado brought suit after he and Chinese resident Felipe L. Jan, as well as police officer Juan S. Gastelum, had walked by a group of men who threatened and insulted López Alvarado. Monroy had yelled, "There goes the *chinero*." López Alvarado had previously endured verbal assaults from Arana's supporters, impelling him to ask the *presidente municipal* for a police escort for safety and to help identify his detractors. When Gastelum arrested Monroy, about forty other men surrounded them, demanding to be told the motive for the arrest. The men kept up the verbal abuse until López Alvarado, who perceived their attitude as "seditious," feared that they would assault him. He sought refuge in a Chinese business, Juan Lung Tain and Company, until government authorities sent enough police to dispel the demonstrators. The mob had targeted him because he regularly represented the Chinese in court. As he testified, the anti-Chinese displays had "no other objective but to demonstrate the hatred and contempt for my defense, which is within the scope of our laws, of the Chinese Fraternal Union association." Moreover, he asserted, his legal representation of the organization had prompted the governor to ban anti-Chinese rallies because they merely caused chaos and incited crimes against Chinese.[42] *Antichinistas* subsequently continued to focus on him and his legal aid to Chinese. Writing again to Arana from Pilares de Nacozari in 1918, Ibáñez referred to López Alvarado as a "chinero" and "robber." "Bad" and "unpatriotic" Mexicans such as López Alvarado offered their services to the Chinese to the detriment of their fellow Mexicans. Nevertheless, López Alvarado continued to defend Chinese. About ten years later, for example, he would represent Manuel Sam Lee against American merchant Frank Bonfiglio in a cross-border fraud lawsuit.[43]

In yet another 1917 court case, Magdalena's *presidente municipal*, Enrique Campbell, accused Arana and his followers of insulting local society. The court tried Arana and his comrade, Francisco Batriz, for offending public morality at their demonstrations. Pointing out that anti-Chinese propaganda had provoked crimes against Chinese in the nearby towns of Ímuris and San Lorenzo, Campbell based his accusations on police officer Jesús Verdugo's account of a recent rally in the community. Arana had publicly declared that 25 to 50 percent of the single and married Mexican women who entered Chinese men's businesses were *chineras* whom the Chinese "fondled." Arana also warned that the Chinese were prostituting "our young and our women" and urged the community to find a quick remedy for the Chinese "fondling" of women. Batriz had said that women who had any pride would refuse to patronize Chinese stores. *Antichinistas* begrudged women's new public roles as consumers in Chinese businesses.[44] Members of Arana's group charged the police officer with using his authority to obstruct their right to gather in public. They maintained that he had threatened them and even shot at participants who spoke against public officials. Campbell, in turn, argued that the anti-Chinese crusaders had directly offended particular members of the community in an obscene manner. Such actions not only represented an infraction of the law but also constituted a blatant social offense. To avoid punishment, Campbell cautioned the group to uphold the dignity and composure required at public demonstrations, especially when they included women and girls, who deserved the utmost respect and consideration. Both Campbell and Arana's faction drew on ideas of proper gender behavior and the protection of women.[45] Together, these cases show that local citizens and authorities either disregarded or publicly disputed the anti-Chinese crusade from the beginning.

Public debate continued as the movement strengthened in the 1920s and early 1930s. Mexicans defended Chinese community members in court, and local and state authorities upheld their rights. In 1932, during the heyday of the anti-Chinese movement, the Supremo Tribunal (the state's highest court) tried José Arrellano, also known as El Machete, for injuring Antonio Jui in Guaymas during the previous year. Jui had been walking home when Arrellano suddenly attacked him with a knife. After the assault, Jui went to Rosaura Osuna de Ahumada's home for help. She and two other witnesses, Francisco Ayala and Rafaela Rivera, described the brutal attack. Rivera had also heard Arrellano yell to another Chinese man on the street, "Come here so I can give you some of this, too." The witnesses in the attack saw no other motive than random anti-Chinese hatred. Nevertheless, Arrellano held that he had simply asked the Chinese man when he was going back to his country, since the expulsions were well under way. The question upset Jui, who tried to burn the defendant with his cigarette, and Arrellano had reacted by taking out his knife. Jui and the other witnesses refuted those claims. The court ultimately ruled that the attack had occurred "suddenly without giving [Jui] a chance to defend himself," found Arrellano guilty, and sentenced him to five months in prison.[46] Even at its pinnacle, the anti-Chinese movement failed to convince all Mexicans to go along, though the division between *antichinistas* and *chineras/chineros* ran deep.

Chinese-Mexican Marriages and Law 31

As the anti-Chinese movement gained ground, Chinese men and Mexican women as well as local officials who flouted the law against Chinese-Mexican unions faced legal repercussions. On 19 March 1931, a criminal court in Alamos tried Ramón T. Mendivil for executing an illegal matrimony. As the civil judge of El Chinal, a small locale in the district, he had married a young Mexican woman, Candelaria Wilson, to an older Chinese man, Manuel Loyetoia, at the request of Loyetoia and the woman's father, Epigmenio Wilson. The judge knew that Chinese-Mexican marriages were problematic and had warned the parties involved. Another local judge, Ramón M. Salazar, had even told Mendivil that it was illegal to authorize such a union. But the woman's father and the prospective groom had insisted; Loyetoia paid the judge fifty pesos to perform the civil ceremony. The court fined Mendivil two hundred pesos and sentenced him to one hundred days in prison. He appealed the case, admitting that he had acted "foolishly" in performing the marriage but nevertheless arguing that the state law prohibiting unions between Chinese men and Mexican women was unconstitutional. The Mexican Constitution of 1917 guaranteed equal protection to foreigners, and its anticlericalism defined marriage as a civil ceremony. In this period, Chinese appealed to the Mexican Supreme Court in *amparo* or civil rights cases challenging the constitutionality of Law 31 and other anti-Chinese measures.[47]

In their zeal to enforce the state law, anti-Chinese crusaders cultivated social stigma. Policing local sexuality, *antichinista* newspapers printed the names and photographs of women who partook in romantic or sexual relations with Chinese men to pressure other women to comply with Law 31. On 24 June 1927, *El Intruso* (The Intruder) reported that police in Cananea, an important mining town near the northern border, had caught Manuela Salcido and Rafael Bio, a Chinese man, breaking the law against Chinese-Mexican marriages and liaisons. The newspaper's name signaled that Chinese were unwanted in Sonora. The editors urged society to shame women such as Salcido and force them to live in separate zones—in small yellow houses to avoid "confusion [and] dangerous contagion"—and argued that authorities should apply corporal punishment in greater proportion to Mexican women who had romantic ties with Chinese men than to the men themselves.[48] On 25 June 1931, the paper reported that officials in the southern city of Ciudad Obregón had apprehended a Mexican woman they caught "in delito infraganti" [*sic*]—that is, in flagrant violation of the law. Police carried the "bad woman" to jail, where a photographer took her picture. *El Intruso* applauded a Ciudad Obregón *antichinista* newspaper, *El Nacionalista*, for printing the photograph, a practice *El Intruso* believed would help to decrease the numbers of Mexican women who unscrupulously gave themselves to Chinese men. The article called on other newspapers to discourage similar transgressions by broadcasting infractions of the law. The *antichinista* newspapers suggested that these women knowingly broke the law and as race traitors were more of a menace than their Chinese partners. Foreigners could (and would soon) be excluded or expelled, but aberrant Mexican women, as members and procreators of the race, represented a deeper problem.[49]

This climate of sexual surveillance permitted some Mexicans to use the stigma on Chinese-Mexican relationships to justify violence against Chinese. In 1929, a court in Cananea tried four Mexican men for the brutal assault of six Chinese men at El Nogal ranch in Cuquiárachi, a community in the municipality of Fronteras, and the murder of three of the men. Survivor Ramón Lam remembered hearing one of the aggressors declare that he had had orders from the *presidente municipal* to search the house for Mexican women. One of the accused, Angel Ocaña, had also heard his companion, Rafael Benítez, state such orders during the assault.[50] Although it is unclear whether the mayor of Cananea or another municipality in the area had actually made such commands, the assailants nonetheless invoked anti-Chinese logic and the ban on Chinese-Mexican unions in their defense.

Sonorans challenged Law 31 in a number of ways. Mexican women wrote open letters published in newspapers in which they claimed the right to enter into relationships of their choosing, a signal of modernity. Some politicians refused to support the measure, and people challenged its constitutionality in court. While Sonoran authorities never officially revoked the decree against Chinese-Mexican unions, they also never consistently enforced it.[51] Mexican women and Chinese men, moreover, continued to form and maintain romantic ties sanctioned by local authorities and communities around the state throughout the period.

The presence of Chinese in Sonora profoundly divided the populace. As revolution swept through northern Mexico, groups of Mexicans vilified Chinese, arguing that they had usurped resources that rightfully belonged to Mexicans. Developing deeply racialized and gendered stereotypes about the Chinese, these anti-Chinese activists also targeted Mexicans contemptuously branded as *chineras* and *chineros*. As *antichinismo* infiltrated state law and found its way onto the national stage, crusaders used social stigma to demean persistent Chinese-Mexican relationships. These activists envisioned destroying Chinese-Mexican ties as a key step on the way to their fundamental goal of removing the Chinese.

Yet other Mexicans kept shopping at Chinese stores, buying from Chinese-operated *carretas* (carts), and forming friendships and romantic unions with Chinese men in spite of the legal repercussions and the social stigma with which *antichinistas* tried to mark those connections. Public debate took place, and citizens used the courts to challenge anti-Chinese activism from the movement's inception through its zenith. *Antichinistas* ultimately would secure the expulsion of the majority of Chinese, but they never fully abolished Chinese-Mexican relationships. People drew on local cultural, economic, and organizational resources to go on living in the face of severe challenges. Such strong ties drove some Mexican women and Chinese Mexican children to follow husbands and fathers out of Mexico or to help them stay in secret after the expulsions began.

PART TWO

Chinese Removal

CHAPTER THREE

The Expulsion of Chinese Men and Chinese Mexican Families from Sonora and Sinaloa, Early 1930s

In 1926, Francisco Martínez wrote to President Plutarco Elías Calles from Nogales, Arizona, attaching a newspaper article, "Mexicans Will Be Kicked Out of California." The piece reported that 75 percent of Mexicans in California had entered the United States illegally and that a campaign to return them to Mexico was to begin immediately. Although the United States would not conduct a massive deportation of Mexicans until the depression years, California undertook smaller deportation campaigns during this time. Drawing on this anti-Mexican backlash to call for the expulsion of Chinese from Mexico, Martínez wrote, "If the Americans can do this to a neighboring country, to Mexicans, why don't we take advantage of this idea—using it against Chinese?" The Chinese "plague," he argued, had "infested and threatened" Mexico.[1] Dwelling on the Arizona side of the border, Martínez may have been an official or a businessman, a Mexican immigrant or Mexican American—or an amalgamation of all these things, as these lines of identity have historically been blurred, especially in the border region. In any case, the borderlands resident's wish would be fulfilled a few years later. Mexican workers, as scapegoats for the Great Depression in the United States, returned to Mexico en masse beginning in

1929. Shortly thereafter, Sonora and Sinaloa carried out massive evictions of Chinese men, who likewise received blame for Mexico's economic and social problems.

The Enforcement of Anti-Chinese Laws

The Great Depression and the economic turmoil it caused in the border region as well as the consequent U.S. deportation of Mexicans invigorated *antichinista* efforts; the larger context ramped up previous sentiment.[2] In 1930, knowing that local authorities inconsistently upheld the ban on Chinese-Mexican unions and other anti-Chinese measures, the Sonoran state government began to pressure municipal governments to more thoroughly enforce the laws aimed at Chinese. On 7 October 1930, a decree from the office of the governor ordered local leaders to enforce the law that prohibited Chinese men and Mexican women from marrying or living together in *amaciato* (as lovers). Authorities in each district were to levy fines and report transgressions directly to the governor. Another edict addressed to local officials of the civil registry stated that the governor's office was aware that Mexican women frequently visited local offices soliciting birth certificates for children born of Chinese fathers—proof, it noted, that people routinely violated the law against Chinese-Mexican unions. Authorities in each district were ordered to report such requests to the head of the local jurisdiction.[3]

In 1931, the Sonoran government carried *antichinismo* into full swing. In August, Governor Francisco S. Elías issued a circular allowing local authorities to close the businesses of those Chinese who had violated the "80 percent labor law."[4] Local and state authorities soon began forcibly removing Chinese men and their Mexican-origin families, sending them north through Arizona or south through Sinaloa.[5] Governor Rodolfo Elías Calles, who assumed power on 1 September, further entrenched the process of expulsion. The son of national political figure Plutarco Elías Calles and like him an affirmed anti-Chinese ideologue, Rodolfo Elías Calles nationalized local commerce, closed Chinese businesses, and legally dissolved Chinese-Mexican marriages and unions.[6]

Unwilling to tolerate municipal officials' incoherent treatment of Chinese, the governor sent a series of communications similar to those from the previous year, ordering authorities throughout the state to execute the central government's anti-Chinese laws. A 14 October 1931 decree instructed local authorities to apprehend and jail Chinese individuals who maintained businesses after the state had ordered them to close. One week later, another edict noted that the governor was aware that Chinese men had not only reopened businesses after officials shut them down but also continued their relationships with Mexican women. Demanding that local governments begin "energetic campaigns" to disband the illicit marriages and unions, the governor instructed authorities in each district to detain and punish anyone who defied the law. If Mexican women resisted the state sanctions, local officials should report those women directly to the governor, whose office could deal with them. The Sonoran government also outlawed women's presence in Chinese businesses.[7]

The missives' special focus on women invoked long-standing *antichinista* concerns regarding Chinese-Mexican ties, anxieties about public space, and the perceived need for gendered social control as society underwent modernization. Lacking steady local enforcement, anti-Chinese edicts had been largely ineffective; municipal officials often tacitly complied with Chinese Mexican disregard for the state laws. People had gone on with their lives and maintained connections with the sanction of the local community.

The Expulsion of Chinese

It would take the power of the central government and a state leader who was an *antichinista* to the core to fully implement anti-Chinese laws and rid the state of the vast majority of Chinese. Sonoran local and state authorities, with the help of vigilantes, drove out the Chinese without uniformity or a clear organization—through mob violence, arrest and deportation processes, and exit deadlines. The process of expulsion varied significantly from town to town as well as from month to month and year to year during the early 1930s.

The brutality and violence of the expulsion period quickly became palpable to Chinese men and their families. According to María del Carmen Irma Wong Campoy Maher Conceição, her father, Alfonso Wong Fang, had to run away from anti-Chinese tormenters who targeted him for being a Chinese businessman. To escape, the Wong Campoy family patriarch climbed a roof; falling off exacerbated his heart problems, and the incident showed him that he could no longer live in peace in Sonora as he had done for years. The same day, he began packing up his family's belongings, and he and his wife, Dolores Campoy Wong, soon took the family out of the state.[8]

As a consequence of the increasingly aggressive vigilantes, Chinese men and their families lived in uncertainty and fear. Chinese testified before U.S. immigration agents that Mexican officials in Sonora had meted out harsh treatment, barring the Chinese from working and stripping them of their possessions. Sonoran authorities jailed the Chinese, forcing them to undress and searching and robbing them. Tucson's *Arizona Daily Star* reported that people in towns around Sonora broke into Chinese homes and businesses, looted them, and forced the owners and their families out onto the street.[9] In some instances, local and state authorities or mobs simply rounded up Chinese men as well as their Mexican wives or companions and mixed-race children and pushed them out of the state, carrying *antichinismo* to its logical conclusion.

In some cases, officials gave Chinese deadlines to leave the state. On 30 August 1931, the *New York Times* reported that Chinese had until 5 September to depart. They could exit as refugees through points on the border with the United States, such as the town of Nogales, or through the Sinaloan port of Mazatlán.[10] Some municipal authorities violated their own deadlines. In early 1932, the *Nogales Daily Herald* reported that officials told a Chinese consul to inform his compatriots living in the northern mining town of Cananea that they had eight days to leave the area but waited only overnight before rounding up and jailing 250 Chinese and deporting 40 others to an unknown place. Officials later released the Chinese they had held captive but told them to depart within the week.[11]

Chinese men and Chinese Mexican families experienced severe economic loss during the expulsions. On 5 September 1931, the *Arizona Daily Star* reported that Navojoa's Ching Chong Company, where Alfonso Wong Fang was an associate, had suffered a loss of 500,000 pesos. Authorities also forced Ng Wo of Nogales, Sonora, to give up a business worth 250,000 pesos. Chinese lost property and earnings as the state took possession of their businesses.[12]

Chinese confronted the acute hatred of the expulsion era by drawing on a number of resources that they had accrued over the years. Some hid in Sonora with the support of family and friends. Others defended their businesses and civil rights in federal court.[13] Some became vagabonds, wandering streets and communities for months, hoping to find respite. Others felt compelled by the harshness of the anti-Chinese movement to leave their homes and communities before authorities or mobs had the chance to remove them. A few of the wealthiest immediately returned to China, while others relocated to the border areas of Baja California and Chihuahua, where anti-Chinese movements were less strong. The differences in individual places' treatment of Chinese rested on their specific racial politics and their connections with the Mexican Revolution. The long presence of diverse foreigners in Sonora pressed local leaders and others to prove racial authenticity, leading to the state's expulsions of foreigners of various nationalities.[14] Among its most pernicious campaigns was the one directed against Chinese. Both Sonora and Sinaloa defied the federal government in carrying out expulsions of Chinese. Baja California and Chihuahua, conversely, had distinct relationships with the nation and revolutionary ideology. Although anti-Chinese movements existed, they never matured enough to carry out massive expulsions. Some Chinese who left Sonora made new homes in these neighboring areas. Still others entered the United States surreptitiously, in violation of that country's Chinese exclusion laws. While some crossed the northern border voluntarily after local persecution became unbearable, others entered the United States by force when Sonoran authorities or mobs literally pushed them across the boundary, where they would soon constitute a refugee crisis.

Mexican women and Chinese Mexican children had a variety of reasons for accompanying Chinese men out of Sonora during the expulsions. When they had the choice, women opted to go out of love and to keep their families unified. Fears that they would be unable to support their families without their spouses or that anti-Chinese proponents would direct their hatred at racially mixed children were also part of women's motivations to leave. *Antichinistas* had portrayed Mexican women who formed relationships with Chinese men as traitors to the race and nation and had cast the children born of those unions as degenerates. Moreover, the dominant gender ideology and citizenship policy defined women's status by that of their husbands. Indeed, in 1930, the Dirección de los Censos (Census Management Office) began listing Mexican women who had civilly married Chinese men as "Chinese" rather than "Mexican" unless the men had naturalized as Mexican citizens.[15]

Some women traveled north with their men: The U.S. Immigration and Naturalization Service (INS) later listed more than a hundred women as Chinese refugees from Mexico. Other victims of the anti-Chinese persecution reported being forced to Sonora's southern borders. Georgina Victorica later told Mexican consuls in China that a mob in Huatabampo, a small southern town near the Río Mayo, had taken her and her husband,

Hanfon, to the port of Mazatlán and deported them to China, where they arrived in the fall of 1931. Her husband died soon thereafter, and she appealed to Mexican authorities for permission to return to Mexico to be with her family.[16]

Antichinismo beyond Sonora

The rise to power of the "Sonora Dynasty" and its dominance in national politics bred *antichinismo*, and by the early 1930s, roughly two hundred anti-Chinese committees or nationalist leagues existed not only in Sonora but also in Sinaloa, Baja California, Chihuahua, Colima, Nayarit, Durango, Nuevo León, Tamaulipas, Veracruz, Chiapas, and Oaxaca and to a lesser extent in Yucatán, Michoacán, Jalisco, and Mexico City.[17] But only Sonora and Sinaloa expelled Chinese en masse. The federal government officially considered the two states in contempt of the revolution for their maverick practices. Even in the absence of large-scale expulsions, Chinese and their families also fled other areas because of growing anti-Chinese activity and because of the looming fear that officials or mobs might eventually forcibly evict them, as in the two northwestern states. As a result, Mexico's Chinese population fell drastically, from nearly 18,000 in 1930 to fewer than 5,000 a decade later. The population decline was most dramatic in Sonora, where the Chinese population dropped from 3,571 to 92 over the period, and in Sinaloa, where the number fell from 2,123 to 165. "To this day," as Roberto Chao Romero has written, "the Chinese immigrant community of Mexico has never recovered."[18]

Effects of the Expulsion

Scholars have argued that the anti-Chinese movement was crucial in the development of the state of Sonora and its connection to the Mexican nation during the revolution. Expelling the Chinese not only was about economic scapegoating and racial panic but also was about proving Mexican racial legitimacy in a state that had a unique ethnic makeup as a consequence of the longtime presence of foreigners. The expulsion of Chinese was one in a chain of related events in the revolutionary making of Sonora—the deportation of Yaquis and the expulsion of Jesuits and Mormons, among other groups of foreigners. These events linked the state to the nation and shaped postrevolutionary Sonora and Mexico. Thus, the Chinese were key in Mexican political history in this era.[19]

Mexicano: El color amarillo que ves en la carta geográfica de tu patria, es la demostración del dominio mongol. Ves a Sonora limpio de la mancha asiática, pues sigue el ejemplo de este pueblo batallador y pronto harás de tu patria chica una entidad que podrás llamar tuya y de los tuyos.

Anti-Chinese map of the Chinese presence in Mexico after the Sonoran expulsion. The anti-Chinese leader José Angel Espinoza attempted to sway *antichinistas* in other states to act swiftly to remove Chinese people, as he and his brethren had done. The caption accompanying the map says, "Mexican man: The color yellow that you see on the map of your fatherland represents the *Mongol* dominion. You see Sonora free of the Asian stain, so follow the example of this fighting people and soon you will convert your homeland into something you can call your own and that of your people." From José Angel Espinoza, *El ejemplo de Sonora* (Mexico City: n.p., 1932).

The Chinese population's economic importance in Sonora meant that their mass expulsion devastated the state. Local economies experienced severe setbacks at the sudden closure of Chinese businesses. Some communities instituted bartering systems because crucial supplies provided by Chinese stores had become scarce.[20] On 3 July 1932, the *San Francisco Chronicle* reported that the expulsion of Chinese from Sonora had proven to be "an economic boomerang." Chinese withdrew their bank deposits and sent money to their compatriots in San Francisco, utilizing the cross-border networks that had helped them settle and prosper in Sonora to salvage their assets during the expulsion. The Sonoran Anti-Chinese League declared that in a single year, the Chinese had taken more than fifty million pesos out of the state. By reducing business activity, the exodus of Chinese also caused an "alarming decrease in State revenues from taxes" during its first and most drastic year.[21] In the end, the Sonoran government nearly went bankrupt after the removal of the Chinese.[22]

The Memory of the Expulsions

Anti-Chinese leader and public intellectual José Angel Espinoza called for the rest of Mexico to commemorate and duplicate the eviction of the Chinese population. His rhetoric embedded racialized and gendered assumptions about not only the Chinese but also Mexican men and women. Espinoza's writing reflected the anti-Chinese movement's class-based anti-Mexican notions. According to Espinoza, the expulsion had placed businesses in the hands of Mexican men who had beforehand led "inactive lives" and survived on widowed women's economic activities. He argued that the expulsion had provided Sonoran authorities with "national capital"—from assets taken from the Chinese—to set up new establishments run by young Mexican men. These men, who were lazy, parasitic, and in dire need of government assistance, could not become economically productive without the state-sponsored expulsion of Chinese.[23]

The removals were abrupt. María Luisa Salazar Corral Navarro remembered visiting Chinese businesses in Navojoa with her father before they vanished "almost all at once."[24] Jesús Verdugo Escoboza recalled how different the landscape appeared without Chinese peddlers and their carts on the streets of Hermosillo.[25] Etched in Gastón Cano Ávila's memory was the virtual disappearance of the Chinese businesses in the capital's commercial district, which he had frequented with his parents as a small child.[26]

The historical memory of the expulsion of Chinese and the government's confiscation and liquidation of their property has survived in Sonora, albeit unevenly. Common understandings and sometimes jokes maintain that certain wealthy families in the state obtained their original capital during the 1930s via businesses and other assets that had once belonged to Chinese. Delfino "Pino" Robles and his family joked about the origins of a hardware store run by the family of a son-in-law, moving him to clarify the history of the family business and its apparent lack of connection with the expulsion. According to Marta Elia Lau de Salazar, people in Navojoa were well aware that some families there and in the nearby town of Bacobampo had become wealthy only after securing Chinese land and businesses in the expulsion period. Manuel Hernández Salomón, the local chronicler of Navojoa, agreed: Authorities in the district had sold confiscated Chinese property at very low prices, allowing certain Mexicans to become upwardly mobile.[27]

While the expulsion of Chinese from Mexico brought some Mexicans economic benefits, it caused others heavy emotional burdens. María Rosario Valdez Rodríguez married José Han in Sinaloa. Shortly after the birth of the couple's second daughter, Rosa María Han Valdez, in 1934, authorities expelled Han, and his daughters never saw him again. To support her daughters, Valdez Rodríguez moved to Guaymas, Sonora, leaving the girls with their grandmother, Enedina Rodríguez de Valdez, for several years. The widowed Rodríguez de Valdez later married Antonio Chang, whom local authorities also eventually expelled. Luisa María Valdez's uncles and aunt from that marriage thus were "in the same boat as I was because their father was sent away," too. Growing up in the company of women and children whose families had been torn apart by anti-Chinese prejudice framed her experiences. Relatives have told Valdez that her father was very hardworking, cared for her mother, and provided for the family. On one occasion when she was doing business by telephone with someone in Los Angeles, she spoke with a man whose surname was Han and asked if he was related to her father: Her "hopes came down" when the man said that he had no relatives named José Han. She has always felt deeply her father's absence, and keeping his memory alive has helped her confront the painful reverberations of the expulsion period.[28]

For Valdez, "Mexico expatriated" the Chinese simply because they were Chinese. Her use of the term "expatriated" communicates that Chinese men had previously been part of the polity. Like other Chinese, her father and second grandfather had contributed economically to Mexico and formed families, thereby becoming part of the local community. Valdez believed that the government rather than the common people had executed the Chinese removal.[29]

Valdez was not alone in this perception of the expulsion. Alfonso Wong Campoy learned from his parents—both of whom taught him to be proud to be Mexican—that the government rather than the Mexican people had been responsible for the anti-Chinese movement. A Chinese woman in Guaymas experienced anti-Chinese hatred at the grassroots level as she walked her children to school each day to help shield them from insults and ill-treatment, yet she blamed the state government for the movement against Chinese.[30]

Such characterizations of the expulsion era notwithstanding, the record tells a more complicated story. While it is true that *antichinismo* was eventually embraced by local and state governments, the campaigns' origins in the 1910s were fundamentally at the grass roots. Although the movement never won over all Mexicans, ordinary working- and middle-class citizens played a crucial role. People first organized at the base and later ran for public office to further their cause. And even though some leaders eventually held local and state government positions, the movement retained a grassroots element. Indeed, when the campaigns peaked in the early 1930s, anti-Chinese leaders and regional authorities as well as throngs of common people together drove out the Chinese and their families from Sonora and Sinaloa.

Nevertheless, Chinese Mexicans' views reveal a great deal about identity and memory. Perhaps locating the blame exclusively on a government long in the past has provided some remedy for the anguish felt by Valdez and the other wives and children who stayed behind as well as the Wong Campoys and other Chinese men and their families who left Mexico. Such a vision of the past may have helped Chinese Mexicans reconcile the highly incongruent aspects of their family histories, making it possible to recognize their ancestors' contributions to the nation and reclaim their rightful place in its memory in spite of the hateful history of expulsion. This viewpoint may also have provided them with a sense of belonging as culturally and racially mixed people despite the anti-Chinese chapter in Mexico's history.

Condemning the Expulsions

Chinese diplomatic representatives publicized their strong objections to the expulsions. Arizona's *Nogales Daily Herald* interviewed consul Yao-Hsiang Peng in Nogales, Sonora, in February 1932, a time of especially pernicious anti-Chinese violence and vigilantism. The consul told reporters that the state's Chinese population had already dropped from three thousand before the expulsion began to fewer than one thousand. Authorities then stepped up their anti-Chinese efforts, compelling hundreds of Chinese to close their businesses and flee the state and forcibly deporting others who had not escaped on their own. Government officials separated Chinese men from their families and took them to unknown destinations, acting on secret orders from Governor Elías Calles. Although American and Chinese diplomatic officers had arranged for ships to arrive in the ports of Mazatlán and Guaymas to transport the refugees, the state leader ordered officials to detain and deport the Chinese immediately. Peng speculated that authorities had expelled these men to Sinaloa, undoubtedly to send them out of the country. Authorities deported seventy Chinese merchants from Hermosillo and hurried out thirty others from Huatabampo. They arrested Chinese consul K. Wong, whose superiors had sent him to meet with the mayor of Cananea. The mayor released Wong, admitting that his detention had been a mistake.[31] Peng lamented that "In Nogales, Sonora . . . many law abiding Chinese were told that they must go to see the mayor. They were then reported missing and later accounts indicated that they were deported." Officials refused to let Chinese liquidate their property, obliging them to leave their families and businesses unprotected. During the expulsion period, Chinese consuls protested the actions of local and state authorities, and the Chinese legation in Mexico City informed the press that it would soon conduct a sweeping investigation of Sonora's maltreatment of Chinese.[32]

Some Mexican citizens also publicly denounced the mistreatment of Chinese in Sonora and Sinaloa. In February 1933, residents of Culiacán, Sinaloa, published a reproving statement in the newspaper *El Pueblo*: "Disgrace to Nation: So many violations against the Chinese have been committed that, as civilized human beings, we must protest so that it may not be said later that we stood silently by and tolerated these inhuman acts." Mexicans who opposed the expulsion and general mistreatment of the Chinese also sent declarations to the president of Mexico and the governor of Sinaloa, firmly voicing their objection to the merciless campaigns against the Chinese.[33]

Chinese men and Mexican women drew on support systems created through their relationships. For example, Chinese registered businesses in their Mexican female companions' names to circumvent anti-Chinese measures and deflect persecution. Francisco López, a Chinese resident of a central town, Ures, listed his shop under his Mexican wife's name in 1931. He and another Chinese businessman, Carlos Ley, also appealed to a federal court to combat the discriminatory local ordinances against Chinese stores during this time. López and Ley argued that authorities had jailed them after their businesses were ordered closed without just cause. When court officials delivered the notice of a hearing, López refused to sign because his "wife might become angry," since the shop was in her name.[34]

Staying in Sonora

Some Chinese men simply refused to leave the state, physically hiding or passing as Mexicans, at times changing their names. Chinese men's integration into communities across Sonora enabled some to stay in Mexico secretly with the help of Mexican families and friends. Despite the rampant violence that anti-Chinese hatred had provoked, Chinese and Mexicans found ways around exclusionary policies. Going to such lengths as physically hiding reflected the strength and depth of Chinese-Mexican ties. Complicit Mexican and Chinese Mexican spouses, lovers, children, friends, and other community members risked punishment to conceal men from local authorities. To be sure, Chinese Mexican community networks were crucial to the endeavors to hide Chinese. Suggesting that this phenomenon was a significant problem for his administration, Governor Elías Calles formed "rural brigades" to search for Chinese hiding in the countryside in the latter part of 1931.[35]

In spite of the government's attempts to find them, Chinese stayed underground and waited out the expulsion period; such stories have become common knowledge in some parts of Sonora. Some Good Samaritan employers helped Chinese stay. Carlos Lucero Aja's grandfather hid Chinese who worked with him on his ranch outside Hermosillo. According to Hernández Salomón, a series of tunnels in Navojoa's commercial downtown hid Chinese from authorities. Marta Elia Lau de Salazar also learned over the years that numerous Chinese, including her father, went underground throughout the Río Mayo Valley in southern Sonora.[36]

With the help of his wife, Preciliana Yocupicio, Concepción Lau Wong hid from authorities in subterranean spaces he constructed in Bacobampo. While her husband lived in hiding, Yocupicio took over the work of supporting the family, cooked, and delivered him food. She raised cows, horses, and other animals and sold milk and cheese to sustain the family. Using rice and beets as her husband did when he cooked, she developed a distinctive Chinese Mexican cooking style.

Lau Wong survived the expulsion period and stayed in Mexico with his family. Their youngest child, Marta Elia, was born in 1935, after the threat of expulsion had largely passed and family life resumed. She recalled seeing him cry profusely as he told her that bombs had destroyed the region where his family lived in Guangdong Province during the Japanese invasion in the late 1930s and early 1940s. She remembered her father very fondly as an honorable man who worked hard and was dedicated to his

Guillermo Chan López, María Elena López Islas, and Luis Chan Valenzuela.
Photograph by author.

family; Sonora had become his second home, so he hid to stay with his family. He adopted local Mexican customs while maintaining his Cantonese identity. He also had children by Mexican women other than Yocupicio and maintained those families as well, although Marta Elia's family was his primary household. Her father remained in Mexico until his death as a result of a heart attack at the age of sixty-five. He had suffered tremendously because of anti-Chinese hatred and the knowledge that war raged in the land of his birth. After he died, Lau de Salazar's mother advised her always to feel proud to be Chinese Mexican.[37]

José Chan also went into hiding to avoid deportation in the expulsion period. His wife, Dolores Valenzuela Romero, took him food while he lived in caves outside Hermosillo. Like Lau Wong, Chan survived the expulsion period with the support of his family. His son, Luis Chan Valenzuela, remembered his parents' stories about his father's experiences during the anti-Chinese movement and shared those tales with his son, Guillermo Chan López.[38]

Mexican women played a key role in concealing their husbands from authorities and sustaining their families. These women took risks and sacrificed to keep their families together. The Chinese who defied the expulsion by remaining secretly were so integrated into local society that the only option was to stay in Sonora. Keeping this memory alive, their descendants have reminded us of a largely forgotten story.

While some Chinese remained in the state by hiding, others did so simply by living discretely or utilizing racial passing, also a common practice among Chinese in the United States during the era of exclusion.[39] Some Chinese altered their identities, replacing their surnames with Mexican ones. José de Jesus Tapia Martens's grandfather, Lau Ket, stayed in Carbó, a small village north of Hermosillo, throughout the expulsion period without much difficulty. Tapia Martens's father changed the family's name from Lau to Tapia many years after the expulsion period in an attempt to prevent discrimination against his children.[40]

Other Chinese made compromised choices. Sonora's self-serving government permitted the continued presence of a few Chinese who had special skills that benefited local and state authorities or the military, although even these men had their property and capital confiscated. Stripped of their resources and fully aware that local officials and common people had rejected most of their countrymen, the Chinese men who remained must have felt humiliated. As for those who hid, deciding to remain under such circumstances echoed the vigor of Chinese Mexican ties and the profundity of Chinese integration into local communities.

The Sonoran government allowed Luis Wong Cervón to stay in Guaymas because of his ability to repair a variety of equipment. Local officials seized his assets, meaning that Wong Cervón gave up his material possessions to be with his family. His granddaughter, María de Los Angeles Leyva Cervón, remembers him as her "hero" and "idol," teaching her the values of love of life, independence, self-sufficiency, and frugality. They remained close until his death in Guaymas in 1983, and the lessons he imparted have remained with her throughout her life. She created an album documenting his life, inscribing it, "For my grandfather to remember him always. He has left, but as long as I live, he shall live in me." Leyva Cervón has shared her family history with her daughter, who proudly claims Chinese heritage and embraces the nickname *china*. Unlike Valdez and others who have gone through life without their Chinese loved ones, Leyva Cervón was fortunate to grow up in the company of her grandfather, and she is well aware of her good fortune.[41]

Domingo Chon Bing also stayed openly in Hermosillo during the expulsion. He had become a naturalized Mexican citizen and owned a local business that officials left alone, although specifically why remains unclear. Like Leyva Cervón, Ignacio Fonseca Chon learned such important values as frugality and saving from his grandfather and cherishes the memory of the older man. Authorities also allowed a doctor, José Chon, to stay in Hermosillo because he had helped cure an outbreak of yellow fever in the area in 1912.[42]

Authorities in Guaymas also permitted one Chinese couple to remain. The woman had arrived in Guaymas in 1927, after her father, a laborer in the port, arranged his daughter's marriage to a young Chinese wholesaler of vegetables. The couple married in accordance with local Mexican custom. Important Guaymas citizens and officials attended their wedding, which included several days of music, feasting, and drinking. The couple soon became naturalized Mexican citizens. During the expulsion, their *compadre* (a good friend through family and baptismal connections) and a well-known lawyer drafted a legal document defending the Chinese man's Mexican citizenship status and arguing that authorities should respect his rights. Although they lost their savings, the couple survived the expulsion period with the help of such friends. The husband considered himself Mexican and refused to leave because his life was in Guaymas. He declined to withdraw his money from the Banco de Sonora, although most other Chinese had done so, and he lost fifty thousand pesos when the bank closed as a consequence of the volume of expulsion-related withdrawals. For three years after the fall of the bank, the family lived in a small room without light that someone had offered them. Taking her two children by the hand back and forth to school each day, the mother tried to protect them from taunts and abuse, as anti-Chinese resentment persisted in Guaymas. In spite of the challenges, she felt at home in Sonora and took on a sense of Mexican identity. As anti-Chinese sentiment declined, the family began to sell fruits and vegetables again. Years later, the family moved to Tucson, Arizona, where most of the woman's friends were Mexican Americans rather than Chinese, who were from regions in China other than hers.[43]

The Chinese who employed diverse strategies to remain in Sonora became Mexican in a deep sense. They endured sacrifices and relinquished material possessions for the chance to stay with their families in the communities they had come to consider as their second homes. At the same time, they retained Cantonese and Taishanese values and fluidly adapted them to local norms, creating hybrid sensibilities. Severe anti-Chinese persecution never prevented them from transmitting ever-changing Chinese and Chinese Mexican culture in all of its complexities to their descendants. In turn, Chinese Mexicans have kept their ancestors' memories alive and created dynamic senses of self.

The early 1930s brought drastic changes for Sonoran Chinese and their families and communities. Although irregularity had characterized the local enforcement of anti-Chinese laws in Sonora in the previous decades, the state government began to coerce municipal authorities to fully implement laws aimed at Chinese. After Governor Elías Calles came to power in 1931, the movement against Chinese reached its highest point. Most Chinese fled or were forcibly deported within a few years, with the most dramatic action against Chinese occurring in late 1931 and early 1932. While in some cases officials uprooted men from their families and communities in Sonora, at other times entire families left the state.

The national power of the "Sonora Dynasty" generated anti-Chinese activity throughout Mexico. Sinaloa mimicked the Sonoran model and also began expelling Chinese, and anti-Chinese campaigns emerged elsewhere. Although *antichinismo* spread to other parts of Mexico, Sonora and Sinaloa were the only states to execute massive removals of Chinese. Still, Chinese from all over Mexico left their communities during the Great Depression. After Lázaro Cárdenas assumed power in 1934, the "Sonora Dynasty" and the anti-Chinese movement in Mexico would begin to decline.[44] But Mexico's Chinese population had already fallen dramatically.

Chinese and Mexicans had formed relationships and maintained them in the face of legal punishment, social stigma, and the threat of violence during the expulsion period. Chinese Mexican families used assorted methods and drew on myriad resources to remain unified. Some Chinese men hid, while other families stayed together but left Sonora. They traveled to China directly from Mexico or crossed illegally into the United States, either voluntarily to escape escalating abuse or when they were forced across the boundary by Mexican authorities or mobs. While some Chinese Mexicans entered the United States without incident, others landed in the custody of U.S. immigration agents enforcing the federal Chinese Exclusion Acts and became refugees.

CHAPTER FOUR

The U.S. Deportation of
"Chinese Refugees from Mexico,"
Early 1930s

After narrowly escaping hateful *antichinista* tormenters who had driven him to run away and climb a roof, from which he fell, aggravating a heart condition, Alfonso Wong Fang knew that he and his family could no longer remain in Sonora as before. They had stayed well into the expulsion period, but in early 1933, the Wong Campoys—Alfonso; his wife, Dolores Campoy Wong; and the couple's children, Alfonso Wong Campoy, María del Carmen Irma Wong Campoy, and Héctor Manuel Wong Campoy—headed north, crossing the border illegally into the United States. The oldest child was only four years old, while Héctor was a mere baby. Enforcing the Chinese Exclusion Acts, U.S. immigration agents apprehended the Campoys and held them in an immigration jail in southern Arizona, labeling them "refugees." U.S. authorities soon put them on a train to San Francisco and deported them to China with other "Chinese refugees from Mexico." For nearly three decades, the Wong Campoy family would remain in China, where Alfonso Sr. would die prematurely as a result of his heart condition.[1]

Facing heightened anti-Chinese persecution in Sonora and Sinaloa as well as elsewhere in Mexico, several thousand Chinese men and their Mexican-origin families entered U.S. territory as illegal immigrants and became refugees from Mexico between 1931 and 1934, complicating Mexican-U.S. relations during the depression era. Attempting to understand and control the situation, the Immigration and Naturalization Service (INS) heard testimony from hundreds of Chinese men who described the brutality they had endured in Mexico. U.S. officials at first perceived Chinese men and Chinese Mexican families from Mexico through the decades-old lens of Chinese exclusion. But after taking testimony, they saw a new pattern: Anti-Chinese hostility had driven these Chinese from Mexico. Thus, these people were refugees whom the agency could neither send back to Mexico in good conscience nor allow into the United States owing to the exclusion policy. The federal Exclusion Acts prohibited Chinese laborers—a broad category that included the vast majority of those who attempted to enter—from migrating to the United States from 1882 to 1943.[2] The United States usually referred to "illegal" Chinese immigrants as "contraband" or "smuggled." In the case of Chinese Mexicans, however, the INS and the State Department utilized the term "refugee," even though nations in the prewar era were not yet in the regular practice of understanding the concept or employing the term in this way. The use of "refugee" pointed to the complexity of the situation and the diplomatic issues it raised.

U.S. immigration agents deployed a gendered rubric of Chinese exclusion as they labeled not only Chinese men but also Mexican women, whether married or unmarried, and Chinese Mexican children as Chinese refugees from Mexico and ultimately deported them to China.[3] The INS avoided sending Mexican women and Chinese Mexican children back to Mexico, even though doing so would have cost the agency far less than the trip to China. Moreover, the United States had already been deporting Mexicans—more than a million Mexicans and Mexican Americans were forcibly "repatriated" during the depression—so returning the women and children would have been a simple undertaking.[4] With few exceptions, U.S. immigration agents did not even take Mexican women's testimony, although they interviewed hundreds of Chinese men who had entered the United States from Mexico, and the men at times discussed their Mexican-origin families in their testimonies. The ideology of men's control over women under coverture and the "feme covert" legitimized the deportation to China of entire Chinese Mexican families, including women in free associations rather than legal marriages with Chinese men. Gender ideology and citizenship policy commonly upheld around the world during this time stripped women of their citizenship when they married or formed unions with foreigners. While men maintained citizenship regardless of marriage, these notions defined women by the citizenship status of their husbands or companions. In 1931, amendments to the U.S. Cable Act allowed women married to "aliens ineligible for citizenship" to maintain U.S. citizenship status. While notions of female citizenship were beginning to change in this period, U.S. agents nonetheless opted to deport Mexican women to China rather than to Mexico. Mexico's anti-Chinese movement made it problematic for the United States to return any of the refugees to Mexico, where they might have faced violence. Concerns about the nation's image abroad as well as the residue of the ideology of coverture trumped nascent concepts of female citizenship that for the first time saw a woman's status as separate from her husband's.[5] In this context, U.S. agents classified Mexican women, by virtue of their associations with Chinese men, initially as "illegal immigrants" and then as "refugees" under Chinese exclusion. Mexican women would fall deeper into the interstices of the nation-state after reaching China, where many Chinese men's previous marriages removed the possibility that authorities would consider the Mexican women to be Chinese citizens.[6]

By pushing Chinese men and their families across the border, Mexican officials forced their wealthier neighbor to the north to pay for the deportations. Although the United States had created the Border Patrol almost ten years earlier, the international boundary was still quite porous. Mexican officials used established networks for illegal entry since cross-border "smuggling" of Chinese people as well as goods, narcotics, and alcohol had become a profitable business enterprise by the turn of the twentieth century.[7] U.S. immigration officials used Arizona courts to try Sonoran authorities who coordinated refugee "smuggling" efforts or acted as "coyotes," taking people across the border.

Mexican-U.S. regional and national competition and overlapping racial ideologies that defined the Chinese as undesirable outsiders framed the contentions over the "refugees." The INS took testimony from Chinese partially to try to establish that Mexican authorities in Sonora and Sinaloa had in one way or another obligated the Chinese Mexicans to cross the border illegally and had thus flagrantly violated U.S. immigration law, which prohibited Chinese entry, a charge Mexican officials routinely denied. At odds with each other, the United States and Mexico attempted to assert national power at the shared border. As Adam McKeown has shown, the rise of nationalism and the nation-state went hand in hand with the legitimization of border enforcement and restrictive migration law around the world. By the early twentieth century, nations and their citizens had internalized the notion that "civilized" countries had the right to delimit borders. A nation's status rested on the existence of laws regulating migration and their implementation—at national borders.[8]

The INS ultimately concluded that in evicting Chinese from Sonora and forcing American agencies to bear the brunt of the removal, Mexican officials had infringed on U.S. sovereignty and damaged relations between the two nations. On 29 November 1932, J. Reuben Clark Jr. at the U.S. Department of State in Washington, D.C., drew on the testimonies of Chinese in a letter to Manuel C. Téllez at the Secretaría de Relaciones Exteriores (Foreign Relations Department) in Mexico City warning that serious international repercussions could arise from the expulsion of Chinese. The United States was aware that Mexican local and state authorities had taken high numbers of Chinese very close to Nogales and given them a short time to leave Sonora; as a result, the Chinese had been unable to meet the official deadlines for departure unless they crossed illegally into Arizona. In other cases, Mexican authorities virtually forced Chinese across the border. Sonora's recent actions, Clark argued, were inconsistent with the neighborly friendliness that had thus far characterized the relationship between Arizona and Sonora and the two countries more generally. Department of State officials and the Department of Labor communicated and filed reports on the expulsion of Chinese and the "refugee" crisis through early 1934.[9]

Crossing into the United States

Chinese passage into Arizona from Sonora increased in the fall of 1931, following the start of the Sonoran expulsions in August and Rodolfo Elías Calles's assumption of the governorship in September.[10] The numbers spiked again in early 1932, when anti-Chinese activity in Sonora became particularly rampant.[11] The District Court of Arizona in Nogales heard cases of "illegal" immigrants and other people who violated the National Prohibition Act, which forbade the entry of alcohol and certain migrants during the early 1930s.

In the summer of 1932, after a year in which INS agents had apprehended hundreds of Chinese crossing the Arizona-Sonora border, the agency began to compile a comprehensive record of the cases and ensuing costs. U.S. officials perceived the situation as an unfolding refugee crisis. Individual immigration inspectors in charge at the U.S. border towns of Douglas, Naco, and Nogales as well as in nearby Tucson sent lists of refugees to superiors at the Department of Labor, which oversaw the INS. After

TABLE 3. Chinese Apprehended and Tried at Nogales, Arizona, for Illegal Entry into the United States, January 1931–July 1932

	Chinese Tried for Illegal Entry	Total Number of Illegal Entry Cases
1931		
January	0	14
February	0	7
March	0	13
April	0	22
May	0	8
June	2	17
July	4	32
August	5	28
September	49	69
October	176	202
November	105	141
December	25	46
1932		
January	30	41
February	208	223
March	0	14
April	0	5
May	0	15
June	0	5
July	0	6

Total Number of Chinese Tried: 604

Total Number of Trials: 908

Source: Box 1 of 1, U.S. District Court (Arizona) Final Mittimus Records, 1930–32, Arizona Historical Society, Tucson.

Note: These numbers are based only on people with Chinese names. Some Chinese may have had documents with Spanish first names and surnames, since some Chinese in Mexico had become naturalized Mexican citizens and adopted Mexican naming practices.

agents completed the first register of Chinese refugees whom they had deported to China between the summer of 1931 and the summer of 1932, twenty "supplementary lists" documented the apprehension and deportation of additional Chinese refugees from Mexico between late 1932 and early 1934. The lists itemized the refugees' names and dates of railroad passage to San Francisco for travel to China; they also included the specific amounts paid in each case for guards at immigration jails, meals, and railroad and steamship fares. The INS spent $530,234.41 to maintain and deport a total of 4,317 refugees. These figures included at least 574 people who were members of 114 Chinese Mexican families traveling as units.[12]

The Refugee Crisis in International Context

The INS considered keeping the refugees in immigration jails for long periods to discourage continued illegal entry; officials also considered simply sending the Chinese back to Mexico to force that nation to pay the costs of deportation. In the end, however, the United States sent the Chinese Mexicans to China and covered the expenses involved. Although the Chinese government made modest attempts at repayment, the Mexican government paid nothing to the United States. As a consequence of Chinese exclusion, authorities detained thousands of Chinese at the immigration facility at Angel Island in San Francisco Bay between 1910 and 1940.[13] In early 1932, for example, the detention center held more than four hundred Chinese refugees from Mexico awaiting deportation to China on Dollar Line steamships.[14]

As the refugee crisis gained international attention, organizations in China and the Chinese community in the United States became involved in the refugees' plight. Home-district associations known as *huiguan* (meeting hall or gathering place) had a long history in China and eventually played a key role in the lives of the Chinese overseas. Chinese brought the *huiguan* system to the United States in the mid-nineteenth century to help establish social, economic, and political stability. Led by merchants, the associations not only provided leadership but also maintained social control in migrant communities. As the anti-Chinese movement gained ground in the United States, the diverse *huiguan* became part of a single umbrella organization to more effectively lead the struggle against discrimination. The Chinese Consolidated Benevolent Association, known less formally as the Chinese Six Companies, played a crucial role in combating anti-Chinese activity in the United States. Based in San Francisco,

Chinese detainees at the Angel Island Immigration Station carved poems, made up of Chinese characters, into the walls of the barracks where they were held. The largest of the carvings is located in a small room separate from the men's barracks; apparently, it was valued so much that it provided a rationale for the preservation of the facility as a museum. Here is a translation of the carving:

Detained in this wooden house for several tens of days,
It is all because of the Mexican exclusion law which
     implicates me.
It's a pity heroes have no way of exercising their prowess.
I can only await the word so that I can snap Zu's whip.

From now on, I am departing far from this building.
All of my fellow villagers are rejoicing with me.
Don't say that everything within is Western styled.
Even if it is built with jade, it has turned into a cage.

—author and date unknown

From Him Mark Lai, Genny Lim, and Judy Yung, *Island: Poetry and History of Chinese Immigrants on Angel Island, 1910–1940* (Seattle: University of Washington Press, 1991), 134–35. Reprinted by permission of the University of Washington Press.

the Six Companies became the central organization of the Chinese not only in the United States but also in U.S. colonies as well as areas of Latin America that lacked Chinese diplomatic representation.[15]

In early 1932, three hundred Chinese refugees awaited travel to China on a combination freight and passenger steamer from San Marcos Island off the eastern coast of the peninsular Baja California territory. The Chinese consul general in San Francisco had made arrangements to cover the passage for Chinese who were destitute; others had the means to pay for themselves. The Chinese originally were to travel on grain carriers that departed regularly from the Columbia River and Puget Sound areas in the U.S. Pacific Northwest en route to Shanghai. The Chinese consul general had reached an agreement with American ship operator W. L. Comyn to offer a minimum passage fee because Chinese were stranded in San Francisco and other Pacific Coast ports, living on the charity of local countrymen who had been in the nation before the exclusion era began or were exempted as merchants, officials, teachers, students, or travelers. Other Chinese who had been unable to enter the United States were stuck in Mexican seaports. When many refugees found themselves unable to travel to the northern ports from which the grain ships departed, the plan was delayed. The Six Companies then made a deal with Comyn so that the ship leaving from San Marcos Island would transport both gypsum and Chinese refugees to Shanghai. The ship was scheduled to travel down the West Coast to La Paz, Baja California, before proceeding further south to the Mexican mainland port of Manzanillo, Colima, and then heading north to collect refugees from the ports in the Gulf of California—Mazatlán and Guaymas. From there, the ship would continue to San Francisco to pick up Chinese and Chinese Mexicans whose permits to remain in the United States were up or about to expire. Only then would the vessel finally head to China. After unloading the gypsum in Shanghai, the steamer was to travel down the eastern coast to drop off the refugees, most of whom were from Guangdong Province.[16]

In 1933, as the anti-Chinese movement reverberated beyond Mexico and the borderlands, the Shanghai press began to cover the expulsions. Local newspapers reported that Chinese organizations had set up relief for desperate refugees from Mexico. An international mutual aid association for Chinese migrants, the Chinese Overseas Union, offered ten dollars to each expelled adult and five dollars to each child. In addition, the Mexican Refugees Maintenance Association worked to help the refugees resettle in China. The Guangdong provincial government also produced reports on charitable operations to help resettle unemployed returning Chinese. One such report sent to Hong Kong described Chinese expelled from northern states in Mexico who had passed through the United States en route to China.[17]

"I Did Not Want to Leave Mexico; I Have Lived There Longer Than I Have in China": Describing the Expulsions

In spite of the existence of Spanish-language interpreters, INS records of the Chinese Mexican refugee crisis contained numerous errors, including Anglicized listings of Mexican names. These mistakes underscore the broader experience of Chinese Mexicans: After being ejected from northern Mexico, they encountered cultural misreading by the U.S. nation-state, which categorized them as refugees and ultimately deported them as part of an excluded group. Chinese often elected the Spanish rather than the

Chinese interpreters the agency provided. The INS may have lacked interpreters who spoke the Chinese men's particular dialects. Nonetheless, the fact that they testified in Spanish was significant. Chinese had undoubtedly become part of local communities in northern Mexico in the previous decades. The Spanish translators who helped immigration agents interview hundreds of Chinese men and an exceptional Mexican woman had Spanish surnames, and some were women. These cultural brokers witnessed the detainment and ultimate deportation of Chinese Mexican families. How did these Mexicans, who probably lived in the United States while they worked as interpreters for the INS, perceive the mixed-race families they encountered in the facilities? Female interpreters watched as the agency deported women with whom the interpreters shared cultural and linguistic commonalities simply because they had entered the United States with Chinese men.

Chinese testimony before U.S. immigration agents brought to light the haphazard nature of the Sonoran and eventually the Sinaloan expulsions. Chinese men described a wide range of situations that had led them to cross the international boundary. Nevertheless, two broad themes emerged. On the one hand, Chinese had entered the United States voluntarily to escape escalating maltreatment in Sonora. In some cases, the only way they could comply with the Mexican-imposed deadlines for leaving the country was by heading north. On the other hand, Mexican officials had transported Chinese to the boundary and forced them across, at times even literally pushing them through gaps in the international boundary fence, a brazen violation of U.S. immigration law and a clear assertion of regional and national authority.[18]

Cho Lai entered the United States of his own volition, traveling north because people in Navojoa had become deeply antagonistic toward him. After immigration agents detained him in June 1932, he testified, "I did not want to leave Mexico; I have lived there longer than I have in China." Cho Lai had been in Mexico for thirty-three years, four in the port of Mazatlán and the past twenty-nine in Navojoa. Cho Lai and other Chinese men had made Mexico a second home and left only because anti-Chinese hatred had become intolerable. The movement against Chinese abruptly broke ties and patterns that had existed for decades.[19]

Another longtime resident of Mexico, Lee Hung Pen, also opted to travel north because of persecution. In September 1932, he told INS officials in Tucson that Sonoran authorities had come to his home in Navojoa the previous July and transported him and twenty-four other Chinese to the state line between Sonora and Sinaloa. Once there, the Chinese had headed in different directions: Lee traveled back to Navojoa on foot because his wife, Francisca Tan, and their six children resided there. Lee had lived in Mexico for thirty-eight years, the last twenty-two of them in Navojoa. After he returned, local officials kept insisting that he should leave Sonora, telling him that the United States would send him to China, so he took his family to Nogales, Arizona. Once they crossed the border, the INS apprehended the family, sending Lee, his wife, and their children—Lee Wen Fee, Lee Wen Lee, Lee Wen Mu, Lee Lo Nue, Lee Chee Nue, and Lee Gee Nue—to San Francisco in October 1932 for deportation to China.[20]

Hong Sheo had also left Sonora to escape abuse. In September 1932, he told U.S. officials that he had lived in the port of Guaymas for eleven years. After Mexicans refused to let Chinese work and took their clothing and vegetables, Hong had to quit farming. Mexicans soon began throwing rocks at Chinese on the streets, and the hostile climate persuaded Hong to make a weeklong journey on foot to Nogales, where he crossed the border.[21]

Felipe Wong Ley also voluntarily left Sonora, taking his Mexican-origin family with him when anti-Chinese forces in the central town of Baviácora confiscated his pharmacy. According to his daughter, Antonia Wong Enríquez de López, some people had told her father to take the family to Sinaloa, where he and his wife, Ester Enríquez Wong, had been married, because the situation was less bad for Chinese there. Instead, his pride led him to take his family to China via the United States. Knowing that his wife would refuse to move to China, Wong Ley took her "engañada" (under false pretenses), telling her that the family was going on a vacation. After they left, a friend warned Enríquez Wong's mother that her son-in-law was "going to take them to China!" Fearing that she would never see her daughter and grandchildren again, the woman traveled from Baviácora to the Nogales border, though she never caught up with the Wongs. The INS deported Felipe Wong Ley, Ester Enríquez Wong, Antonia Wong, Elodia Wong, Felipe Wong, and María Ester Wong as part of a group of refugees from Mexico in the summer of 1933; however, Enríquez Wong and her daughters would soon return to Sonora.[22]

In other cases, local police and other authorities in Sonora rounded up Chinese and compelled them to travel north on trains or sometimes in trucks and cars. Officials either obliged Chinese to buy railway passage with their own money or purchased tickets for them. In some instances, military escorts made sure that the Chinese remained on the trains until

Nogales. Authorities around Sonora collaborated with police in Nogales, Sonora, and certain Mexican, Chinese, and American businessmen on the border. Officials or private citizens sometimes met Chinese at the Nogales train station and held them in jails or boardinghouses before escorting them to the international boundary. In other instances, Chinese were free to leave the Nogales train station and stayed with friends or acquaintances or in rooming houses before finding the border on their own or asking Mexicans on the street for directions. Chinese described a range of experiences in their testimonies.

Chinese border businessmen aided and profited from the expulsion, escaping eviction because the services they provided facilitated the removal of their countrymen. These Chinese possessed language skills and cultural capital that Sonoran officials valued. Chinese refugees testified that in Nogales, they paid around two pesos to stay at the Hotel Pacífico, run by a Chinese man, Ng Bak. Ng Bak and his associates charged another two pesos to help the Chinese cross the border into the United States. Some Chinese voluntarily went to the hotel after hearing that the owner could help them enter the United States. In other cases, Mexican authorities conspired with Ng Bak to take Chinese to the hotel, lock them in rooms, and then transport them to the border after nightfall.[23]

Other sites also offered accommodations to the expelled. Some Chinese stayed at a rooming house owned by a naturalized American citizen known as Captain Baker, while others lodged at an establishment next to Hotel Pacífico owned by a Mexican citizen, José Ramírez. Chinese, Mexican, and American entrepreneurs worked with Sonoran officials to increase profits in a border economy beset by depression.[24]

Longtime Sonoran resident Lo Ping Som was among the Chinese who left Sonora by force and stayed as a captive at Ng Bak's hotel before entering the United States under duress. He had been a farm laborer in Guaymas for twenty-five years. Having "lived longer in Mexico than I did in China," Lo did not want to leave. He and his wife had married in Guangdong Province, but their seven children were born in Guaymas, and "this is their home," he told INS officials in Nogales, Arizona, in August 1932. Nevertheless, the local chief of police ran the family out of Sonora, ordering them to depart for the United States. Lo asked for a month to prepare; the chief gave him a week.[25]

On the day of departure, the chief kept Lo and his family in jail until the train arrived and then took them to the station and bought their tickets. Lo's "children did not want to leave and they began to cry." The family had friends and acquaintances in Guaymas, and he testified, when people in the crowded depot "heard my children cry, they came over and asked what was wrong." Perturbed by the commotion, the chief angrily told Lo that if the "children did not stop crying, he would slap them across the face." He soon put the family on the train and instructed them to stay aboard until Nogales, where a police officer was waiting to transfer them to Hotel Pacífico. After depositing them at the hotel, the officer returned the next morning with a Mexican customs agent, who loaded the family into one car and put a group of seven Chinese who had been in jail in another vehicle. Again, Lo testified, his "children began to cry because they had been woke [sic] up out of their sleep." The unsympathetic customs officer "kept saying to them, shut your mouth." Before transporting them to the international boundary fence, the official demanded one peso from each person in the two cars. At the border, the agent told everyone in the group to get under the wire. Once the rest of the group had gone, Lo and his wife passed through the fence; the officers then shoved their children across.[26]

The INS apprehended and separated the family, taking Lo's wife and children to Tucson and keeping him in Nogales to give testimony. The agency deported him to San Francisco and eventually to China in the fall of 1932. It is unclear whether officials deported his wife and children with, before, or after him, since their names do not appear on any of the INS lists.[27]

Chang Chow had lived in Mexico for thirty-eight years, the past three in Navojoa, before he entered the United States under pressure. Several Mexicans wearing anti-Chinese campaign buttons had come to his home in mid-1932 and told him that the governor had ordered him to leave. Four Mexicans then took him, his wife, and their three children to the train station; he was unsure of who had bought their tickets. After Chang and his family arrived in Nogales, three Mexicans with pistols transported them to a small vacant house at the edge of town, locked them inside, and periodically brought them meals. Two days later, three Mexicans took Chang and his family on foot to the boundary, raised the wire for them, and told them to pass through a gap in the fence.[28]

Sonoran officials or police robbed Chinese and compelled them to enter the United States illegally as penniless refugees. Huey Pin had lived in Mexico for twenty-three years and peddled vegetables with a wagon from house to house in Empalme, as other Chinese had done across Sonora for decades. But harassment by local authorities and ordinary citizens soon became unbearable. He traveled north in the summer of 1932 and was jailed in Nogales, Sonora, where officials took "all my money and forced me to come through the fence. I did not want to come this way, but I could do nothing else." Corrupt officials justified stealing from the Chinese on the grounds that they had earned their money in Sonora unfairly, at the expense of Mexicans, an argument that *antichinistas* had made since the 1910s.[29]

Sonoran authorities treated poor peddlers and middling business owners with equal inhumanity. For thirteen years, Chie Ming had lived in Navojoa, where he operated a grocery and clothing store with two partners. As anti-Chinese sentiment grew stronger, Chie planned to return to China by his own means and traveled to Culiacán, Sinaloa, to gather money for the trip from associates. He and two compatriots bought train tickets to Nogales in the summer of 1932. When the train arrived in Empalme, a group of Chinese from Guaymas boarded the train with guards, who forced Chie and his companions to join the group. In Nogales, police officers took his possessions and jailed him, even though he tried to explain that he had come as a passenger rather than a prisoner and could pay his own fare to China. Local police stole from him $165, a new bedroll, and a silk shirt as well as other items, and they later obliged him to cross the border into the United States with the other captive Chinese. After the deeply degrading experience, Chie told INS agents, "I did not want to come to the United States this way. I had bought this new bedroll intending to go steerage on the ship from San Francisco, and had brought sufficient money to pay my way home. But now the Mexicans have taken my money and forced me into the country. I could not help it." Compelling the Chinese to become destitute refugees regardless of their class status in Mexico, Sonoran officials cared little about Chinese dignity.[30]

Further complicating the refugee crisis for the United States were several hundred Chinese Mexican children. Sonoran authorities expelled Roberto M. Fu, who entered U.S. territory a widower with seven children in 1933. He had married Ana María Domínguez in Aconchi, a town in the central district of Arizpe, nearly fifteen years earlier, but she died shortly after their youngest child was born, just before officials expelled the family. A Chinese Mexican compatriot would later write from Macau that the anti-Chinese movement had caused her great stress and was a factor in her death. The United States apprehended and ultimately deported Fu (whose Chinese name was Fu Gui) and his young children, Roberto Jr., Manuela, Jacinto, Tomás, Ventura, Amelia, and baby Maximiliano. Within a few years, the family would be split by exclusionary Mexican repatriation policies, struggling for years to be reunited. Lázaro Cárdenas eventually attempted to repudiate the anti-Chinese movement by welcoming Mexican women and Chinese Mexican children back into the nation, but his administration barred Chinese men, causing the Fu family and many others great heartache.[31]

Officials in Sonora also expelled Ho Ping and Celsa Echeverría and their children, Miguel Ho, Reinalda Ho, Alfonso Ho, Dolores Ho, José Ho, Roberto Ho, Celsa Ho, and Jesús Ho from the small central town Esperanza. After detaining them, the INS sent the family to San Francisco for deportation to China on 20 March 1933. Another child would be born in China, and Echeverría and her children would wait nearly thirty years to return to Mexico during the second official repatriation under the administration of Adolfo López Mateos.[32]

Mimicking Sonoran policy, local and state authorities in Sinaloa also expelled Chinese men and their families. Antonio Yee had arrived to work in the mines in Culiacán in 1928. With the help of the local Chinese community, he soon opened a small store and met Cruz Arredondo. They married and had three sons, Alfonso "Poncho" Yee, Jacinto Yee, and Antonio Yee Jr. In 1932, authorities rounded them up and expelled them to Arizona with other Chinese Mexicans. Arredondo de Yee's granddaughter, Conchita Villalba Yee, recalled that "given the choice to go with their husbands or stay and raise their children alone, many women, like Abuelita Cruz, chose to go." After the Yees crossed into the United States, immigration agents apprehended and eventually deported them to China with other refugees from Mexico in January 1933. Embraced by Cárdenas, the mother and children would soon return to Mexico.[33]

Sinaloan officials also expelled a Chinese man and his Chinese Mexican son, Francisco Chong López, in 1932. During the same year, Rafael Wong and his wife, Manuela González de Wong, left the state. Both had been born in Dorado, Sinaloa, and were twenty-four years old: Even Mexican-born Chinese found it difficult to remain during the expulsion era. The following year, authorities forced out of the state Chong Chin, Rosaria Luque de Chong, and their sons, Ramón Antonio Chong, Cirilo Chong, and Arcadio Chong. U.S. immigration authorities apprehended and eventually deported them to China in April 1933. Chong López, González de Wong, and the Chong Luque family would remain in southeastern China for three decades.[34]

INS records include almost no Mexican women's accounts. The focus on Chinese exclusion, the attempts to prove that Mexican officials had violated U.S. sovereignty, and the ideology of coverture together precluded immigration agents from systematically recording the women's testimonies along with those of their husbands and companions. Some women would later relate to Mexican consuls in East Asia that they had crossed into the United States because their men claimed that they had obtained permission. The women soon discovered that their families had entered illegally. After being detained by U.S. authorities, the women had no choice but to accompany their romantic partners to China as refugees.[35] Since women and children entered the nation with Chinese men, U.S. agents felt compelled to deport the families as units to China rather than split them up.

Cross-Border Chinese Smuggling

The INS accused Sonoran governor Elías Calles of flouting U.S. laws by ordering Mexican authorities to force or help Chinese refugees across the border with the United States. Calles denied the allegations.[36] Using its court system, the United States tried to prove that the governor and other Mexican officials had acted disingenuously. In late 1932, Alcadio García, a Nogales, Sonora, police officer, stood trial in Arizona for breaching U.S. immigration policy by obliging Chinese to enter the nation. García denied the charges, but the evidence against him included photographs and maps of the border that showed points where García and others had allegedly "smuggled" Chinese refugees from Mexico into the United States. In early 1933, the United States tried Alejandro Ungson (also known as Ung Son, Ng Hom, and Ng Ham), a witness in the García case, for aiding Chinese who crossed the border illegally. Ungson purportedly worked as a coyote for the accused police officer.[37]

Chinese testified that they had paid Ungson between two and five pesos each to help them enter the United States. Some characterized Ungson as a good man whose uncompromised loyalty to his countrymen had driven him to assist them, especially when they had had no money to pay for food, shelter, or his border-crossing services and he offered them at no cost. Ungson told a few of these Chinese to convey to their companions in U.S. immigration jails that he had helped them in an effort to boost his reputation. He knew that he had made enemies of some of his compatriots. Other Chinese, however, depicted Ungson as a brutal villain who had betrayed them by cooperating with the police in Nogales to profit from their expulsion. A few even testified that they were infuriated with Ungson and that if he should ever travel to China, he would have to contend with countrymen who wanted revenge. Like the Chinese hotel owner, Ungson forestalled his expulsion by offering crucial aid to Sonoran officials.[38]

"Free Trippers"

The INS persistently denounced Mexican officials' actions in forcing Chinese and Chinese Mexican families across the boundary. At the same time, the agency became convinced that some Chinese entered the United States for reasons unrelated to anti-Chinese activity and fabricated stories about their oppression in Mexico to gain passage to China. Immigration officials labeled these individuals "free trippers" and tried to distinguish them from the true "refugees." Chinese testimony fed officials' fears that word had spread in Mexico that the United States would shelter, feed, and transport Chinese. Chu Man Kam told U.S. authorities that although no one specifically had advised him to enter the country, "all the Chinese in Mexico knows [sic] that when we cross over in the United States, the American Immigration will send us back to China for nothing. The Chinese what [sic] are already in jail here, send letters to us in Mexico and tell us how good you treat the Chinese." Cho Lai testified that he and other compatriots "know how good the United States has been to all the Chinese, they have fed them and then sent them to China." Chu Fon stated, "Every Chinese in Mexico knows what the United States is doing for us, they are our good friends," and Quan Kiu told U.S. authorities, "We knew that the United States is our friend and they would take care of us."[39] Even in the era of Chinese exclusion, the United States enjoyed a certain reputation for benevolence in light of Mexico's brutal expulsion.

The word also spread in print. Ho Chung had heard from friends who read in a Chinese newspaper that if they went to Nogales, Arizona, they "would be able to get back to China without trouble." He had lived in several places including Sinaloa after arriving in Mexico seven or eight years earlier. In Los Mochis, where he had resided for the past three years, he had been unable to find work, and Mexicans treated him badly, so he settled on traveling north to the United States in the spring of 1933.[40]

Immigration inspectors used probing questions when they believed that people had suffered no ill treatment in Mexico and simply sought a free trip to China. In May 1933, agents questioned separately Ng Pak (an individual unrelated to Hotel Pacífico owner Ng Bak) and his wife, Atilana Tovar de Ng, after their family entered the United States east of Nogales.

In a rare instance of testimony by a Mexican woman, Tovar de Ng told U.S. officials that her children, Seferino Ng, who was seven, and Juvencio Ng, who was two, were born in Tampico, Tamaulipas, but the family had lived for the past two years in Culiacán, Sinaloa, where the anti-Chinese movement was strong.[41]

Ng testified that he had entered Mexico at Manzanillo, Colima, thirteen or fourteen years earlier and had lived in Monterrey, Nuevo León, and Mazatlán, Sinaloa, as well in Culiacán. When the immigration agent asked how long Ng had lived in each of the other places, he said he was unsure, prompting the inspector to note that the Chinese man had tried to evade the question. When the official inquired whether Ng had ever lived in Tamaulipas, he responded that he had been there only for a short time and did not remember when. But his wife, the agent informed him, had testified that their two children were born in Tamaulipas. Ng was unsure why she had said that but suggested that she could not recall where the family had lived. The inspector then asked for proof that they had lived in Culiacán. Ng said he had none, adding, "Mexicans treated us bad and told us to get out of Mexico." The agent prodded, "But why did you come to Nogales, Mexico, instead of going to some other part of Mexico?" Ng made no reply. The inspector continued, "Is it not a fact that you came here for the purpose of securing free transportation to China?" The agent noted that Ng failed to give a direct answer but said only that he had had no money left after paying for his family's passage north, to which some of his friends contributed. Despite official misgivings, on 11 April 1933, immigration authorities sent Ng, Tovar de Ng, and their two children to San Francisco for deportation to China.[42]

Mexican-U.S. Relations

The Mexican expulsion and the refugee problem it created in the United States weighed heavily on dealings between the two nations. U.S. diplomats complained to their Mexican counterparts that the Sonoran expulsion had compelled the United States to use its scarce resources in a depressed economy to deport to China refugees who entered its territory illegally at the behest of Mexican regional authorities. While it critiqued Sonora, the INS relied on the assistance of the Mexican federal government to curtail the influx of Chinese from Mexico. As a result of the "free tripper" problem, authorities at the U.S. embassy in Mexico City asked Mexican officials to bar nonrefugee Chinese from proceeding to the northern border unless they had papers from the American consulate—the same arrangement that applied to European immigrants.[43]

During this time, Governor Elías Calles tried to maintain a facade of cooperation with the United States. He communicated with officials at the Secretaría de Relaciones Exteriores regarding the flow of Chinese from other areas of Mexico through Sonora with the intention of crossing into the United States for free passage to China. He reported to federal officials on groups of Chinese who arrived in Sonora from Sinaloa and further south and suggested setting up a surveillance system in Navojoa to stop them from entering the state from the south. Sonoran officials had already approached Nogales, Arizona, authorities to deal cooperatively with the problem of several hundred Chinese who were in Nogales and planned to cross into the United States in the spring of 1933. Having been key in orchestrating the expulsion from the moment he took office, Elías Calles spoke out of both sides of his mouth.[44]

Although it never secured any reimbursement from Mexico, the United States obtained partial repayment from China for deporting the "Chinese refugees from Mexico" during the early 1930s. Minister Sao-Ke Alfred Sze sent the United States $4,170.94 in October 1932 and an additional $10,443.26 a year and a half later, after the refugee crisis had passed. With the second payment, the foreign minister included a letter that read, "I take this opportunity to express to you the sincere thanks of my Government for the considerate treatment shown by the American Government to the Chinese refugees who have been forced to flee from Mexico."[45] Mexico's chaotic, aggressive expulsion of Chinese helped shine a positive light on the United States in spite of its own policy of Chinese exclusion, now in effect for half a century, and the anti-Chinese sentiment and violence that had characterized the U.S. West in particular throughout the era.

By early 1934, the INS had become concerned about growing anti-Chinese activity in the northwestern peninsular border territory of Baja California. Anti-Chinese crusaders there were quite vocal and organized during this time and maintained communication with their brethren in Sonora. Alfredo Echeverría, a leader in the Hermosillo campaign, had repeatedly traveled to Mexicali, Baja California, to give speeches.[46] But neither high-level government officials nor the press there supported the movement, thus preventing it from gaining the strength to carry out a massive expulsion of Chinese. In February 1934, when violence against Chinese erupted in the northern port of Encenada while the governor was away, the local press condemned the anti-Chinese crusade. Using his national connections to combat the anti-Chinese movement in his area, Eduardo Guajardo, a lawyer for local Chinese, sent his brother-in-law, President Abelardo Rodríguez, several communications asking for his support. These efforts apparently helped even though Rodríguez was under the watchful eye of *jefe máximo* Plutarco Elías Calles.[47] The anti-Chinese movement in Baja California never gained significant traction. Nonetheless, the INS kept abreast of developments as a precautionary measure in light of the Sonoran and Sinaloan expulsions.

U.S. officials also followed anti-Chinese activity in other northern states. In the summer of 1932, some Chihuahua residents considered holding anti-Chinese demonstrations. But in light of the economic woes that took hold in Sonora after it started expelling the Chinese, Chihuahuans did "not take very readily to the viewpoint of their neighboring state."[48] Nevertheless, organized anti-Chinese activities erupted in Chihuahua the following spring. In a demonstration in the border city of Ciudad Juárez, across from El Paso, Texas, members of the National Defense League picketed Chinese stores and placed Mexican flags across the establishments' entrances. The mayor publicly stated his regret that the protesters had obtained the flags from his office "under misrepresentation," and both he and the governor of Chihuahua offered the local Chinese protection from anti-Chinese forces. Activists boycotted Chinese merchants in the weeks leading up to the protest, but authorities provided Chinese with ample security. The lack of government support notwithstanding, anti-Chinese organizing continued in Ciudad Juárez. In July, El Paso's *El Continental* reported that the Juárez campaign had promised that all of the Chinese in Mexico would soon be expelled. Concerned about the potential expenses of another refugee crisis, U.S. immigration officials investigated and found that maintaining and deporting the thousand or so Chinese who lived in Ciudad Juárez would cost the United States between $130,000 and $150,000 if they crossed into Texas or New Mexico.[49]

Mexico's International Reputation

Newspapers in the United States and China portrayed Mexico unfavorably as a result of the maltreatment of Chinese in the northern states.[50] The Shanghai press informed readers that not only Chinese men but also numerous Mexican women and mixed-race children had arrived in China as a result of the expulsion of Chinese from Mexico.[51] Furthermore, the

United States rather than Mexico had paid the refugees' passage, and "the returning Chinese were very grateful for the generous and kind treatment accorded them" by American immigration authorities. According to the Shanghai press, Mexican authorities ordered another twenty thousand Chinese to leave Mexico by the end of June 1933.[52] Ironically, the U.S. policy of racial exclusion earned the country positive depictions for its willingness to accommodate and deport refugees to China. Indeed, coinciding racial ideologies and negative views of the Chinese in the United States and Mexico led to the interconnected expulsions and deportations from the borderlands.

While the United States and China criticized Mexico, Mexican officials argued that American shipping companies had failed to respect Mexican immigration policies regarding the Chinese during the early 1930s. The Mexican consul in Yokohama, Japan, Manuel Tello, communicated with the Mexican consulate in San Francisco regarding the American Dollar Steamship Line's transportation of Chinese to Mexico. Tello also met with a Canadian Pacific shipping line agent regarding Chinese passengers to Vancouver or Seattle, since these travelers proceeded to the Mexican border by train.[53] Shipping companies had certainly benefited from the illegal movement of Chinese in the late nineteenth and early twentieth centuries; the steamship fares to transfer Chinese men and Chinese Mexican families to China during the expulsion period only added to those profits.

After decades of being part of local communities in Sonora and Sinaloa, the Chinese faced expulsion from the places they had claimed as second homes. Mexican women and Chinese Mexican children accompanied these men for diverse reasons, sometimes by choice and other times by force. The Chinese men and Chinese Mexican families who entered U.S. territory during the expulsion period did so under different circumstances but invariably complicated Mexican-U.S. relations. As part of a longer chapter of contention with the northern neighbor, Mexican authorities handed the United States a refugee crisis, forcing that nation to bear the better part of the cost of ridding northern Mexico of the Chinese and their Mexican-origin families. When U.S. immigration agents apprehended Chinese Mexicans, the long-standing U.S. policy of Chinese exclusion guaranteed that they would soon travel to China.

Since women and children entered the nation with Chinese men, the INS was obliged to send the refugees to China as family units rather than separate them. By deporting Mexican women and their children, the

United States folded into Chinese exclusion the era's dominant gender ideology and citizenship codes of coverture and the "feme covert" that stripped women of their citizenship when they married foreigners. But what happened to these Mexican women and their Chinese Mexican children in China during a time when a woman's citizenship status hinged on that of her husband?

PART THREE

Chinese Mexican Community
Formation and Reinventing Mexican
Citizenship Abroad

CHAPTER FIVE

The Women Are Neither Chinese
nor Mexican

Citizenship and Family Ruptures in Guangdong
Province, Early 1930s

Rosa Murillo de Chan arrived in Guangdong Province in southeastern China with her husband, Felipe Chan, and their children in 1930. Even though the mass eviction of Chinese had not yet begun, growing anti-Chinese activity in Sinaloa had been a factor in the family's departure. Once in China, Murillo de Chan discovered that her husband had another wife, although he had told her otherwise in Mexico. It shocked and appalled her to live next door to the Chinese wife, whose side she perceived her in-laws had taken. She had hoped that her sons would receive a good education in China but soon became disenchanted with their schooling in her husband's village, Kaw Kong (also written as Kau Kong). In light of these difficulties, she appealed to Mexican officials for permission to return. At first they told her that they could do nothing: She had lost her Mexican citizenship when she legally married Chan in Mazatlán, Sinaloa, in 1929, just before their trip.[1]

Murillo de Chan and Mexican women facing similar plights concerned Shanghai businessman and honorary Mexican vice consul Mauricio Fresco. In a 1932 letter to the Secretaría de Relaciones Exteriores (SRE) in Mexico City, Fresco described the problems facing Murillo de Chan and hundreds of other Mexican women and Chinese Mexican children in

Southeastern China

Guangdong Province as well as in Portuguese Macau and British Hong Kong. The women were in a severe bind. Chinese law recognized only the first wives as legitimate, and many Mexican women were married to men who already had wives in China. Mexican law held that women lost their citizenship when they married Chinese nationals. Legally, therefore, these women were in effect stateless, wrote Fresco, since "once in China, the women are neither Chinese nor Mexican."[2] Women and children under these circumstances had no legal right to protection by either Mexican or Chinese authorities. Fresco urged his superiors to engage in diplomatic negotiations to encourage Chinese officials to assist Mexican women in China. The women had sought Fresco's aid because they wanted to repatriate to Mexico, but citizenship issues complicated their ability to return.

In China, Mexican women re-created their identities and challenged notions of Mexican citizenship. Most of the women who appealed to Mexican officials to repatriate were unable to return right away. To survive, they created networks and congregated in cities. As they met other families from different parts of Mexico and tried to return home, Mexican women would become increasingly steeped in Mexican national identity. Mexico, in turn, would eventually redefine the citizenship of women who married foreigners.

Mexican citizenship law and marital practices were historically patri-archal. They were guided by long-standing European principles of cover-ture, whereby married women lost legal status and rights and were effec-tively "covered" by their husbands. Mexican law first officially expatriated women married to foreign men in 1854. An 1881 Supreme Court case and the 1886 Law of Alienage and Naturalization passed by the Mexican Con-gress upheld this policy. Although the revolutionary Constitution of 1917 brought about many striking legal changes, it failed specifically to address the citizenship of women married to foreign men. Thus, the previous stat-utes that explicitly expatriated women married to foreigners continued to guide authorities. Mexican law also recognized as aliens the Mexican-born children of foreign fathers. Legal scholars argued that this principle applied even when the children were born out of wedlock as long as the men acknowledged paternity.[3] In spite of these legal precedents, Mexican women and Chinese Mexican children in China would challenge officials to rethink conventional notions of citizenship.

Arriving in China

Hundreds of Mexican women came to reside in southeastern China by the early 1930s. Some had migrated there in the first decades of the twen-tieth century, before the expulsion era, with husbands and companions who chose to move their Mexican-origin families to the communities from which they had emigrated. Wanting to secure entry back into Mexico, Chi-nese men and their Mexican spouses requested visas from the consulate in Hong Kong and appealed to Manuel Tello, the Mexican consul in Yoko-hama, Japan. In 1930, Tello wrote to the SRE several times to inquire about whether the men could travel to Mexico with tourist visas but no passports.[4]

María Teresa Guadalajara de Lee had arrived in China with her hus-band, Eugenio Lee, in the 1920s. She appealed to authorities to repatriate because he had abandoned her and returned to Mexico City by himself in 1926. She remained in China five years later because she had lost her pass-port and neither Mexican nor Chinese authorities would grant her another one. When she appealed again, the Secretaría de Gobernación (the Mexi-can government's internal affairs branch) denied her reentry because she had been away for more than five years. Nevertheless, Mexican authorities tried to help her. They pursued her husband in Mexico to obligate him to pay for his family's return and provide any documents in his possession. With the help of her brother, Benito Guadalajara, authorities repeatedly looked for Lee, but to no avail. In spite of the lack of documentation, Mexican officials ultimately approved Guadalajara de Lee's repatriation after her brother acted on her behalf. Federal authorities told local officials in Nogales, Sonora, to permit her and her children to enter Mexico via its border with the United States in the early 1930s.[5]

María Pérez traveled to Guangdong Province with her husband and their children in the spring of 1930. Like Murillo de Chan, she lived in the small community of Kaw Kong. Pérez began appealing to authorities to repatriate to Mexico about a year after she arrived. She was unhappy because her husband had brought her to China "engañada" (under false pretenses), having told her that they were going on a vacation. He had taken out a passport with permission to reenter Mexico within six months and, since it had expired, she and her children could not return. Pérez's husband had two other spouses in China. After she made known her discontent with the situation, he took her children and threw her out. Though he gave her a very small pension, it was not enough to sustain her. He did, however, agree to pay her passage back to Mexico if she obtained government permission to return.[6]

Hundreds more Mexican women would travel to China during the expulsion years. By Fresco's accounting, more than six hundred Mexican women as well as their Chinese Mexican children arrived in China by 1933, either with the mass expulsions of Chinese men and their families from Sonora and Sinaloa or fleeing anti-Chinese activity in other areas of Mexico.[7] While some women chose to follow their husbands or companions to keep their families together, in other instances authorities simply rounded up the women and sent them out of Mexico along with their partners because mixed-race families were perceived as non-Mexican.

The Geography of Chinese Mexicans in China

ARRIVING IN VILLAGES

Chinese Mexican families at first lived primarily in villages in Guangdong Province. Antonio Yee had brought Cruz Arredondo de Yee and their children to live in his hometown, where he already had a wife and children, in early 1933, after Sinaloan authorities expelled the family and the United States deported them. Arredondo de Yee was miserable in China. Her sons felt ill at ease because they were different from their classmates and at first spoke poor Cantonese, although they improved. The mother and children would in time return to Mexico.[8]

Mexican women were profoundly dismayed at the gender norms in their husbands' or companions' communities. These practices overlapped in some ways with Mexican customs but also diverged in others, and the departures became acute in China. Historically, men in Mexico, as in China, could have only one legal wife. If they had the ability to support additional dependents, however, both Mexican and Chinese men could have concubines and additional children. Although the Chinese Revolution of 1911 had outlawed concubinage, it was still widely practiced until the Communist Revolution and the creation of the People's Republic of China in 1949, when Chairman Mao Zedong would impose a strict ban on the ancient custom. The 1950 Marriage Law sought to enforce monogamous unions.[9] Similarly, although Mexican law historically outlawed bigamy, men openly maintained multiple households. The families might even have been privy to each other's existence, but the topic was not discussed explicitly. Contrary to common practice in China, however, Mexican men's multiple households were not generally in close proximity.[10] As a consequence of this key difference in Mexican and Chinese marriage and sexual norms, Mexican women vociferously objected to having to live with or near their partners' Chinese wives. Mexican women also balked at the loss of their previous status as primary spouses and at becoming concubines in a foreign land. Moreover, they resented their ignorance of the other spouses before leaving Mexico.

After returning to their country of origin, Chinese men had to contend with conflicting sets of social and gender expectations. For those who had lived in Mexico for long periods, reintegrating into Chinese society was particularly trying. Furthermore, Chinese men's extended families pressured them to readjust to Chinese gender obligations. Local cultural imperatives held that Chinese men should seek to marry Chinese women and continue their family lines, even though Chinese overseas routinely brought home foreign wives.[11] The return of Chinese men with Mexican spouses and mixed-race children during the expulsion period sent shock waves through families and communities. Further complicating matters was the fact that the returning Chinese and their families brought back few resources, since Mexican authorities had confiscated Chinese possessions. Some Chinese men's relatives reacted with dismay and disapproval.

The situation presented intense trials for Chinese Mexican families, and most split apart after their relocation to China. Ester Enríquez Wong soon became disgruntled after her husband, Felipe Wong Ley, brought her and their children to live with his family in Guangdong Province in mid-1933.

Their eldest child, Antonia Wong Enríquez de López, who was five years old at the time, remembered her parents constantly arguing for a year before the couple separated and the mother and daughters returned to Mexico with the financial assistance of their extended family in Sonora.[12]

Although a few women and their children returned to Mexico within a short time, most Mexican women and Chinese Mexican children remained in China for years. Some continued to live with Chinese men and their families in Guangdong Province. Others separated, refusing to share space with and give up status in favor of the Chinese spouses or having been abandoned or forced out by their men. To survive, these women forged relationships with women in similar situations and appealed to Mexican consuls. Mexican women lived together or near each other, caring for their children communally.

In 1932, Euselia de Lasala wrote to Fresco and Tello on behalf of Mexican women married to Chinese men. She had become concerned about the dismal conditions in which the women lived in Jiangmen, near Guangzhou, and other towns, as well as in Macau and Hong Kong. She hoped that a consular representative would travel to the area to investigate the cases. She, her mother, and her husband, who was well known throughout Guangdong Province, offered to help the consul.[13]

But Mexican women in China did not always write to consuls to help each other. Piedad Becerra in Kaw Kong believed that her compatriots' complaints were lies. All of the other Mexican women were "much happier than me . . . living in luxury . . . in need of nothing." Yet they dared to bother Tello simply because they "quarreled" with their husbands. Removed from the situation in Yokohama, Tello worried that some Mexican women might indeed have exaggerated their situations. As he noted in one communication, Becerra must have known the women who had directed themselves to his office, since they lived in the same area.[14]

Fresco was more inclined to believe the women with whom he communicated in China. He relayed to Tello and officials in Mexico Mexican women's stories about their abuse and abandonment in China. He sought to persuade the Mexican government to act swiftly on behalf of these women, whose situations were becoming ever more unbearable. He recognized early on that Mexico's brutal treatment of the Chinese had spawned increasingly negative images of that nation in China. Consequently, he believed, Chinese men found it easier to mistreat and desert Mexican women. Mexican women and Chinese Mexican children in China paid a steep price for the expulsion of their families from Mexico. As one scholar has put it, the women "pagaron los platos rotos de la campaña antichina," or, suffered the damages wrought by the anti-Chinese campaign.[15]

Fresco had heard about the women in Guangdong Province from women he met in Shanghai. In 1931 and 1932, he repeatedly appealed to the SRE to sponsor a trip so that he could investigate the problem. The agency replied that it had no resources for such an undertaking but would grant him permission to do so on his own. Fresco had no means to travel in China, but Trinidad Lacayo at the Mexican embassy in Manila visited Guangdong Province sometime in the early 1930s, after Mexican women who lived there appealed to his office. Fresco continued to communicate with women in Cantonese villages, mainly through letters.[16]

Murillo de Chan frequently wrote to Fresco, Tello, and officials in Mexico from Kaw Kong throughout the early 1930s. While local anti-Chinese activity in Sinaloa had prompted the Chan Murillos to move, so too did the desire to educate their sons, one of whom had been in China for a decade before the rest of the family arrived. In keeping with an overseas Chinese custom, the couple had sent their eldest son, Ramón Felipe Chan, to China from Mazatlán around 1920, when he was five years old, to live with his father's Chinese relatives, one of the many kinds of transpacific households that overseas Chinese established.[17] The parents wanted their son to go to school in his father's country because Chan believed that the child could receive a good education there; the couple also hoped to send their other sons to school in China. But after seeing for herself, Murillo de Chan bitterly told Mexican consuls that in China, her sons could expect to receive schooling only in vice.[18]

Compounding her dissatisfaction with her sons' education, Murillo de Chan had become distressed because her husband had another wife living next door. Adding insult to injury, Chan's family treated his Mexican wife unkindly. Accustomed to being the only wife, as she had been in Mexico, she refused to adapt, which soon led to marital disputes. In retaliation, she told consuls, Chan had beaten her, kept her children from her, and kicked her out of the house. Her husband had also kept her passport and refused to give her any money. Even though she and her husband had been married only a few years, they had been together much longer. Chan's behavior toward her had changed dramatically in China. "I have lived with him for twenty years," she wrote in one letter, "and in all those years, sir, he never treated me as badly as he does now that he is in his own country." The move to China and competing gender norms and expectations had caused the family great stress and quickly deteriorated the couple's bond.[19]

Murillo de Chan believed that her husband was angry with her partially because he thought she had persuaded another Mexican woman to repatriate to Mexico. She denied the accusation: She lived on the outskirts of the village, while the woman who returned to Mexico had resided in the center, and they had had little chance to communicate. Nevertheless, Chan blamed his wife for her compatriot's departure and resented it because he did not want Mexican women to return and relay to people in Mexico "how base Chinese customs were," Murillo de Chan wrote to Mexican officials.[20]

In fact, the Overseas Chinese Association expressed concern about the ways Mexican women depicted China in these years. Newspapers in the United States picked up reports that Mexican women who had accompanied Chinese men out of Mexico were "suffering severe hardships in their adopted land." Dispatches from Guangzhou reported that the Overseas Chinese Association had "urged Mexican deportees to prevent their wives from writing 'wrong impressions of China' to their former homes."[21] The expulsion of Chinese from Mexico and the presence of their Mexican spouses in local communities, as well as the women's efforts to repatriate to Mexico, caused anxiety regarding China's international image. Felipe Chan and other Chinese men had to negotiate multiple pressures from local institutions—including the Overseas Chinese Association's entreaties to men to help keep their wives' negative views from getting out— as well as their unhappy spouses. In turn, Rosa Murillo de Chan and other women had to navigate the conflicting sets of objectives that tore through expelled families in China.

Felipe Chan had applied for a permit to return to Mexico within two years of their departure, and his wife wanted to repatriate before it expired. Since she had no funds, she urged the Mexican government to compel him to pay for her return. As the principal associate of a Mazatlán-based business, El Palacio de Hierro, her husband had resources. But Mexican officials denied Murillo de Chan's repeated entreaties in 1931 and 1932 on the grounds that she had neither the necessary funds nor her husband's permission. The Mexican government had no power to grant her a passport as a Mexican citizen because she had relinquished her citizenship rights by marrying Chan.[22]

In time, Murillo de Chan's case pushed authorities to rethink Mexican exit/reentry rules and change the nature of citizenship policies regarding women married to foreigners. Her letters led officials to try to prevent other Mexican women from being caught in similar binds. Authorities informally discouraged women from leaving Mexico with Chinese men and denied Chinese men's reentry without their Mexican wives and children. On 10 March 1932, a government edict officially required Chinese men who departed Mexico with Mexican-origin families to deposit in cash the amount necessary for their families' return and barred them from reentering Mexico without those families. The mandate noted explicitly that the "obligatory" and "indispensable" deposit of five hundred pesos for each adult applied even though Mexican women had surrendered their citizenship rights by marrying Chinese nationals. Circular 94 soon reached local governments around the nation. The Chinese legation in Mexico City called for the measure's repeal on the grounds that it violated the rights of Chinese immigrants in Mexico. For their part, authorities at Mexico's Consular Department defended the decree, noting that its provisions complemented rather than conflicted with the Ley de Extranjería y Naturalización (Law on Aliens and Naturalization) and the Mexican Constitution regarding the nationality of Mexicans who had obtained another citizenship through marriage. Its sole aim, they argued, was to help protect Mexicans in unfortunate situations in China—whose numbers had increased with rather alarming frequency—and to prevent future problems. Pointing to the flexible nature of Mexican nationality in the postrevolutionary era, Mexican women's appeals spurred officials to create a caveat in gendered citizenship policy.[23]

During this time, Felipe Chan appealed to consuls to return to Mexico because he needed to check on his business in Sinaloa. Tello denied Chan's visa and informed him of the new policy stipulating that he could return only with his Mexican wife and children. Chan had wanted to travel alone and subsequently returned to Kaw Kong. Suspicious that he might try to get to Mexico another way, Tello asked officials in Mazatlán and at the consulate in San Francisco to notify their superiors if Chan attempted to reenter Mexico without permission via those ports. Chan presented Tello with a letter in which Murillo de Chan asked the consul to allow her husband to return. Committed as she was to educating her children in China, she wrote, she wanted her husband to travel to Sinaloa without the family because he had to make sure that the business was secure. However, Murillo de Chan later told Tello that her husband had forced her to write that letter, and Mexican authorities thenceforth perceived Chan as a "pernicious foreigner" who should never receive a visa to travel to Mexico.[24]

CREATING ENCLAVES IN CITIES

Over time, Mexican women and Chinese Mexican families gravitated to the cities of Shanghai and Nanjing and to the foreign colonies of Macau, a Portuguese holding since 1557, and Hong Kong, a British colony since 1842. Greater economic opportunities were available to Mexican women in urban settings, where they could work as domestic servants or in Catholic churches and other institutions. Mexican diplomatic representatives were housed in Shanghai and Nanjing during the early twentieth century. Furthermore, women drew on newly created Chinese Mexican systems of support. For those who wanted to repatriate, moreover, ships traveling to Mexico departed regularly from the port of Hong Kong.

Though Fresco knew that Mexican women had traveled to China with Chinese partners, he did not encounter one of these couples personally until April 1931. One day on a Shanghai street, he overheard a Chinese man speaking Spanish to a woman. Fresco approached her, they spoke for a while, and she invited him to her home and then took him to another Mexican woman's house. He thus observed firsthand the miserable conditions in which these women lived. One of them rarely went out because she felt desolate and afraid, especially as she had no mastery of Chinese languages. He then started communicating with others, beginning to grasp the deeper troubles of their circumstances. He lamented to officials in Mexico that poverty and desperation characterized these women's experiences in China, leading them to want to repatriate. He sought to resolve the problems of lack of resources and citizenship that would prevent them from returning home.[25]

CONGREGATING IN MACAU

Macau's cosmopolitan flavor and familiar Latin, Iberian, and Catholic traditions attracted not only Mexican women who had separated from their spouses in China but also Chinese Mexican families who had remained unified. They formed close-knit ties with other Latin Americans in Macau as well as in Hong Kong, ultimately creating a vibrant, coherent community that would foster diasporic Mexican national identity formation and become the foundation for struggles to repatriate to Mexico.[26]

Georgina Victorica was drawn to Macau in the fall of 1931. She was from the northern Mexican state of Durango, but her family had moved to Huatabampo, a small community in southern Sonora, where she had lived with her Chinese spouse before authorities expelled the couple. Her husband, Hanfon, died soon after they arrived in China. His family was unsupportive and mistreated her, so she moved to Macau. Seeking repatriation to Mexico, she lived on the charity of local Portuguese authorities.[27]

The members of the Wong Campoy family stayed together through their expulsion from Sonora, the passage through the United States as refugees, and the move to China in 1933. Dolores Campoy Wong had decided to follow her husband out of love and devotion and to keep the family together. Once in China, however, she had a difficult time with linguistic and cultural differences and became deeply unhappy. Her daughter, María del Carmen Irma Wong Campoy Maher Conceição, recalled experiences that terrified her mother and the family in the father's village. One day, after Alfonso Wong Fang left town to go to a meeting, tigers circled the lagoon that surrounded their house, leaving his wife and children feeling trapped and fearful. Even more frightening, one of the bandits who roamed the countryside in those years tried to kidnap the family's oldest son, Alfonso Wong Campoy, although Dolores foiled the attempt. After that incident, the Wong Campoys left Guangdong Province and resettled in Macau, where the father conducted business and later worked for the government and the mother performed domestic services in people's homes. She was much more at ease in the Portuguese colony as a result of its Latin and Catholic flavor and the strong friendships she formed with other Mexican and Latin American women. Two of the couple's children, Antonio René Wong Campoy and Raquel Wong Campoy, were born in Macau.[28]

Refashioning Mexican Citizenship

As Mexican women forged networks in cities and communicated with consuls, Mexican officials became more and more concerned about the women's plight. Fresco and Tello at first asked the SRE whether they could even advocate for women such as Murillo de Chan without their husbands' permission since they were no longer Mexican citizens. Mexican authorities researched citizenship law and created guidelines for the varied cases. In time, they circumvented gendered citizenship policy by helping Mexican women in diverse situations. Frequent official exchanges regarding foreign policy and international jurisdiction in these cases helped shape

Mexican citizenship and nationality as well as Mexico's participation in the global landscape during the formative postrevolutionary period.

The most straightforward cases were those of free association, in which the women had without a doubt retained Mexican citizenship. In 1932, Emilia García, who was living in Hong Kong and wanted to return to the southern Mexican state of Chiapas, told Mexican consuls that her children's father was Chinese, but she had never married him. The children's birth certificates listed them as "hijos naturales" (children born outside of marriage) and recorded the father as unknown.[29]

Mexican women who had legally married Chinese men were more problematic. Mexican authorities consulted Mexican, Chinese, and international marriage and nationality law to help plan a course of action for women in these circumstances. As one official noted, the Ley de Extranjería y Naturalización stated that "the Mexican woman who does not acquire her husband's nationality upon marriage to him in the laws of his country, shall conserve hers." In response to Mexican authorities' inquiries, Samuel Sung Young of the Chinese legation in Mexico City relayed that a foreign woman married to a Chinese citizen acquired Chinese citizenship unless her country's laws established that she should keep her citizenship after such a marriage. Mexican officials also observed that Article 8 of the 12 April 1930 International Convention on Nationality held, "If national law causes a woman to lose her nationality upon marrying a foreigner, the consequence shall be conditioned by and subject to the acquisition of her husband's nationality." Thus, Mexican, Chinese, and international law agreed that Mexican women lost Mexican citizenship and became Chinese citizens upon marrying Chinese nationals.[30]

The common practices of dual marriage and concubinage in China both further complicated matters and opened loopholes for Mexican women and the consuls assisting them. Chinese men's families arranged marriages in China, both before the men departed and after they returned from Mexico and even if they had married abroad. But civil codes enacted after the Chinese Revolution of 1911 made concubinage a crime in China, as in Mexico. As Sung Young relayed to Mexican officials, Article 985 of the Chinese Civil Code held that a person who had a wife could not obtain another, even if one of the marriages was performed overseas. Thus, when Chinese men had married in China before wedding in Mexico, the latter marriages were null and void. In such cases, under the laws of both nations, Mexican women retained their citizenship and had the "full right to protection by the Mexican government" and its consular representatives abroad. Children followed their mothers, gaining status and rights as well. In cases when Mexican women were the first wives, either the Mexican or the Chinese wife could appear before Chinese courts to report the unlawful bigamy, unless Chinese authorities had already canceled one of the marriages for being between two relatives or failing to be an "open ceremony" before two or more witnesses under Article 983 of the Chinese Civil Code. Insight into Chinese law clarified whether Mexican women had legally retained—and could therefore claim—Mexican citizenship. If such status could be affirmed, the consuls had an easier time assisting the women, especially those who wanted to return to Mexico.[31]

By late 1931, the SRE sent Fresco and Tello a set of guidelines on the assorted cases of Mexican women in China and the research officials had conducted on citizenship law. The women married to Chinese men with previous marriages in China undoubtedly retained Mexican citizenship. After ascertaining that such was the case, consuls could authorize the women's return and grant passports without the permission of the husbands or the Secretaría de Gobernación. If the Mexican women were the first wives, the husbands' approval was still unnecessary; clearance from the Secretaría de Gobernación, however, was required, and consuls could only approve identification cards for these women. Consuls had authorization to negotiate with shipping companies for discounted fares no matter the circumstances.[32]

Mexican first wives whose husbands had remarried in China needed to prove that bigamy had occurred to establish that they maintained Mexican citizenship and thus could seek the protection of the nation's representatives abroad. Consuls worried that Mexican women were deficient in the language and social skills necessary to report their husbands to Chinese authorities. Fresco noted that most Mexican women in China barely knew how to write in Spanish, let alone communicate in Chinese dialects. Mexican authorities argued that the vast majority of women who had formed romantic unions with Chinese men in Mexico were "mujeres del pueblo" (unprivileged women from the countryside) who lacked the education and experience necessary for their own defense. Most of the women indeed came from lower-class families that had no resources to help pay for passage back to Mexico. Yet Mexican women in Guangdong Province, Shanghai, Macau, and Hong Kong advocated for themselves by visiting and writing letters to consuls and other officials to appeal for repatriation.[33]

Tensions between Mexican states and the federal government and changing circumstances in China kept Mexican women on uncertain ground, especially when they could neither claim Mexican citizenship nor rely on the assistance of Chinese authorities. Although the Mexican federal government had expressed concern for them and Circular 94 included provisions to protect women and children, Sonora and Sinaloa disregarded outright the federal statute and continued to expel Chinese Mexican families for almost two years after the measure's passage.[34]

Fresco kept working on behalf of Mexican women in China and became increasingly fearful as their situations grew ever more precarious. A legal change threatened in particular those Mexican women who were first wives and whose husbands had not remarried in China. In November 1934, the Shanghai press published an official Chinese communication mandating that foreign women married to Chinese men had to solicit naturalization to gain Chinese citizenship. The Chinese government no longer automatically recognized them as Chinese citizens simply because they were married to Chinese nationals. Under the new decree, Mexican women who had relinquished citizenship through marriage lost Chinese citizenship, and with it the possibility of protection by local authorities. Now they were truly in between nation-states—neither Mexican nor Chinese. Mexican law's provision that women married to foreign men who did not acquire their husbands' nationality retained Mexican citizenship made little practical difference to Mexican women in China, who nonetheless found themselves in the murky waters of interstitial citizenship. Fresco urged Mexican officials to take further measures to prevent Mexican women and children from traveling to China with Chinese men and adding to the numbers of those already in tough situations. He warned the SRE that increasingly negative anti-Mexican propaganda in local newspapers indicated that Mexican women, regardless of marriage or citizenship status, would face a difficult climate.[35] Some Mexican women, in turn, had made angry declarations to the local press against the Mexican government for sending their families away from Mexico.[36]

Mexico in the Global Arena

In the 1930s, Mexico wanted both to nationalize Mexican resources and gain worldwide recognition.[37] The expulsion of Chinese impinged on the nation's international goals. In the interest of Mexico's image abroad, Fresco attempted to counter the mounting negative publicity in China. In the spring of 1933, he declared to the Chinese press that the Mexican federal government had not ordered the expulsion of Chinese. The Chinese

Overseas Union soon publicly refuted his claims. At around the same time, the Chinese Ministry of Foreign Affairs and the Overseas Chinese Affairs Commission collaboratively agreed to send a diplomatic representative to Mexico to further investigate the anti-Chinese movement there.[38]

During this time, the federal government tried to curtail anti-Chinese activity in the states, at least superficially. At the behest of Mexico City, on 1 March 1933, the Campaña Pro-Raza (Pro-Race Campaign) announced that it would suspend the deportation of Chinese. As a result of hostilities between Japan and China in the early 1930s, Mexican officials temporarily lifted the deadlines for Chinese to leave. Sonoran anti-Chinese activists Juan de Jesús Bátiz and José Angel Espinoza declared to Mexican newspapers that the group wanted to work in solidarity with the Mexican government on this issue. The two men noted, however, that their campaign would change not its attitude toward the Chinese but rather the methods by which it confronted the Chinese "problem" in Mexico. As long as the Chinese complied with the Federal Labor Law, which held that Chinese businesses had to employ 80 percent Mexicans (defined by both birth and nationality), and the Sanitary Code, authorities would cease to take drastic measures, such as deportation, against the Chinese. Denouncing Japanese imperialism in China, as other "civilized" nations had done, the Mexican government vowed to "save Mexico's moral interests in future possible cases similar to this one."[39] Mexico wanted to foster international goodwill through camaraderie with other democratic nations.

Nevertheless, Mexican states continued to expel Chinese. Less than two months after the announcement of the cessation of Chinese deportations, a government bus carrying twenty Chinese under the charge of a rural police force passed through Empalme, Sonora, on its way to San Blas, Sinaloa. Having been ousted by authorities in Sinaloa, the Chinese had dispersed among towns in the central Río de Sonora area, where state officials eventually apprehended them. Local authorities had decided to take the Chinese back to Sinaloa because transporting them to the northern border with the United States would cause problems with that nation. When the Chinese returned to Sinaloa, authorities likely deported them to China.[40] As late as 1933, newspapers reported that the anti-Chinese campaign was thriving in Mexico. The movement also targeted the Mexican wives of "Asiatics": Mexican authorities had advised Mexican women to refrain from marrying Chinese men, since doing so would cause them to lose their civil rights and suffer boycotts. The force of racism became all the more evident as Mexican women married to men who had naturalized still lost their Mexican citizenship. Anti-Chinese activists saw these women as race traitors. The movement's searing sense of racial panic bore on the legal standings not only of the Chinese but also of the Mexican women with whom they formed romantic unions.[41]

Chinese men, Mexican women, and Chinese Mexican children arrived in China directly from Sonora and Sinaloa as expelled persons or via the United States as refugees until at least early 1934. Local and state authorities thus violated Circular 94, which had attempted to prevent Mexican women and children from leaving national territory. Anti-Chinese policy held considerable sway in the two northern states, and crusaders had important allies in the federal government. Although the Mexican government paid lip service to solidarity with China, the complexity and uncertainty of the relationship between the states and the nation allowed the expulsions to continue. While some national politicians scorned the Sonoran and Sinaloan expulsions, others quietly supported it. The most important figure to back anti-Chinese politics in the national arena was Plutarco Elías Calles. Calles had had strong *antichinista* leanings since his days as a Sonoran state politician almost two decades earlier. His powerful position as the *jefe máximo* (supreme chief) of the Mexican Revolution in the late 1920s and early 1930s, a period known as the Maximato, helped individual states expel Chinese with impunity.[42]

Officials and private citizens outside of Mexico bemoaned the expulsions and the problems Mexican women faced as a result as well as Mexico's consequent negative reputation in China and beyond. In late 1932, a number of Spaniards, including a prominent citizen and former consul in Peru, visited Fresco in Shanghai to express their dismay at the situation. The men were especially concerned about the plight of Mexican women in southern China but hesitated to offer any assistance because of the possible diplomatic repercussions for their nation. The expulsions had cast a shameful light on Mexico. As he relayed the incident to Mexican officials, Fresco regretted that consuls from other countries had similarly refused to become involved in Mexican women's struggles.[43]

When hundreds of Chinese Mexican families arrived in China in the early 1930s, they found that Mexican gender customs collided with those prevailing in China and presented formidable challenges to family cohesion. Chinese men had to contend with local customs and institutions that pressured them to reintegrate into the societies they had departed years earlier. Competing pressures squeezed Chinese Mexican families in China, and although some remained unified, most split apart.

Mexican women who separated from their spouses as well as families who stayed together formed networks in villages and cities and appealed to Mexican consuls and other authorities to repatriate. Thorny questions arose concerning the citizenship of Mexican women who had married Chinese men and these women's right to protection by authorities in both nations. By urging the Mexican government to help them, Mexican women challenged the country's dominant notions of nationality and helped refashion citizenship in the postrevolutionary period. These women and their complicated situations would eventually spur Lázaro Cárdenas to reincorporate them into the nation as war broke out between China and Japan.

CHAPTER SIX

Mexico in the 1930s and Chinese Mexican Repatriation under Lázaro Cárdenas

Complex and contradictory currents ran through Mexico during the 1930s. On the one hand, individual states expelled Chinese while national leaders tacitly supported these efforts or turned a blind eye. On the other hand, the federal government—with the goal of making Mexico visible in the global political arena—officially supported China and condemned Japanese aggression early in the decade. When Lázaro Cárdenas (1934–40) came to power, the anti-Chinese campaigns began to lose momentum. To repudiate the movement's expulsions of Mexican citizens, his administration ultimately sponsored the first official repatriation of Mexican women and Chinese Mexican children when war between China and Japan formally broke out in the latter part of the decade.

The Cárdenas repatriation privileged women and children who had already become separated from their men. Families that had not split up had to decide whether to do so, since Chinese men remained barred from returning to Mexico. The choice brought immense heartache to families who had wanted to stay unified but saw no other option than to be divided for the well-being of the women and children in a climate of war and uncertainty in China. Even though *antichinismo* lost significant sway under his administration, Cárdenas's exclusionary repatriation policy precluded him from halting Mexico's anti-Chinese moment. Moreover, once in Mexico, mothers had to prove that their mixed-race children belonged in the nation, as people they encountered made them feel otherwise. Claiming a place for their families in Mexico was never easy.

Yet Mexican women and children insisted on repatriating. Some returned to Mexico before the Cárdenas repatriation as a consequence of the work of Mexican consuls in East Asia and relatives in Mexico. In addition, the creation of Mexico's National Committee on Repatriation to help Mexicans whom the United States expelled during the Great Depression offered aid to the women and children returning from China. The U.S. repatriation of Mexicans had transnational and transpacific reverberations. It had helped spur the Chinese expulsions from northern Mexico; in turn, the support system Mexico established in response to U.S. policy assisted women and children who had departed Mexico with Chinese men. Adding another transnational dimension, a Japanese shipping company provided significant discounts to Mexican women and Chinese Mexican children, allowing them to resettle in Mexico.

The journeys of Chinese Mexicans are part of the interlinked global phenomena of state-sponsored expulsions during the depression era and admissions of refugees in the World War II era. The expulsion of Chinese from northern Mexico occurred as the United States deported not only Mexicans but also Filipinos. As colonial subjects, however, the latter group received distinct treatment: The United States argued that returning Filipinos to their home country was in their best interests. Like Filipinos, Mexicans were unwanted, but no such colonial benevolence framed their expulsion. Numerous countries admitted "refugees" during the World War II era, when the concept first came into wide usage. Mexico was among the few countries to accept Spanish Republican refugees, including intellectuals and orphans, during the Spanish Civil War, and this influx of Spanish citizens coincided with Mexico's first official repatriation of Mexican women and Chinese Mexican children. In the next two decades, the United States and countries in Latin America and elsewhere would admit Eastern Europeans and Korean orphans.[1]

Returning to Mexico after the Chinese Expulsions

The Mexican women who sought to repatriate to Mexico soon after they arrived in China did so out of desperation. They had become so deeply unhappy with their lives in their husbands' or companions' communities that they saw no other option but to return to Mexico. Furthermore, those whose unions had broken apart had very limited resources with which to care for their families.

After undergoing forced expulsions and deportations, families found it difficult to deal with the abrupt transition to life in China. In their letters, Mexican women described the drastic changes that had occurred in their romantic relationships and family dynamics. Chinese-Mexican bonds had become strained or broken as Chinese men negotiated Cantonese and Tai-shanese customs to reintegrate into the places from which they had emigrated years earlier. Karen Isaksen Leonard has described the difficulties cross-cultural Punjabi Mexican families faced in twentieth-century California. As a consequence of significant ethnic differences, forces beyond individual families both created close ties and caused incredible conflict. Families had to negotiate gender norms and power relations and notions of ethnic identity both within and outside of the family. Punjabi Mexican families adjusted to a family life that was anchored around both coinciding and diverging notions of family and economic disparity. While some marriages were long lasting, others ended in divorce or violence.[2]

For Chinese Mexican families, overlapping value systems opened possibilities for negotiating gender and cultural norms in Mexico; once in China, however, cultural difference reached a breaking point. After living in Guangdong Province for about a year following her family's expulsion from Mexico and deportation from the United States, Ester Enríquez Wong became so profoundly disenchanted with her marriage and the family's life that she found it impossible to imagine remaining in China. She took her children back to Sonora around mid-1934 with the financial assistance of her sister. Life had been too hard in China, and the marriage had fallen apart; in Mexico, at least she and her children would have the support of her extended family. Before she departed, her husband asked her to leave their son, Felipe Wong Enríquez. The decision was painful, but she acquiesced, understanding the significance of father-son bonds in China, which were comparable to those in Mexico.[3] But she soon regretted that decision, and more than forty years would pass before she again saw her son.

While Enríquez Wong and a few other women returned from China quickly and fairly easily with the help of their families, others had to wait to gather resources and to contend with Mexican federal authorities regarding their citizenship status. Rosa Murillo de Chan learned just how complicated negotiating Mexican law could be for the spouse of a Chinese man. Local Mexican authorities had stripped Chinese men of their civil liberties during the expulsion period. In the following years, however, the Mexican federal government tried to uphold their rights to equal treatment under the Constitution of 1917, at times creating problems for wives and children who wished to repatriate.

Mexican women urged consuls and religious aid workers from other countries to pressure Mexican authorities; such appeals struck a chord with officials as a consequence of Mexico's concern for its international image. After several unsuccessful attempts to repatriate by appealing to her own government, Murillo de Chan asked U.S. consul and honorary Mexican consul in Shanghai Norwood F. Allman for help in 1932. Invoking notions of American benevolence in the world, she wrote, "Knowing that Americans have such noble hearts, I confidently hope that you will not ignore the prayers of a frenzied woman, surrounded by five suffering children in a foreign country."[4] Allman soon contacted Mexican officials to recommend that they assist their compatriots in China, noting that Mexican women could rule out the possibility of protection by Chinese authorities. Manuel Tello, the Mexican consul in Yokohama, complained to his superiors that Allman had failed to keep him apprised of matters concerning Mexico; perhaps irritated by the American consul's admonishing tone, Tello explained that he had not deliberately overlooked Murillo de Chan's case.[5] Murillo de Chan subsequently sought help from another American, Bishop James E. Walsh of the American Catholic mission in Jiangmen, Guangdong Province, who also appealed to Mexican authorities on her behalf. Walsh recounted the abuse she had suffered at the hands of her husband, Felipe Chan, and suggested that "we devise some means to repatriate the women," offering his organization's assistance.[6]

Walsh soon provided Murillo de Chan with financial aid; a Japanese shipping company and Mexico's repatriation committee also helped facilitate her return to Mexico. Fresco and Tello had negotiated with Nippon Yusen Kaisa for reduced steamship fares for women whose spouses had abandoned them in China. "Abandoned" was broadly conceived to include deserted women as well as those who had become secondary wives or concubines and objected to living with or near their husbands' primary Chinese wives. The trip from Hong Kong to Manzanillo, Colima, cost approximately sixty-five dollars, and the Japanese company's ships made the voyage monthly.[7] Nippon Yusen Kaisa agreed to offer a 50 percent discount to Murillo de Chan and other women whose husbands had become abusive and to women such as María Refugio de Lee, whose husband had left her and remarried after the family arrived in China. Even though its main goal was to assist Mexicans returning from the United States during the depression years, the National Committee on Repatriation helped Murillo de Chan resettle in Mexico.[8]

With the committee's assistance, Murillo de Chan arrived in Mazatlán, Sinaloa, on 21 April 1933. She had traveled alone: Unable to finance passage for her five children, then aged between nineteen and seven, she had left them at the Freng Convent on the Causeway Bay in Hong Kong, vowing to work for their repatriation after she was back in Mexico. The convent allowed children to stay for up to three months before putting them up for adoption. At the end of that time, the children moved into their father's home in Hong Kong. One son, Arnulfo Juan Chan Murillo, later reported to Mexican authorities that Chan had shown little interest in taking care of his children and that their Chinese stepmother had on numerous occasions thrown them out with no food or clothes. At such times, the children had taken advantage of local Chinese Mexican networks and stayed with Mexican women, including María Viuda de Leyton. The Chan Murillos and other children of mixed-race unions bore the brunt of the Mexican expulsion of Chinese and its aftermath.[9]

Back in Mexico, Murillo de Chan kept her promise, working ceaselessly for her children's repatriation and challenging Mexican authorities' perceptions of her hybrid family at every turn. Her three daughters returned to Mexico by 1935. She then wrote to Mexican consul Armando C. Amador, Tello's successor in Yokohama, urging him to deny her husband custody of their two sons. Reminding him that Chan had refused to care for the boys, she begged him to help them repatriate to Mexico, as he had done for her daughters. Amador at first refused, citing the Mexican concept of *patria potestad* (parental legal custody), which upheld a father's right to his sons, another part of the complex tangle of laws that Mexican women confronted after marrying Chinese men. Nevertheless, the consul ultimately advised her to send $145 for her sons' passage. Once she submitted the payment, Amador would arrange for their travel.[10] In the end, Chan's lack of interest in keeping his children trumped Mexican officials' adherence to patriarchal legal codes. Moreover, Chan was a Chinese man who was a Mexican citizen by naturalization rather than birth, so he did not fit with Mexico's dominant notions of race. Murillo de Chan was now free to bring her sons to Mexico if she could gather the money to do so.

Chan soon died. Lacking any inheritance in China, Murillo de Chan tried to claim his assets in Mexico to finance the return of her sons but once again ran into legal obstacles. In 1935, Murillo de Chan sued Carlos

Ley, her husband's business partner in Mazatlán, for taking possession of all of Chan's capital to establish a large linen and drapery business even though two-thirds of the business rightfully belonged to her family. Chan had hoped to leave his two sons his share of the Mexican business, but he had been away from Mexico for more than five years and had never given his wife permission to represent him, so authorities in Sinaloa decided that she had no legal grounds on which to claim any of his assets.[11]

Mexican Politics

In this decade, Mexico was concerned with the intertwined projects of nationalizing Mexican resources and seeking international recognition. Conflicts between China and Japan had forced Mexico to consider the negative political implications of the deportation of Chinese from Mexican states, and the federal government at least paid lip service to solidarity with China before Cárdenas came to power. Japan invaded Manchuria in September 1931, and relations between China and Japan became increasingly hostile as Japan seized control of parts of northern China. Mexico soon officially voiced its support for China and opposed Japan's imperial aggression.[12]

Imbued with postrevolutionary ideology, Cárdenas strengthened the central state and worked to fortify Mexico's relationships with other nations, a process that had begun under earlier administrations. Focused on national interests and putting revolutionary ideology into practice, Cárdenas continued to divest foreigners of their power in the nation. At the same time, Mexico sought international legitimacy for its revolution partially by drawing connections with similar struggles against imperialism. In a key move in this direction, Mexico accepted thousands of refugees from Spain during the Spanish Civil War.[13]

Cárdenas repudiated the exclusionary policies of the "Sonora Dynasty." He and other key Mexican politicians had considered Sonora and Sinaloa in contempt of the revolution for executing the expulsions. Indeed, under his administration, the anti-Chinese movement in Mexico would lose significant influence both at the state and national levels. He would eventually bring home several hundred of the previously expelled Mexican women and numerous Chinese Mexican children.[14] His administration would also offer some protection to Chinese men who had remained in Mexico. By forbidding the return of expelled Chinese men with their families, however, his policies ultimately endorsed the localized anti-Chinese movements that had removed Chinese Mexican families. The repatriation movement also embedded anti-Chinese sentiment in its views of the repatriates as diseased. Chinese Mexican families still stood on uneven ground in Mexico.

Heightening tension in the global arena tested the Mexican president's international aims. As relations between Japan and China became overtly hostile by the mid-1930s, future military conflict between Japan and the United States likewise seemed inevitable. Mexico became ever more worried about its "strategic vulnerability" as a consequence of its proximity to the United States. Mexican planners feared that the United States would ask Mexico to become part of a U.S. alliance against Japan. Mexico's geographic location would make it difficult to refuse such an agreement, which would in turn trap Mexico in a confrontation between its northern neighbor and the growing fascist power. The stakes grew higher after Japan stationed naval and military attachés in Mexico, surpassing even the U.S. military presence there. When officials came across unidentified ships they perceived as Japanese vessels assessing the Mexican coast in 1936, the military prepared the Acapulco harbor for a possible coup de main in the advent of aggression between the United States and Japan. Armed conflict between Japan and China was imminent; the Second Sino-Japanese War officially broke out in July 1937. Japan's attack on Nanjing beginning the following December "left a deep impression on the Mexican public and the Mexican leadership." Cárdenas feared that the world was on the brink of war.[15]

Mexico became increasingly visible on the international scene as it strengthened its relationships with other nations. In October 1937, Belgian diplomats staged an international convention on the Sino-Japanese conflict, with Mexico and Brazil the only Latin American countries invited to Brussels: Cárdenas sent Mexico's representative to the League of Nations to participate.[16]

The Cárdenas Repatriation

As armed conflict loomed in East Asia, Cárdenas learned that Mexican women and children were stuck in China. Mexicans urged authorities to take action, and newspapers began pleading with the government to "rescue" its citizens in China. Eduardo Miller, the member of a distinguished Mexican family and a merchant in China, helped broadcast the plight of hundreds of Mexican women who begged for charity in the streets of

Shanghai and elsewhere because their spouses had abandoned them. Urging the Mexican government to repatriate them, Miller argued, "Each day that passes is in fact a day in hell for those women." Overlooking the expulsions, he argued that Mexican women and children had left Mexico in search of a better life, only to find misery, desperation, and death in China. Newspapers reported that Chinese men had deserted their Mexican spouses in China with "Asiatic indifference." In response, the Mexican government planned a major repatriation. Officials remitted ninety-four thousand pesos to the Mexican consul in Yokohama to feed and repatriate approximately four hundred Mexican women and hundreds more Chinese Mexican children by the spring of 1937.[17]

Despite the hardships of life in China, Mexican women felt some trepidation about returning to Mexico. They would need to renew ties with their families and reintegrate into the communities from which they had been expelled. Those whose relationships remained intact would have to sever those bonds to return to Mexico. On 9 March 1937, Soledad Duarte wrote to Margarita de Campbell from Honam, in Guangdong Province, to thank her for helping to arrange the return of Duarte and her daughters. Duarte and her husband had decided that she and the girls should return to Mexico, and once there, they would need financial assistance to buy clothes: After living in China for several years, "poverty and the need to conserve has made us dress in the manner of [the] country." Duarte had not been in contact with her family in Magdalena, Sonora, for five years, so she asked Campbell to let her relatives know that she would soon return so that she would have a place to stay. Duarte knew of other Mexican women in Guangdong Province who wanted to repatriate but hesitated to leave their husbands.[18] As during the period of expulsion, these families faced difficult choices with the prospect of full-scale war approaching.

Although some Mexican women whose relationships had not already collapsed decided to stay in China with their men, most took their children and repatriated to Mexico. In March 1937, the first group of eighty-nine women and several hundred children departed Hong Kong on a steamer and arrived in Mexico via the Pacific port of Manzanillo, Colima, where an immigration delegate met them. The federal government had ordered local authorities to facilitate the repatriates' travel from the port to their home communities, mostly in Sonora and Sinaloa. Two hundred more families would soon arrive in Manzanillo, and others followed through 1937 and into 1938.[19]

Although Duarte and her husband had jointly agreed that she and their children should return to Mexico, other Mexican women surreptitiously left their husbands in China. Cruz Arredondo de Yee "packed up her three sons and snuck away in the night" from a village in Guangdong Province because she knew her husband would have refused to let her leave. Her husband also had a Chinese wife, and Arredondo de Yee's four years in China had been unhappy. After she learned from a local newspaper that the Mexican government would repatriate Mexicans who recounted the story of their arrival in China and named the president of Mexico at the time of their departure, she resolved to return to her country. Seven months pregnant, Arredondo de Yee traveled with her sons to Shanghai, where they boarded a ship that left just before war broke out. Throughout the two-month journey, she was sick and worried about going into labor, but her daughter was not born until after the family reached Sinaloa.[20]

While some women embraced the opportunity to return to Mexico, other families experienced profound grief and trauma as a result of the exclusionary policies of the Cárdenas repatriation. Widower Roberto M. Fu had worked as a porter at the Seminario San José in Macau since he arrived with seven young children following the family's expulsion from Sonora in the early 1930s. Fu was a longtime resident of Mexico who had married in Sonora in 1919 and had made it his second home. In 1937, he sent his six oldest children back to Mexico, but because he was Chinese, he could not accompany them, and his youngest child, Maximiliano, was too young to travel without his father. The Cárdenas repatriation thus split the family, and reunion would prove difficult.[21]

Other families, including the Wong Campoys, chose to stay in China rather than be separated.[22] Still others found that they were not eligible under Cárdenas's repatriation program because they had traveled to China of their own volition. Ramón Lay Mazo's family was considered to have freely chosen to leave Mexico (although they faced the threat of expulsion) and so was denied permission to return.[23]

Other Chinese Mexicans missed the opportunity to repatriate before the program ended in mid-1938. In June of that year, María Sam in Santa Ana, Sonora, appealed to Mexican officials to repatriate her father, Juan Sam. Seven months later, Rafael Ramos in Culiacán, Sinaloa, made the same request on behalf of his father, José Rodolfo Ramos, who was in Shanghai.[24]

Some Chinese Mexicans had little or no desire to return to Mexico until their Chinese spouses or fathers died. After the Cárdenas repatriation was over, families appealed to return on these grounds. On 19 August 1938, Al-

Seminario San José in Macau. Photograph by author.

bina Fregoso Viuda de López wrote to Cárdenas from Mazatlán, pleading for the return of her three children, Roberto López Fregoso, María Jesús López Fregoso, and Esteban López Fregoso, who lived in Sung Ping, Chonsamg, in Guangdong Province. The children's father, Roberto López, had died during a trip to San Francisco. In May 1940, relatives of Juana Trujillo Viuda de Chiu in Chiapas also appealed to authorities to repatriate her and her children because their father had recently died and the family now lived in poverty. Mexican officials replied that the federal government had exhausted its budget for repatriation.[25]

In other cases, families split by the repatriation asked the Mexican government to reunite them for economic reasons. Ranjín Chá wrote to Cárdenas from Hong Kong in August 1939 requesting that Mexican authorities either allow him to enter Mexico to support his family or send his wife, Josefa Montiver, and their child back to China. Chá and Montiver had married in Hong Kong before she and their daughter repatriated to Mexico. But Montiver had found it difficult to sustain herself and her daughter, and they were living in misery in Manzanillo. The following month, Agustín Lanuza Jr. replied to Chá that the president's office was unable to approve or finance his request.[26]

In the end the Cárdenas repatriation was both incomplete and narrow. Some Chinese Mexican families would wait until the decades after World War II to return to Mexico, either under the second official repatriation or in smaller unofficial waves. Others would simply remain in China. After the creation of the People's Republic of China in 1949, and especially during the Cultural Revolution two decades later, people with mixed racial and cultural backgrounds may have found remaining in China more difficult, although some Chinese Mexicans, especially those with Mexican indigenous heritage, may have blended into local society with ease. Chinese Latin American families, particularly those from Peru and Ecuador, increasingly gravitated to Portuguese Macau and British Hong Kong, where some of their descendants still reside. Although Peru repatriated women and children in the early twentieth century, Ecuador evidently never orchestrated an official repatriation of its citizens in China. Chinese Peruvians who missed the opportunity to repatriate as well as Chinese Ecuadorians who lacked the resources to return of their own accord remained and integrated into local society. Although Mexico ultimately repatriated most of its citizens, a few remained. Luis Ruiz, a Spanish Jesuit priest who lived in Macau for more than sixty years and helped the Chinese Mexican community, remembered a Mexican man who never repatriated, ultimately becoming "more Chinese than Mexican."[27]

Reintegrating into Mexican Society

Despite its limitations, the Cárdenas repatriation brought numerous grateful Mexican women and Chinese Mexican children back to Mexico. Their relief, however, was often short-lived. In addition to economic difficulties, these families confronted residual anti-Chinese prejudice and discrimination. Children who had spent little time in Mexico or who were born in China had the most trouble adjusting. Yet Mexican mothers refused to accept the ill treatment of their families, appealing to authorities on behalf of their racially mixed children and thus reclaiming their Mexican identity.

People in Mexico perceived Chinese Mexicans as carriers of Asian diseases. Such fears kept many of the repatriates from reuniting with their families for weeks or months after they returned as public health authorities held repatriates in Manzanillo during the summer of 1937. These detainees included Ramón Felipe Chan Murillo and Arnulfo Juan Chan Murillo, who repatriated in June and were eager to join their mother and sisters. After more than two months of Murillo de Chan's pleas for the release of her sons, government officials still held the boys in custody and had not developed a clear timeline for their release. Four years after she had last seen her sons, and even with them on Mexican soil, she still had no access to them.[28]

Some of the repatriates sent letters of protest during their detainment. On 14 July 1937, Juana Rivas, Juana López, and Piedad Argüellas wrote to Cárdenas. Authorities had held them and other repatriates at the Hotel Manzanillo for thirty days. They argued that most of the repatriates were in good health, and officials had done nothing to help those who were ill, giving them prescriptions but no medicine or medical attention. The writers demanded care for the sick, the release of the healthy, and an investigation of the situation. On 26 August, the head of Mexico's public health department, Julio César Treviño, responded that the government had mistakenly expedited train passage for other people and inadvertently prolonged the women's stay in Manzanillo. Treviño assured them that their release was imminent and they would soon reach their homes.[29]

Anxieties about disease were based both on anti-Chinese prejudice and on actual reports of contagion in China. Cholera in particular provoked fears because it often emerged without warning and spread rapidly. Prevalent in southern China especially during the summer, cholera outbreaks had taken thousands of lives in the 1930s. In October 1937, the League of Nations approved plans to send a team of medical experts to China to assist the government with recent epidemics. At the same time, Mexican doctors found that Chinese Mexican repatriates had brought a cholera epidemic from China. Physicians Eduardo Suárez and José Siurob requested 115,000 pesos to establish a lazaretto in Mazatlán to treat the problem.[30]

Lingering anti-Chinese racism was most powerful in Sonora and Sinaloa, the two northern states that had carried out massive expulsions of Chinese. In December 1935, Murillo de Chan wrote to Cárdenas to ask him to help her daughter, Graciela Chan Murillo, obtain work at a library; she had been unable to find employment because people in Mazatlán defined her as a foreigner. Two years later, the mother was trying to persuade authorities to release her sons and other repatriates perceived as diseased. Also in 1937, Chinese in the town of El Dorado, Sinaloa, urged Mexican authorities to protect them against persistent local anti-Chinese activity. Sonora's teachers called for a renewed Chinese expulsion in 1936, and miners in the state expressed strong anti-Chinese sentiment throughout the latter part of the decade.[31]

Mexicans in other regions also denied the repatriates opportunities to reestablish themselves. María Teresa Guadalajara de Lee appealed to federal authorities to help her sons open a bakery in the northern state of Durango in January 1940, two years after she had repatriated. Local officials accused her sons of failing to comply with bakery regulations but also informed the family that local labor organizations opposed the creation of such a business, suggesting that anti-Chinese elements were alive there.[32] Although the climate for Chinese Mexican families had improved by the late 1930s, their reintegration into Mexican communities remained complicated. Acting as brokers on behalf of their mixed-race families, Mexican mothers pushed the nation to widen its notions of who belonged.

Chinese Mexicans repatriated to Mexico both in small groups and as part of a larger repatriation effort in the 1930s. The main goals of Cárdenas's repatriation program were rescuing Mexican women from a war zone and remedying some of the wrongs of the expulsion era. The reincorporation of previously excluded citizens helped shape postrevolutionary Mexico and its growing international reputation. Although the anti-Chinese movement lost sway under his administration, Cárdenas maintained a limited vision of who fit into the nation-state, and Mexican women and Chinese Mexican children still encountered social and economic barriers to reintegration.

Mexican women and Chinese Mexican families created new relationships and networks in Asia that laid the groundwork for the process of becoming Mexican over the next two decades. As they forged a community and maintained ties with people in Mexico, including those who had repatriated under Cárdenas, a diasporic Mexican national identity began to crystallize. Dreaming of Mexico from abroad, Chinese Mexicans worked tirelessly to return to the place that they would soon come to see as their homeland.

CHaPTeR seven

We Want to Be in Mexico

Imagining the Nation, Performing Mexicanness,
1930s–Early 1960s

On 12 May 1960, the Chinese Mexican community leader in Macau, Ramón Lay Mazo, wrote to a prominent Mexican widow, Concepción Rodríguez Viuda de Aragón, in Tampico, Tamaulipas, Mexico. Seeking her continued support for the Chinese Mexican repatriation cause, he conveyed the deep, devoted love Mexican women living in China felt for their nation—Mexico. When he asked Mexican women in China whether they wanted to move to other countries, they replied, "Not even if they gave me a palace there, I prefer Mexico, even if I have to live under a mesquite." Disheartened by the Mexican government's disregard for them and their desperate situations, Lay Mazo tried to convince Mexican women to consider living elsewhere. He warned them that Mexico might not be the same as it once was and that it might be more difficult to survive in the communities where they had once lived. To this the women responded, "Even if we have to dig for bitter sweet potatoes in the sierra, we want to be in Mexico." The conditions, where in the nation they might live, and how long they might have to wait were no matter. They wanted to return to a Mexican homeland for which they longed.[1]

A romanticized notion of the Mexican homeland had begun to emerge in the 1930s as Chinese Mexican families from diverse local communities in Mexico met in Guangdong Province, Shanghai, Macau, and Hong Kong. Their love for Mexico was both genuine and strategic. As with other diasporic peoples, their identification with the nation they had left became stronger once they were away. Devotion to Mexico was conditioned by a sense of alienation compounded by social and political turmoil in China. Because they wanted to leave China, Chinese Mexicans claimed Mexico as their homeland and argued that their families belonged there. After the formation of the People's Republic of China in 1949, Cold War politics framed Chinese Mexicans' rhetorical strategies and nationalistic fervor. As culturally and racially mixed people, they perceived a need to perform Mexicanness. At the same time, their longing for the nation was heartfelt. They believed their lives would improve if they could return to their land of origin. Chinese Mexicans thus idealized Mexico and forged a deep connection with an imagined homeland across the Pacific. When they eventually returned, it would be difficult if not impossible for the actual Mexico to live up to three decades' worth of expectations.

The Chinese Mexican Community in Macau and Hong Kong

Concentrating in the two foreign colonies in close proximity to one another on the southeastern edge of Guangdong Province on the South China Sea, Chinese Mexicans forged a vibrant, coherent enclave from the early 1930s to the early 1960s. Mexican women formed the heart of the community. They found Macau especially attractive for its Catholic roots and its population of residents with mixed racial and cultural identities, a cosmopolitan atmosphere into which Chinese Mexican families could blend.[2] Founded by merchants in the sixteenth century, Macau was under the control of a Portuguese colonial administration through most of the twentieth century. People spoke Cantonese and other Chinese dialects there, but the official language was Portuguese. A "Macanese Creole" vernacular known as Patoá had emerged, influenced not only by Cantonese but also by the languages of navigators and merchants from India and Malaysia. In Macau, Chinese, Portuguese, and other cultures, languages, and political styles had coexisted and blended for more than four hundred years.[3]

Early in the twentieth century, numerous refugees from China came to reside in Macau, whose population doubled from about 75,000 in the early 1900s to 150,000 by the early 1930s. A host of economic and political problems besieged the Chinese republic after the Sino-Japanese War broke out in the summer of 1937 and fifty million refugees fled the northern war zones into the interior of China within a few years.[4] Macau received an overwhelming influx of refugees from diverse areas of China, especially after the fall of Shanghai in late 1937. The colony's population grew to 350,000 by the beginning of the following decade. During World War II, thousands more refugees entered Macau, bringing the population to 600,000 by 1945. Although Japan occupied Hong Kong and forced the British colony to surrender in 1941, the Japanese took a different course in Macau because Portugal, unlike Great Britain, remained neutral in the war. Nonetheless, Japanese soldiers maintained a presence in Macau, and Japan's policy toward the colony became harsher as World War II progressed.[5] Still, Chinese Mexicans as well as other groups felt more at ease and found opportunities in Macau.

Alfonso Wong Campoy, who arrived in Macau with his family in the mid-1930s, recalled that ships constantly docked there, bringing people from all over the world. He became fluent not only in Spanish and Cantonese but also in Portuguese and Italian, which he learned at an Italian school.[6] Chinese Mexicans became cosmopolitan people by necessity, as they negotiated their diasporic realities after the Mexican expulsions, the complexities of life in mainland China, and the consequent attractiveness of the foreign colonies. Indeed, they can help us historicize cosmopolitanism as a phenomenon that has reached beyond the privileged families of diplomats and merchants in the modern era.[7]

Wong Campoy also studied in mainland China, in keeping with Chinese custom for firstborn sons. But Alfonso Wong Fang soon brought his son back to Macau when Japan launched its full-scale invasion of China. Despite the difficulties of life in a wartime colony besieged by refugees, the Wong Campoy family was better off than most Macau residents because Wong Fang worked for the government. The eldest daughter in the family, María del Carmen Irma Wong Campoy Maher Conceição, recalled that foreigners had greater status than Chinese people in the colony, a benefit they enjoyed since Wong Fang spoke Spanish very well and the family counted as foreigners.[8] However, Alfonso Wong Fang died of a heart attack in March 1945. His young sons began working to support the family, and his widow, Dolores Campoy Wong, found solace in the other Mexican and Latin American women with whom she had formed close ties.[9]

Mexican women and some Chinese men were the center of Macau's Chinese Mexican community. They taught their children the Spanish language, passed on Mexican cultural traditions, and kept alive memories of community life in Mexico, which many of the children had left when they were very young. These parents taught their children that there was more to Mexico than the anti-Chinese movement that had orchestrated their expulsion. Wong Campoy recalled that both his mother and father taught him to love Mexico and that Wong Fang, like other Chinese Mexicans, believed that the Mexican government rather than the Mexican people had expelled the family. Wong Campoy also identified with Mexico through magazines and movies that circulated in Macau and Hong Kong. He grew up with a persistent desire to "get to know Mexico."[10]

Macau's Latin, Iberian, and Catholic traditions gave Chinese Mexicans a sense of familiarity and fostered the process of becoming Mexican abroad. They met other Latin Americans who had been drawn to Macau for similar reasons, including Ecuadorian and Peruvian women who had formed romantic ties with Chinese men in Latin America and later traveled with them to China.[11] People on the margins have in diverse ways created networks for acceptance and survival. Karen Isaksen Leonard has shown that barriers to entering both Anglo and Mexican society led Punjabi Mexican families to rely heavily on each other and the community they established in California's Imperial Valley in the twentieth century.[12]

For Chinese Mexicans in Macau, Catholic institutions were critical in the formation of community bonds. Churches and other organizations offered places to meet, connections with Mexico through foreign missionaries and clergy, emotional and spiritual support, economic assistance, and even jobs. Catholic sites constituted bases from which Chinese Mexicans conducted their struggle for repatriation to Mexico, thereby reinforcing the community's cohesion. Catholic organizations also linked the Macanese enclave with Mexicans and other Latin Americans in British Hong Kong. People traveled between the two colonies to celebrate Catholic and Mexican (or Latin American) traditions and to strategize about repatriation.[13]

Underscoring the significance of Catholic symbols, the Latin American Association of Hong Kong, a social, political, and religious club that became important for Chinese Mexicans in the postwar era, was known in Spanish as the Asociación Hispano-Americana de Nuestra Señora de Guadalupe (Our Lady of Guadalupe Hispanic-American Association). One of its founders, Manuel León Figueroa, had left Mexico at the age of seven with his mother, Luz Figueroa de León, and sister, Lupe León Figueroa, to live with their father in Guangdong Province. The family suffered numerous hardships, and after World War II and the death of his father, León Figueroa moved to Hong Kong.[14] Members of the Asociación gathered at

Virgen de Guadalupe at Santa Teresa Church in Hong Kong. Photographs by author.

Hong Kong's Santa Teresa Church, which still houses a shrine to the Virgen de Guadalupe that was dedicated the group. Chinese Mexicans and other Latin Americans celebrated 12 December, the feast day of the Virgen de Guadalupe, in addition to other events at the church.[15] The name Nuestra Señora de Guadalupe indicates the strong ties to Catholic traditions specific to the Americas, for this indigenous icon of the Virgin Mary originated in colonial Mexico.[16]

Alfonso Wong Campoy belonged to the Asociación and remembered gathering often with other Chinese Mexicans and Latin Americans in Macau and Hong Kong. He traveled to Hong Kong with compatriots to watch a Mexican soccer team play and to see a Mexican singer perform. When Mexican countrymen passed through Hong Kong on business or for other reasons, the community eagerly received them. Chinese Mexicans also organized dances in Macau and Hong Kong, celebrating with a classically Mexican beverage, tequila.[17]

Although Chinese Mexicans enjoyed each other's company and found ways to survive, life was filled with challenges. The war and postwar periods were particularly trying times for Chinese Mexicans, as most lived in misery and had trouble communicating with relatives in Mexico.[18] Macau's refugees from World War II and the Communist Revolution in

TABLE 4. Lay Mazo's List of Mexican Families Residing in Macau, 1959

| Name of the Head of the Household | ADULTS | | MINORS (A) | | Total | Observations |
	Masc.	Fem.	Masc.	Fem.		
Lucina Cuevas	2	2		1	5	Widow
Carolina Beltrán	1	2	1	1	5	Abandoned by her husband
María Ramos	1	2	1		4	Idem
Dolores Campoy	3	1			4	Widow
María del Carmen Lugo	3	3	1		7	Husband still living
Lucía Lugo de Ley	1	1	2	2	6	Idem
Ramón Lomas Olivas	2	2	3	2	9	Police officer
Federico Vong Córdova	1	1	3		5	Idem
Antonio León Sosa	1				1	He has recently been murdered by communists. His family is in Guangdong, China.
Juan Francisco Wong Martínez	1	1	1		3	In Hong Kong
Julia Sánchez	2	5			7	Husband still living
Jorge Yee Sánchez	1	1	2	1	5	Mechanic
Clotilde Morales de Lau		3		1	4	Husband still living
Maylo Roberto Lau Morales	1	1	1	1	4	Servant at the captaincy
Juan Chiu Trujillo	1	1	3	1	6	Police officer
Timotea Valdés de Pun	1	2	1	2	6	Widow. Has additional family members in Hong Kong.
Josefina Pun Valdés de Fok	1	1	4		6	Husband still living
María Consuelo P. Valdés de França	2	1	2	1	6	Husband is Portuguese
Florinda Gerardo	1	1	2		4	Husband still living
Eduardo Gerardo Auyong	1	1	1		3	Painter

Name of the Head of the Household	ADULTS		MINORS (A)		Total	Observations
	Masc.	Fem.	Masc.	Fem.		
Berta Manuela Gerardo de Wong	3	1	1		5	Husband still living
Carlos Gerardo Auyong	1	1	2		4	Police officer
Francisco Lay Mazo	2	2	3		7	Scribe at the Ecclesiastic Chamber
Ramón Lay Mazo	2	3			5	Idem
Sum total	35	39	34	13	121	

Source: Secretaría de Relaciones Exteriores, Archivo de Concentraciones, OM-149-5, 1960.
Lay Mazo's Note: (a) People younger than twelve years old are considered minors, as this is the criteria for shipping companies. This is to facilitate the calculation of fares.
Macau, 12 May 1960

China formed especially strong bonds, as the colony became an important sanctuary for political opponents or resisters. On occasion, however, China cut off Macau's food supplies.[19]

The size of the Chinese Mexican community in Macau fluctuated as some moved to Hong Kong or mainland China and others returned to Mexico. By 1959, the enclave consisted of twenty-four households with a total of 121 people. Sons and daughters born of Chinese Mexican unions had formed their own families in Guangdong Province or the colonies, at times choosing marital partners from within the community. Some women were married to Chinese, Chinese Mexican, or foreign men; others had been widowed, had separated from their spouses, or had been abandoned. Some Mexican and Chinese Mexican women such as Campoy Wong performed domestic service in homes or religious institutions. Alfonso Wong Campoy was a businessman who for a time also held a position in a Portuguese colonial fiscal office. His brother, Antonio René Wong Campoy, traveled regularly between Macau and Hong Kong, where he worked for the police. Other men were servants for the local captaincy, painters, mechanics, and porters at the Catholic seminary. Ramón Lay Mazo and his brother, Francisco Lay Mazo, worked as scribes for the Ecclesiastic Chamber. Chinese Mexican households ranged from three to nine people; most had several children. Some families were spread among Macau, Hong Kong, and villages in Guangdong Province, often moving among these locales. Travel to the mainland became more complicated after 1949, yet people continued to move back and forth. In doing so, Chinese Mexicans traversed metaphoric and geographic borders; even though they were geographically close, these areas were quite distinct political and cultural entities.[20]

Chinese Mexican Identity

Mexican and Chinese culture and language fused over the decades. Embodying such hybridity, Lay Mazo's complex Chinese Mexican identity emerged in his letters. Born in Mocorito, Sinaloa, he arrived in Taishan County in Guangdong Province with his family around 1933, when he was four years old. He moved to Macau after World War II. Writing letter upon letter on behalf of Chinese Mexicans while he worked as a scribe in Macau's Ecclesiastic Chamber, he became the leader of the repatriation movement. Associated with the church, he was an important figure in the community. His connections with Spanish-speaking clergy allowed him to become highly articulate in Spanish. Indeed, his Spanish was eloquent and well written. The church, moreover, helped him become Mexican. In time, he expressed a strong sense of Mexican nationalism and would ultimately lead his compatriots back to the Mexican homeland.[21]

Yet Lay Mazo also invoked Chinese language and culture. In letters to family members and other compatriots in Mexico, he imparted Cantonese and Taishanese tradition. A 1959 letter described and celebrated the Festival of the Seven Sisters. He lamented that the communist regime sought to eradicate such customs but rejoiced that the government would never succeed because they had such deep roots in China. He closed the letter with words of a song people traditionally sang on the seventh night of the seventh moon during the festival.[22] Lay Mazo also transliterated Chinese phrases into Spanish in letters to compatriots in Mexico. A gesture of cross-cultural communication, his transliterations offered aspects of Chinese culture to people he hoped to enlist in the repatriation struggle. Writing to a sympathetic Mexican widow named Rodríguez Viuda de Aragón, he opened by stating that he had his hands in a fist over his chest, in the ancient Chinese manner, to ask her in Cantonese, "Sek-pau-fan-mei-a?" which he translated as "¿Ya está llena de arroz? [Have you had your fill of rice?]." She had learned this custom on a recent visit to China, and Lay Mazo reminded her that the phrase was a common Chinese greeting and a wish for good health, invoking the importance of basic subsistence.[23]

After sharing the cultural practice, however, Lay Mazo set aside the greeting, saying it might seem comical to a Westerner, and moved on to the discussion he and Rodríguez Viuda de Aragón had begun on the veranda of the S.S. *Fat Shan*, the Macau–Hong Kong ferry, in the spring of 1960.[24] Aware of the deep divisions between East and West, he exhibited his own Chineseness but then made light of it. He was careful not to paint himself or his compatriots in China as "too Chinese," since their long-term goal was to return to Mexico. Renouncing or disregarding their Chineseness was part of the rhetoric of nationalism that Chinese Mexicans elaborated as they attempted to return to Mexico in the Cold War era. In a 1959 letter to President López Mateos, Lay Mazo wrote that even though they had been in China for so long, Mexicans living there knew neither the language nor the "exotic practices and customs of these people whose mentality is so opposite ours." He declared that the members of his community, whom he presented as Mexicans trapped in a foreign land, had the right to return to their homeland. Although he had a Chinese father, was fluent in Cantonese and Taishanese dialects, and had lived in Guangdong Province and Macau for most of his life, he emphasized his Mexicanness. Well aware that the formation of the People's Republic of China and its communist foundation had caused great anxiety in the West, he thought it best to set himself and his compatriots apart from the Chinese. In such ways, Chinese Mexicans performed Mexicanness.[25]

While both real and imagined divisions existed between Mexicans and Chinese, mixed-race people participated in the local culture and blurred existing social and political borders in Guangdong Province. Antonio León Sosa Mazo, the son of Lay Mazo's cousin, Valeriana Sosa Mazo, became a respected dancer in Guangdong Province, where he lived with his family through most of the 1950s.[26] The young man taught ballet and classic Chinese dances in Cantonese social and cultural centers and was recognized as one of the five best dancers and instructors in South China. But his mixed-race status eventually became a liability during the Communist Revolution. León Sosa Mazo had wanted to study medicine but was barred because his father was a "well-off property owner" who had returned from foreign lands and his mother was a "Mexican devil." After his rejection by the university, he wrote a controversial book whose title his uncle transliterated as *Chau-t'in-lui-tek-tung-t'in* and translated into Spanish as *El invierno de otoño* (The winter in the fall). The book described a student's experience of the sudden changes in government as well as private and public life and how texts, materials, professors, and discipline at the university had been transformed. The book survived Communist Party censorship, and the government published fifty thousand copies. Nevertheless, during a campaign to purge intellectuals a few months later, authorities denounced the book as damaging to the mental health of the people because it espoused capitalist and bourgeois ideology. Communist officials condemned León Sosa Mazo as a traitor to the party and an agent of North American imperialists and their puppet, Chiang Kai-shek.[27] Associating the book with the imperialist-supported Nationalist regime in Taiwan, Communist Party authorities ordered all copies of the book burned and the author confined in a mental institution.[28]

León Sosa Mazo escaped to Macau in April 1958 after his friends in the government informed him of the order for his arrest. After he fled, he told Lay Mazo that communist authorities had written to him in Macau offering money and other material benefits if he returned to Guangdong Province, where people missed him at popular dance festivals and social centers. The letters became threatening when he failed to return. Concerned about León Sosa Mazo's safety, Lay Mazo wrote repeatedly to Ambassador Carlos Gutiérrez Macías at the Mexican embassy in Manila during 1958 and 1959, pleading with officials to allow León Sosa Mazo to return to Sinaloa to live with his extended family. The Reverend Lancelot Miguel Rodrigues, the National Catholic Welfare Conference and Catholic Relief Services representative in Macau, offered to pay León Sosa Mazo's passage, but he never obtained permission to enter Mexico and was killed in Macau sometime in 1959.[29]

By the late 1950s, the plight of Chinese Mexicans in Macau and Hong Kong had become so well known that it penetrated the local vernacular in the expression "being like a Mexican," which meant being poor and stateless. Calling this linguistic turn "a disgraceful ridicule of the sacrosanct name of our beloved Nation, of our adored Mexico," Lay Mazo argued that pride in their country should move Mexican authorities to "rescue" their compatriots in China so that neither Mexicans nor Mexico could be characterized in such degrading ways.[30] In their struggle to repatriate, the Chinese Mexican community in China played on Mexico's newfound concern for its image abroad.

Anticommunist Ideology

Fear of communism framed Lay Mazo's pleas with the Mexican government to repatriate his compatriots in Guangdong Province and the colonies in the 1950s. He contended that the situations of Mexicans both on the mainland and in Macau and Hong Kong had worsened after 1949. Chinese Mexicans in the colonies lived in poverty and survived on handouts. The few who had jobs earned barely enough to sustain themselves. Chinese Mexicans in Guangdong Province had suffered even more, especially as the communist regime grew harsher during the 1950s and communist officials cut off people's water supply, stopped the delivery of wood and coal, and limited their rations.[31]

Although he had moved from Taishan County to Macau after World War II, Lay Mazo kept abreast of the mainland Chinese Mexican community as compatriots fled to Macau and Hong Kong or moved between the colonies and Guangdong Province. He drew on the stories he heard from countrymen to appeal to the Mexican government to "liberate" Mexicans from communist China, describing the hardships and persecution some had faced under the new regime.

The Cuevas Ley family experienced difficulties under communism in Guangdong Province. Clemente Ley and Lucina Cuevas had arrived in China in 1933. A successful businessman, Clemente Ley returned to Mexico to attend to his business just before the Japanese invasion, and his family in China never heard from him again; years later they would learn that he had died in Mexico and that his estate there was transferred to another Chinese immigrant. Ley had had a wife in China who died and left him with a daughter before he first emigrated to Mexico. Once abroad, he married Cuevas, and by the time he brought her to China, Ley's mother had taken into the home another Chinese wife for her son. Eventually, Lucina Cuevas would take care of her children and their half-siblings, as well as her husband's granddaughter from the first marriage. Cuevas had wanted to return to Mexico since the 1930s, and the obstacles to repatriation only increased with the Communist Revolution. The family's documents went missing, along with hundreds of others, from the Mexican embassy in Nanjing after communist liberation forces took the city in 1949 during the Chinese Civil War.[32] By the following year Cuevas and her daughter, also named Lucina Cuevas, were living in Macau. Her son Liman Ley soon escaped to the colony by swimming across the boundary waters; Portuguese authorities detained him for a few months before finally releasing him at his mother's insistence. Another son, Clemente Ley, had health problems but nonetheless used his bicycle to run errands for customers in China before he moved to Macau. Clemente Ley Sr.'s daughter from the first wife died in 1952, leaving behind a little girl, Elisa Ley. Communist authorities imprisoned Roberto Ley, the son of the third wife, after he tried to escape mainland China, although his time in prison was brief. The other members of the Cuevas Ley family lived in the Portuguese colony for the remainder of the decade, hoping to repatriate. Ultimately, in 1960 Lucina Cuevas would bring to Mexico her daughter Lucina and sons Liman and Clemente, as well as her husband's granddaughter Elisa Ley, passing as her uncle Clemente's daughter so that authorities would grant her departure. The family would later sponsor Roberto, who joined them in Mexico the following decade.[33]

Lay Mazo also wrote about his own relatives who suffered in Guangdong Province. Since communist authorities confiscated both incoming and outgoing mail, he was unable to communicate with his cousin, Valeriana Sosa Mazo, but he learned about her family from friends who moved to Macau. After Antonio Léon Sosa Mazo fled, local officials punished other family members for his actions, condemning his brother, Enrique Sosa Mazo, to eight years of forced labor and his Chinese brother-in-law to five. Officials banned his sisters from working in and receiving rations from government cooperatives and ultimately forced them to work as slaves in local communes.[34]

Such stories helped Lay Mazo argue that Mexico should "save" its citizens from communism in China. Even Chinese Mexicans who had escaped to the colonies were in danger, he warned. Macau and Hong Kong had become more and more chaotic and unsafe as they drew diverse refugees and expelled persons not only from mainland China but also from North Korea, North Vietnam, and other states. By 1959, the colonies were the only refuges left, but Lay Mazo feared that they too would soon fall to communism, since the Chinese government had issued calls for "total territorial integrity for China" and expressed the desire to take back Macau and Hong Kong.[35]

The Struggle to Repatriate to Mexico

Many of the Chinese Mexicans who had been drawn to Macau in the 1930s and 1940s returned to Mexico either during the Cárdenas repatriation or in small groups after World War II. Others remained in Macau and waited for years to repatriate because they were unable to establish Mexican citizenship. For three decades, these Chinese Mexicans incessantly appealed to individuals, organizations, and officials in Mexico and abroad for permission to repatriate.[36]

Relatives of Chinese Mexicans in Mexico wrote to officials and other compatriots on their behalf. In the late 1950s, Gregorio Luque in Ahome, Sinaloa, worked for the repatriation of Rosaria Luque de Chong (also known as Rosario Luque Cheung Fan Hing), eventually motivating members of the Partido Nacionalista de México to call for her family's return. Luque de Chong had arrived in China with her husband, Chong Chin, and their children, Ramón Antonio Chong, Cirilo Chong, and Arcadio Chong, after their expulsion from Sinaloa and their deportation from the United States in 1933. Another son, José Rosario Chong, was born in China. The family still resided in the mainland during the Communist Revolution, when officials confiscated and destroyed their documents. By the late 1950s, after becoming either widowed or separated from her husband, Luque de Chong and her children lived in Sham Shui Po, Hong Kong, where they were in extreme poverty and unable to prove Mexican citizenship. Pointing out that her husband had become a naturalized Mexican citizen before the family left Sinaloa, she argued that she and her children were legally Mexican citizens. The Partido Nacionalista urged the Mexican government to furnish the family with the necessary documents and offer economic assistance to repatriate them to Mexico.[37]

Lay Mazo's work brought a number of people in Mexico into the repatriation movement. After communicating with him, Mexico City resident María León Viuda de Carriedo became deeply concerned about the welfare of Chinese Mexicans. On 21 January 1959, she wrote to President López Mateos on behalf of ninety-six Mexican women who resided in Macau and wished to repatriate. The women had been in China for twenty-six years, and their lack of documentation precluded repatriation. She had been in contact with them as well as with Mexican authorities on their behalf since she became aware of their plight three years earlier. Even though the previous administration's head of the press for the Secretaría de Relaciones Exteriores had assured her that the problem would be resolved, the government had not done so. Claiming her place in Mexican society and invoking her own citizenship and civic participation, León Viuda de Carriedo wrote as a citizen, a bureaucrat, a woman, the "Queen for a Day" on a local television program, and the president of a district electoral office. Although she was a modest public health employee with few resources, she was "very happy because I live in my Country." Her female compatriots who lived in foreign lands without the documents to prove that they were Mexicans could not say the same; the people and the government bore responsibility for correcting this "error of the revolution."[38] Even though the

Mexican Revolution should have brought change for the good of all Mexicans, it failed women who had formed families with Chinese men.

Other women in Mexico City also became involved in the Chinese Mexican struggle for repatriation. In 1959, Professor Sara Cantú requested a meeting with López Mateos regarding Mexican women in Hong Kong and Macau who wished to return to Mexico; the office of the president thought she should instead interview officials at the Secretaría de Relaciones Exteriores. Teresa Tallien also wrote to Mexican authorities on behalf of three hundred Chinese Mexican families who had been in China since 1932 and wished to return to Mexico from Macau and Hong Kong.[39]

By the late 1950s, the Mexican Lions Club became involved in the repatriation effort. The organization's chief objectives included pushing Mexico to demonstrate its national sovereignty and international standing by protecting its subjects overseas. Indeed, by the mid-twentieth century, the activities and experiences of a nation-state's citizens abroad played an important role in defining its international image.[40] In Mexico, the Lions Club was historically conservative, and most of its members were middle-class professionals, businessmen, and local officials—the same segment of society that had led the anti-Chinese campaigns.[41] By midcentury, however, conservatism in Mexico, as elsewhere in the Western world, had become synonymous with anticommunism. Thus, the traditional association could take on the project of "liberating" Mexican women, Chinese Mexican children, and even some Chinese men from communist China, especially in light of the perception that Mexico needed to continue to establish itself on the world scene during the Cold War. The Lions Club in Tampico, Tamaulipas, began the national campaign to help Chinese Mexicans return to Mexico. Officers and leading members of branches in several states, including Tamaulipas, Guerrero, Jalisco, Nayarit, Chihuahua, and Coahuila, wrote letters during late 1959 and early 1960 urging federal officials to document and repatriate Mexican citizens in China.[42]

The Lions Club used three interrelated tactics. The first turned on Mexican gender norms and the importance of guarding Mexican women. Dr. Luis G. López O. wrote to President López Mateos on behalf of the Lions Club in Hermoso, Tamaulipas, concerning the tragedy of the "abandoned Mexican women who live in China alone." He called on the president to urge the appropriate government offices to open "the doors of our nation to those Mexican women." Also writing to the Mexican president, Dr. Alfredo Ortega Rivera of the Lions Club in Pachuca, Hidalgo, argued that Mexican women had been "faithful to hearth and home" when they chose to accompany their husbands to China. Alluding to the importance of Mexican women's role in forming families, Ortega Rivera pointed out that Mexican authorities had punished those women who chose to fulfill these duties with Chinese men by forcing them out of the country to keep their families intact.[43]

The second strategy appealed to Mexican patriotism. Invoking ideas of sameness, President Dr. Javier Elizondo Otañez and Secretary Antonio López Alatorre of the Lions Club in San Blas, Nayarit, wrote to López Mateos on behalf of the Mexican "families that long to be in the Nation, who share our language and religion, and find themselves far away, sad, and bitter, but nevertheless continue to be our compatriots." Employing the concepts of Mexican citizenship embedded in the Mexican Constitution of 1917, Lions Club members argued that the women and their children, even those born in foreign lands, were Mexican and had the right to protection by their government. In their letter to the national leader, President Armando C. Flores Peña and Secretary Alejo Carrillo Sánchez of the Lions Club in Monclova, Coahuila, cited Article 30, Section 2a of the Mexican Constitution: "Those who are born in foreign lands of a Mexican father and foreign mother or a Mexican mother and an unknown father are Mexicans." Under the law, therefore, the Mexican government needed to grant its citizens in China the documentation they would need to return.[44]

Not only did Chinese Mexicans have the right to protection, but the nation had an obligation to safeguard its citizens on foreign soil. The third tactic evoked the poverty that Chinese Mexicans faced in China, the fear of communism abroad, and the desire to convey Mexican national power to the international community. Dr. Ildefonso Lozano Bosque and Roberto Santos Ibarra of the Lions Club in Ciudad Acuña, Coahuila, lamented that Chinese Mexicans in Macau and Hong Kong lived in misery and worked in the worst jobs—an embarrassment to Mexico. Ortega Rivera used the same line of reasoning, adding that the Mexican government should seek to save from communism its citizens who lived in mainland China along with those who had sought refuge in the colonies. Suggesting that Chinese men had contributed to the development of a number of Mexican states, Ortega Rivera included them in his vision of the nation-state as well. Many of these men had been businessmen in Mexico, and the communist regime, he contended, persecuted and excluded them for their capitalist ideas. Jorge B. Cuellar Arocha and Leopoldo S. Villarreal Corona of the Lions Club in Sabinas, Coahuila, defended the women who were "disliked for being Mexican" in Hong Kong and Macau and "persecuted by communism" in mainland China. Mexico needed to bring them back to the homeland for their safety and to preserve its reputation in the world.[45]

To help the thousands of people seeking refuge from war and poverty in mainland China, Catholic Relief Services opened an office in Macau, providing crucial resources and services. The office was staffed by the Reverend Lancelot Miguel Rodrigues, who was born in Malacca, Malaysia, and arrived in Macau in 1935. He and Ramón and Francisco Lay Mazo became good friends after Rodrigues met the brothers when they worked in the local bishop's office. Rodrigues remembered them as intelligent, good-hearted people who taught him to play the guitar so that he could entertain the refugees, a much-needed distraction for those who were battling depression and trauma. Among the groups with whom Rodrigues worked were several thousand Portuguese Chinese who came to Macau after fleeing Shanghai in wartime. Rodrigues's organization offered to pay passage for Chinese Mexicans after they received the proper documentation, but Mexico's strict requirements for citizenship documents forestalled repatriation.[46]

Ramón Lay Mazo persevered, reminding Mexican officials that his countrymen lacked citizenship documents because they had left Mexico under trying circumstances and because of the hardships they had endured in China. It was absurd, he wrote, to ask for passports documenting when these people had left Mexico: Officials had driven them out precisely because anti-Chinese activists did not perceive their families as Mexican. The only crime Mexican women in China had committed was romantic involvement with Chinese men, and their innocent children's sole offense was the "Chinese blood in their veins." In light of Chinese Mexicans' difficulty in proving their citizenship, Lay Mazo and other activists entertained the possibility of sending Chinese Mexicans to other nations, including Brazil and Canada, which were accepting refugees from China. The Chinese Mexicans, however, preferred Mexico.[47]

Lay Mazo thus depicted Chinese Mexicans as "true patriots" who upheld a strong, deeply rooted Mexican nationalism in spite of being ignored by their government for so long and living as "stateless pariahs." It would not be easy, he wrote, to find people with such fierce patriotism and profound love for their homeland. Indeed, Chinese Mexicans' devotion to Mexico would surpass that of anyone lucky enough to live in the nation that they only dreamed of seeing. Lay Mazo's mother and many other Chinese Mexicans had died far away from their homeland with "Mexico on their lips." Some of his friends in China opined that it was "true insanity" to claim a country that had for so long disregarded its citizens, but Lay Mazo and the other Chinese Mexicans remained resolutely loyal to Mexico. Reclaiming a place in the nation and performing Mexicanness, Lay Mazo was compelled to lead the Chinese Mexican repatriation struggle "como mexicano que soy"—because first and foremost he was Mexican.[48]

The Chinese Mexican families who congregated in Portuguese Macau created spaces for themselves in the interstices between Mexican and Chinese cultures and the nation-state. Strong connections helped them survive. The Catholic Church in Macau and Hong Kong not only provided spiritual support and basic sustenance but also facilitated Mexican identity formation and ties with the homeland. Chinese Mexicans forged culturally hybrid identities while developing a strong sense of Mexicanness.

Although local and regional Mexican identities had once been primary, Chinese Mexicans came to identify with a Mexican nation they reinvented during their years across the Pacific. As people on the fringes of Mexican identity, they perceived the need to perform Mexicanness and develop an illustrative nationalism. Genuine longing for the nation after removal was shot through with strategic impulses during a time of intense and rapid flux in China. As time passed, Chinese Mexicans' love for an imagined homeland solidified. Never losing sight of Mexico, they held onto the dream of one day returning.

PART FOUR

Finding the Way Back
to the Homeland

CHAPTER EIGHT

To Make the Nation Greater

Claiming a Place in Mexico in the Postwar Era

On 7 December 1960, Dolores Campoy Wong wrote to Mexican president Adolfo López Mateos from the small southern town of Navojoa in the northern border state of Sonora. She and her sons—Alfonso Wong Campoy, age thirty-two; Héctor Manuel Wong Campoy, twenty-seven; and Antonio René Wong Campoy, twenty-six—had repatriated to Mexico from Macau the preceding month. Urging the government to help them secure employment or offer the family economic assistance, she told López Mateos that her sons had been unable to find jobs even though Mexican officials had promised the family aid upon their repatriation. The Wong Campoys had spent almost thirty years away from Mexico, most of that time in Portuguese Macau, and had longed and worked to return to Mexico. But when they finally repatriated, they found readjusting to Navojoa more complicated than they had anticipated, and the government's assistance ended when their feet landed on Mexican soil. Extended family members and Chinese Mexican compatriots, however, would provide the Wong Campoys with crucial support and facilitate their reintegration into Sonoran society.[1]

Chinese Mexican repatriates found a Mexico quite different from the one for which they had yearned. To survive they forged new networks in

Mexico, helping each other readjust. Mexican mothers battled residual anti-Chinese prejudice and fought for the full inclusion of their children and families. Repatriated Chinese Mexicans maintained transpacific ties and at times families; in doing so, they carried on the long Chinese tradition of maintaining households split by the Pacific. As they became Mexican abroad, Chinese Mexicans expanded the idea of Mexicanness: Their national identity had a transpacific foundation and a distinctly cosmopolitan flavor.

People began returning to Mexico in small waves in the years after World War II. In 1960, the López Mateos administration (1958–64) orchestrated a second official repatriation that was more inclusive than the first, allowing Chinese men to travel to Mexico with their families. The Mexican government announced that it would cease to repatriate people from China following the end of the 1960 program, but with Chinese Mexicans continuing to stream into Macau from mainland China seeking to return to Mexico, authorities provided assistance until at least the 1980s.

The repatriations of Chinese Mexican refugees from mainland China via Portuguese Macau and British Hong Kong helped Mexico situate itself as a democratic nation on the world scene during the Cold War era. The repatriations offer further understanding of how Mexico became part of the international community and constructed itself in a global arena that turned on newly formed divisions between communist and noncommunist countries.[2] Examining the reincorporation of people the anti-Chinese movement had excluded in the early 1930s and the ways they negotiated their return complicates our understanding of postrevolutionary Mexico. The story sheds light on conflicts between Mexican states and the federal government and the ways these relationships changed as the central state became stronger. Furthermore, this history offers insight into Mexico's complex, incoherent treatment of Chinese men and their Mexican-origin families; the nation's practices reflected larger patterns of changing foreign policy toward China and the Chinese as the era of U.S. Chinese exclusion came to a close.[3]

Repatriation after World War II

Several hundred Chinese Mexican families had either missed the Cárdenas repatriation or chosen to remain in China, Hong Kong, or Macau. As World War II brought additional challenges, some Chinese Mexicans decided that returning to Mexico was a better option. Those who could prove Mexican nationality returned in small groups either by paying their own way or by raising money for their travel expenses through family and friends. Some Chinese men received permission to return at this time in part as a consequence of China's position in World War II and the support it received from the international community during the Japanese invasion.

Nevertheless, Cárdenas's successors over the next two decades never conducted another official repatriation, despite the near-constant pleas from Chinese Mexicans. The administrations of Manuel Ávila Camacho (1940–46), Miguel Alemán Valdés (1946–52), and Adolfo Ruiz Cortines (1952–58) were preoccupied largely with domestic affairs and promoted business-oriented policies that fostered corruption. The Mexican economy and national infrastructure nonetheless grew. Ruiz Cortines moved through Congress legislation that fully enfranchised Mexican women. In the context of the Cold War, he argued against communist intervention in Latin America at the 1954 Caracas Conference by urging fellow national leaders to work for economic progress and increased social justice, even though in practical terms, the latter issue took a took a backseat to economic development projects.[4]

Chinese Mexicans with Mexican citizenship documents and the necessary resources repatriated in small groups in the post-Cárdenas era. Antonio Chua Wong returned to Mexico with his wife, Wong Oi Tai, in 1948 after having lived most of his life away. He was born in Nogales, Sonora, in 1927 to a poor Mexican family. When he was around three years old, the Chinese owners of a local business adopted him because they had no children of their own and his birth family was unable to support him. Fully Mexican by birth and parentage, he left Mexico when local authorities expelled his adoptive parents in the early 1930s. The family lived at first in Kaiping, Jiangmen, Guangdong Province, his adoptive parents' birthplace, but later moved to Hong Kong, where he eventually married. He and his wife traveled to Mexicali, Baja California, and eventually to Hermosillo, Sonora, where their son, Cristóbal Chua Wong, was born in 1949. Since Antonio Chua Wong had the documents to prove that he was Mexican, authorities allowed him to reenter, along with his wife, who was deemed a Mexican citizen by virtue of her marriage to a Mexican man. Chua Wong's case thus contrasts starkly with those of the women who found themselves with murky citizenship status as a consequence of their ties with Chinese men. Chua Wong and his wife soon separated, and she and their young son returned to Hong Kong. More than two decades later, however, father-son bonds and a strong sense of wifely duty would draw Wong Oi Tai and Cristóbal Chua Wong back to Mexico.[5]

Fernando Ma's family was also able to prove Mexican citizenship and departed Hong Kong for Mexicali in 1956. Fernando Ma was born in Herrateña, Durango, in 1937, the oldest son of Chapo Ma, as he was known in Mexico, and his wife, Modesta Machado Ma. Chapo Ma had emigrated from Taishan County and established a small restaurant; the couple met when Machado worked there. Anti-Chinese activity in Durango prompted the family to move to Mexicali, but Modesta was unhappy there. The family traveled to China when Fernando was still very young. Living in Guangdong Province, Macau, and Hong Kong, he and his siblings attended a number of schools. During World War II, the family was unable to leave China or communicate with people in Mexico. By the 1950s, the Mas had few resources, but they returned to Mexico after a relative or an acquaintance sent Chapo Ma money for their trip. The family traveled to Guadalajara by plane and then on to Mexicali by bus. Fernando Ma's paternal grandparents, who had emigrated from China years earlier, had stayed in Mexico and were still living in Mexicali when their son and his family returned. Although Fernando Ma eventually moved to Hermosillo, his parents remained in Mexicali, where Chapo Ma died in 1995 and Modesta Machado Ma took care of her in-laws well into their old age.[6]

The lack of citizenship documents complicated or prevented the repatriation of Chinese Mexicans who had left as children and wanted to return in the postwar era. Felipe Sánchez Chi and Samuel Sánchez Chi exited Mexico through the Ciudad Juárez–El Paso border in 1927, when they were eight and four years old, respectively. Agustín Jim was three years old in 1928 and Arturo H. Yee was six in 1936 when they left at Nogales. In mid-1951, the Secretaría de Relaciones Exteriores sought the help of the U.S. Immigration and Naturalization Service in identifying them because they wanted to return to Mexico from China, but U.S. immigration officials could find no record of these individuals.[7]

After Roberto M. Fu's children repatriated under Cárdenas, they worked to obtain the documents needed to bring their father and youngest brother, Maximiliano, back to Mexico. As part of their efforts, they liquidated their store, leaving them "poor but happy," as they wrote to Ramón Lay Mazo, when they finally obtained permission. Before Maximiliano could return, however, he died in a mental institution in Macau in the early 1950s, leaving his father even more desperate to reunite with his older children. Lay Mazo pled with authorities to allow Roberto Fu to return to Mexico.[8]

Such pleas, combined with the work of supporters in Mexico, particularly the Lions Club, and the internationalist politics of President López Mateos finally triggered the second official repatriation in 1960.

Mexico under López Mateos

Assuming power on 1 December 1958, López Mateos was the first president since Cárdenas to reinvigorate the nation's revolutionary fervor. López Mateos's innovative domestic and international policies brought social and political change, and he sought a tighter relationship between the global and the domestic. Establishing Mexico as a legitimate, democratic nation on the global landscape was a top priority. Moreover, López Mateos's political style was new in its embrace of internationalism as a form of Mexican patriotism. Not coincidentally, he was the first Mexican president to carry out a diplomatic trip to Asia. From 3 October to 24 October 1962, he visited India, Japan, Indonesia, the Philippines, and Hong Kong, where he met Mexican residents.[9]

López Mateos's presidency occurred at a time of stark and vigorous change throughout the world. The global balance of power shifted as the People's Republic of China became stronger and Mao Zedong and the communist leadership formed alliances, although tenuous at times, with Soviet Prime Minister Nikita Khrushchev. Further complicating international politics, important Third World leaders emerged, including Indian Prime Minister Jawaharlal Nehru. China increasingly saw revolutionary potential in the Third World, and the new communist state sought both recognition and alliances elsewhere in Asia as well as in Africa and Latin America. Cuba soon demonstrated that socialism was a viable alternative to capitalist development in Latin America.

López Mateos's policies vis-à-vis socialism and communism were complex. Like his predecessor, Ruiz Cortines, López Mateos argued against communist influence in Latin America and removed communist leaders from Mexican teachers' and railroad unions. He imprisoned (but later pardoned) globally recognized muralist David Alfaro Siqueiros on charges of communism. More important, López Mateos continued Mexico's refusal to establish formal ties with China.[10] Mexico also maintained a critical stance toward the Soviet Union. However, López Mateos engaged in diplomatic relations with Cuba. He had assumed Mexico's presidency just before Fidel Castro and the 26th of July Revolution removed Cuba's right-wing dictator, Fulgencio Batista, and López Matos refused to endorse a policy of total nonintervention in the socialist state, a stance that displeased the United States. Mexico refused to denounce Castro's regime but condemned the Soviet Union for positioning offensive missiles in Cuba in 1962. López Mateos voted against expelling Cuba from the Organization of American States and rejected economic sanctions, making Mexico the only nation in the Western Hemisphere to retain air service and formal ties with the island.[11]

Both increasing Mexico's autonomy and visibility on the world scene and pushing the Mexican Revolution "back to the left" on the domestic front, López Mateos has been called Mexico's "most revolutionary president" since Cárdenas. He revived Mexico's land distribution policy, which the previous administrations had all but forgotten. During his six-year term, he dispersed about thirty million acres; no president since Cárdenas had distributed more land. López Mateos also expanded medical care and old-age pensions, and his public health campaigns went far to tackle disease. Since Mexico's urban population exceeded its rural population for the first time in 1960, his policies focused on problems in cities with efforts including the creation of low-cost housing projects. López Mateos also renewed the emphasis on rural schools. Education became the largest expenditure in the Mexican budget by 1963 as he sponsored literacy programs and a system of free and compulsory textbooks to keep up with Mexico's dramatic population growth. The "most fondly remembered president of the postwar era," López Mateos "was eulogized as a nationalist who defended Mexican interests in the world community and a humane statesman who appreciated the concerns of the powerless masses at home."[12] It was not happenstance that Chinese Mexican families in China would finally repatriate during his administration.

The López Mateos Repatriation

Because of the Mexican president's strong internationalist politics and the Cold War ideology that began to grip the West at midcentury, the 1960 repatriation would be more inclusive than the first, allowing Chinese men to return with their families. In June 1959, the Secretaría de Relaciones Exteriores authorized the official in charge of business relations at the Mexican embassy in Manila to travel to Hong Kong and Macau to interview Chinese Mexican families. Early the next year, the Mexican government permitted Mexican ambassador to the Philippines Carlos Gutiérrez Macías to document people who could confirm Mexican nationality. That spring, Concepción Rodríguez Viuda de Aragón, a widow whose husband had been a prominent citizen of Tampico, Tamaulipas, visited Macau and Hong Kong shortly after the Lions Club campaign began in her hometown; she met with Lay Mazo and others. After she returned, she conveyed information about the Chinese Mexican community to Mexican government authorities with whom she had connections. A series of official communications on the matter ensued, and in May 1960 the government announced that it would document and repatriate its remaining citizens in China.[13]

The news brought hope to many divided families. On 24 May 1960, Juana Trujillo Viuda de Chiu eagerly wrote to the office of the president from Coatzacoalcos, Veracruz, after hearing López Mateos's repatriation order on the radio. She urged the government to include her sons, Juan Chiu Trujillo in Macau and Emmanuel Chiu Trujillo in Hong Kong, in the repatriation. Similarly, on 30 June 1960, Lorenzo Alvarado and other family members in Pichucalco, Chiapas, appealed to the president on behalf of an elderly relative, Mercedes Alvarado Méndez, a longtime resident of Hong Kong.[14]

Other Mexicans responded less favorably to the announcement. In Sonora, where anti-Chinese elements remained active, some people spoke out against the return of Chinese Mexicans. On 28 June 1960, Alfredo G. Echeverría, Professor Eduardo Reyes Díaz, and other members of the Campaña Nacionalista (Nationalist Campaign) in Hermosillo wrote to the office of the president about the "problem" that repatriating these families represented for the nation. Echeverría had been a leader in Sonora's anti-Chinese movement during the 1920s and 1930s.[15] He and the others sought to convince authorities to confine the repatriates to La Isla del Tiburón, an island off the coast of Sonora historically occupied by the racially excluded and marginalized Seri, an indigenous people, much in the way that Angel Island contained Chinese in the United States.[16] These Sonorans argued that there were economic possibilities within the island's *ejido* (community land and farming) system and fishing industry, but in reality, Tiburón had limited resources and arable land.[17] These men worried that the people who returned would become economically successful in Sonora, as some of their Chinese relatives had been prior to the expulsions decades earlier. Continuing to define Chinese Mexican families as non-Mexican, the nationalist campaign had kept alive anti-Chinese ideology for more than four decades, and for these activists, this ideology outweighed anticommunist fears. The influence of the Lions Club campaign and the larger repatriation effort, however, ultimately trumped the proponents of exclusion.[18]

In the fall of 1960, the Mexican government created a repatriation commission to be headed by Dr. Bernardo Bátiz. Bátiz arrived in Hong Kong to document and repatriate Chinese Mexicans living both there and in Macau. The commission circulated a notice in Spanish, Portuguese, Chinese, and English, announcing that the program would "finish definitively the repatriation and naturalization problem of Mexicans residing in the East." The repatriation would also occur "without intervention or contribution from anyone."[19] Although a number of groups had appealed to the government on behalf of the Chinese Mexican community and Catholic Relief Services had offered to pay travel expenses, the Mexican government wanted sole responsibility for the return of its citizens in the effort to build Mexico's international reputation. The repatriation would demonstrate the nation's concern for its subjects overseas and its commitment to the Cold War politics that denounced communism.

On 3 October 1960, Ramón Lay Mazo wrote to López Mateos that some women were apprehensive about returning to Mexico because Bátiz had told them that his goal was to "repatriate Mexicans, not insert foreigners into the country," and the women thus feared that their Chinese husbands would not be allowed to repatriate with them. Whereas in Antonio Chua Wong's case, his wife had automatic citizenship through her marriage, gendered citizenship policies did not apply the same rules toward Mexican women with foreign husbands. Lay Mazo noted that the number of Chinese men married to Mexican women was quite low—nine in Macau and only a few more in Hong Kong—and only two of the Macanese men were under age sixty, meaning that most of them were well above the normative working age and would thus not compete with Mexicans for jobs. Drawing on Mexican family and gender norms as well as those in China, Lay Mazo pointed out if husbands were allowed to accompany their wives, families would not have to break up. There would be no need for the "painful and atrocious sacrifice of the wife, or a son, or perhaps the entire family, remaining in China, simply because a part of the family, or more accurately, its chief member, cannot go along."[20] Bátiz's superiors acceded to this argument, allowing the Chinese men to return to Mexico, where they lived the rest of their lives.[21]

Between 250 and 350 Chinese Mexicans repatriated to Mexico under López Mateos. Departing Hong Kong on 7 November 1960, A. Vargas led a group of 13 repatriates, telling *Excélsior* that they were happy to be returning to Mexico and hoped to be well received. Another group of 113 repatriates, led by Ramón Lay Mazo, traveled from Macau to Hong Kong and ultimately reached Mazatlán, Sinaloa, on 16 November.[22] Grateful to President López Mateos for facilitating their return, Lay Mazo told *Excélsior* that the repatriates "would work 'to make the nation greater.'"[23]

Dolores Campoy Wong and her three sons were among the repatriates in Lay Mazo's group. Alfonso Wong Campoy and his adult brothers chose to leave their jobs in Macau and Hong Kong to accompany their mother, live in the country of their birth, and become acquainted with their extended family. The two Wong Campoy sisters did not repatriate. María del Carmen Irma Wong Campoy married a Portuguese Chinese man who had arrived in Macau as a refugee from Shanghai during the Sino-Japanese conflict. After his death, she married a Macanese man, and they later moved to San Francisco. Raquel Wong Campoy married a Portuguese man and eventually moved to Lisbon.[24]

Those who repatriated to Mexico traveled on Pan-American Airlines from Hong Kong to Mazatlán, stopping in Los Angeles en route. Once in Mexico, the families boarded buses and went their own ways. Dolores Campoy Wong and her sons were one of two families in their group to return to Sonora. The other family was headed by Celsa Echeverría de Luján, who had been expelled from Sonora with her romantic partner, Ho Ping, and their eight children in 1933. Echeverría de Luján and six of her children—Reinalda, Dolores, José, Celsa, Roberto, and Teresa—returned to the mother's hometown, Esperanza.[25]

Paul Tsang's family arrived in Sonora with another group of repatriates in 1960. His grandfather, whose surname was Chan, had migrated to Mexico and married Anita Durán, a Sonoran woman of Yaqui indigenous heritage, before their expulsion. Their Chinese-born daughter learned five Chinese dialects as well as Portuguese and eventually married a Chinese man who came from a wealthy family that lost all of its resources during the Japanese invasion, when the man was in college in Hong Kong. He remained there, quit school, and lived on the streets before becoming a porter in a Catholic seminary. Their Hong Kong–born son, Paul Tsang, was one year old when the family traveled to Mexico under López Mateos's repatriation program.[26]

Reintegrating into Mexican Society

The repatriates once again found themselves facing a difficult adjustment. Children who had left Mexico when they were very young or were born in China had particular trouble becoming part of Mexican society. As in the late 1930s during the Cárdenas repatriation, Mexican mothers combated residual anti-Chinese prejudice and fought to secure a place in the nation for their families.

Alfonso Wong Campoy described returning to Navojoa as "a little strange." When he and his brothers were unable to find jobs and the assistance promised during the repatriation had not materialized, his mother wrote to the Mexican president requesting help.[27] But that help came not from the government but from family members and other Chinese Mexicans. The family lived with Dolores Campoy Wong's brother, Pedro Campoy, for nearly a month. They were visited by compatriots they had met in Macau as well as by one man whose father they had known in the colony. The father had remained behind when his wife and children returned to Mexico during the first official repatriation, and the man frequently wept about his divided family, though he appreciated hearing the Wong Campoys' stories about his father. The Wong Campoys also received a visit from the Chon family, which had returned to Mexico during the Cárdenas repatriation and resettled in Bacobampo, a small town near Navojoa. The Wong Campoys soon went to live with the Chons in Bacobampo, where Campoy Wong worked making *aguas* (water-based fruit drinks) at the Chons' store. According to Alfonso Wong Campoy, the family's readjustment problems eased after they reunited with their *paisanos* (compatriots).[28]

Wong Campoy's use of the term *paisanos* is significant. Both the Wong Campoys and the Chons had made their way to Macau after being expelled from Sonora. They were compatriots in a profound sense of the word. Removed from Mexico and neither fully Mexican nor fully Chinese, they were mixed, in-between, without a country.[29] They had made each other *paisanos* in the new community they created abroad. Such Chinese Mexican families formed relationships that persisted over years and across oceans. After living far apart for more than twenty years, after only a brief friendship in Macau in the 1930s, the two families renewed their close ties in Sonora. The Chons' assistance proved critical to the Wong Campoys' reintegration into Sonoran society. Because their compatriots treated them well, Alfonso Wong Campoy noted, he and his family stayed in Bacobampo for years, returning to Navojoa only later in the decade when it began to grow into a larger town.[30]

The Wong Campoys' strong sense of Mexican identity and culture ultimately helped them become part of Mexican society. Alfonso Wong Cam-

The Wong Campoys in Mexico: (from left) Alfonso Wong Campoy, María del Carmen Irma Wong Campoy Maher Conceição, Dolores Campoy Wong (seated), and Héctor Manuel Wong Campoy. Photograph used with permission.

poy has remained in Navojoa, the same town from which local authorities expelled his family when he was a young boy. Following in his father's footsteps, he began a family and established a business, selling fruits, vegetables, salsa, honey, nuts, and goods, at his Navojoa *mercado* (central market) stand, which attracts customers from the community as well as the surrounding towns and rural areas. Over the years, he has earned a reputation as a fair and kind businessman. He believes that he has a duty to treat his customers well because they are hardworking, especially the indigenous people from the surrounding rural areas who come to Navojoa to shop.[31] Alfonso Wong Campoy has thus kept alive his father's legacy.

The rest of the Wong Campoy family has had varying degrees of connection to Sonora. Héctor Manuel Wong Campoy lived there until he died. Antonio René Wong Campoy stayed for a time and eventually relocated to San Francisco, where he went to school and worked. Dolores Campoy Wong lived in Sonora for more than a decade before moving to San Francisco to live with her elder daughter, María del Carmen Irma Wong Campoy Maher Conceição, and be near her son, Antonio. Dolores ultimately disliked her life in Sonora, particularly the intense heat, and preferred San Francisco, where she remained until her death in the 1990s. Conceição has remained in San Francisco, Antonio René Wong Campoy now resides in Florida, and Raquel Wong Campoy continues to live in Lisbon; the siblings have kept in regular touch and on occasion have visited each other.[32]

Some Chinese Mexicans resettled in Mexican communities other than those they had left years before. Although he was born in Sinaloa, Ramón Lay Mazo and his brother, Francisco, and their families made homes in Guadalajara, Jalisco, after they repatriated. Ramón was at first unable to find employment, but his connections eventually secured him a position. Chinese Mexican Wong Castañeda bought the Mexican newspaper *El Occidental* and offered his compatriot a job writing international political commentary. Lay Mazo's two daughters, Juanita Lay Mazo and María Asunción Lay Mazo, eventually received scholarships to study at the Colegio de Guadalajara. Both Ramón's and Francisco's families fared well in the large, diverse Mexican city. Like the Lay Mazo brothers, Lucina Cuevas was born in Sinaloa, yet she and her children settled in Guadalajara after they repatriated in 1960. Later they moved to Mexicali, where the large extended family lived in one big compound that was attached to their restaurant.[33]

Commemorating the Repatriation of 1960

In 1961, Alberto Antonio Loyola wrote *Chinos-mexicanos cautivos del comunismo: su repatriación fue una gran proeza* (Chinese Mexican captives of communism: their repatriation was a great feat), a booklet intended to memorialize the Chinese Mexican struggle and honor the heroism of the people in Mexico who helped in the repatriation. Mired in Cold War ideology, the booklet highlighted the hardships people suffered under communism in China and their efforts to escape. For Loyola, local newspaper coverage of the repatriation the year before had merely given the simple facts; his work would detail his compatriots' odyssey in China.[34]

The booklet noted that Chinese immigrants had settled in Baja California, Chihuahua, Sinaloa, and Sonora starting in the mid-nineteenth century and later in some regions of Chiapas. After the migrants had amassed wealth, Mexican officials unjustly expelled them to China. Some of the repatriates recounted stories of their lives in China in interviews with Loyola and others for the booklet. Rosario Luque de Chong described the difficult choices she had faced. After working under harsh conditions on a commune, she had had to sell one of her children as a slave so that she and her two other children could escape "the red tyranny." They fled to Macau and became part of the Chinese Mexican community there and in Hong

Kong, where they lived for a time. A month after repatriating to Mexico, Luque de Chong died; her friend, Mercedes Alvarado Hunken, told Loyola that Luque de Chong had been deeply content to finally be in Mexico once again. Although she had died at peace, she remained plagued by the pain of having sold her son, whom she never regained.[35]

Loyola named Ramón Lay Mazo as the key leader in the repatriation struggle and honored his selflessness. Ambassador Gutiérrez Macías in Manila had authorized Lay Mazo and his family to repatriate in 1958, but he refused to return without his compatriots. Over the years, even as the Mexican government repeatedly said it lacked the financial resources to bring home the Mexicans in China, Lay Mazo never gave up his vision.[36]

Lay Mazo also advocated on behalf of other Latin Americans. In April 1958, he wrote to the Guatemalan government to plead the case of the only Guatemalans in Macau, María Felipa de Jesús Meléndez Quinteros and her children, Rodolfo Meléndez Quinteros, Dora Meléndez Quinteros, and Araceli Meléndez Quinteros, who were ages sixteen, thirteen, and ten, respectively. The mother had performed arduous labor under the Chinese communist regime and was destitute when she and her children arrived in Macau. The Macanese community offered its assistance, and the two girls soon went to live in a convent operated by Canossian religious sisters, while María and Rodolfo moved in with another Latin American family. Lay Mazo's efforts persuaded the Guatemalan government to repatriate the family.[37]

Lay Mazo's numerous letters drew diverse individuals and groups into the struggle. By appealing to elite Mexicans, Lay Mazo persuaded Jesús González Cortazar, the son of the governor of Jalisco, José de González Gallo, to become involved. González Cortazar formed the Comité de Ayuda (Help Committee), which circulated propaganda among influential citizens to garner support for Chinese Mexicans in China. The political upheaval brought by the 1958 election, however, impeded any direct action.[38]

Mexico City widow María León Viuda de Carriedo, a member of the working class, was Lay Mazo's key supporter in Mexico. Affectionately calling her "Mamacita Carriedo," Loyola admired the "abnegated woman's" unending work, "valuable assistance, and strong will," all of which he believed had played a role in breaking "Mao's communist barriers." A newspaper report on Mexicans in China in the late 1950s had deeply moved León Viuda de Carriedo, who wrote to Lay Mazo and then circulated his return letters to authorities. She participated in a Mexico City television program, *Queen for a Day*, to bring attention to the plight of Mexicans in

China. After winning, she traveled to Los Angeles to appear on the same program and again emerged as the winner. When the repatriation began in 1960, she visited returnees and continued to work on their behalf, securing food donations from Catholic organizations.[39]

Some of the repatriates came back from China with diseases. Francisco Chong López had contracted tuberculosis in China and was still being treated at the Hospital Regional del Pacífico in Zoquipan, Jalisco, when Loyola published his booklet. Chong López blamed the communist regime's program of forced labor for his and other compatriots' illnesses. The Sinaloa-born Chong López had been very young when he moved to China with his father and spoke only Chinese dialects, so the Lay Mazo brothers, who spoke Cantonese and Taishanese, provided translation for his interview with Loyola. When Chong López mentioned that his wife, who remained in China, had recently written to ask for money, Ramón Lay Mazo interjected that communist leaders demanded cash from certain families to secure funding from their relatives in foreign lands. He told Chong López that he needed to get well so that he could work and send money to his family in China: Only then would the "devilish communists" cease to bother them.[40]

Loyola concluded by both praising and critiquing the Mexican government. Of the 267 people who returned to Mexico in 1960, he contended that 80 percent had trouble sustaining themselves and their families in Mexico. He commended Mexico for pouring more than two million pesos into the repatriation but lamented that Bátiz and other government employees had embezzled some of these funds and faced no punishment. Loyola urged the government to repatriate the seventy Chinese Mexicans still living in communist China both to complete the process begun during the previous year and to wash away "the stain" that Bátiz's actions had "cast on this grand gesture."[41]

In addition to pocketing some of the money intended for repatriation, Bátiz sold documents and told some Chinese Mexicans to falsify their papers. According to Manuel León Figueroa, one of the founders of the Asociación Hispano-Americana de Nuestra Señora de Guadalupe in Hong Kong, when he obtained a $380 loan from a Catholic aid group, Bátiz embezzled $300 of the sum. Celsa Echeverría de Luján told *Novedades* reporter Luis Spota that Bátiz demanded $380 for her family's repatriation and had made similar requests of other families. Serafín Anaya, a missionary and priest at Rosary Church in Kowloon, Hong Kong, beginning in 1976, heard many stories about Bátiz's corruption.[42]

Repatriation after 1960

Having promised to "finish definitively" the problem of citizens residing in the East in 1960, the Mexican government would never again orchestrate an official repatriation. Nevertheless, Chinese Mexicans whose families had been expelled from the nation decades earlier continued to stream into Mexico until at least the 1980s. People who had stayed in mainland China after the second repatriation for whatever reason traveled to Macau or Hong Kong and sought assistance from religious aid organizations, Mexican consuls, and others who worked on behalf of refugees.

Luis Ruiz, a Spanish Jesuit priest at Santo Agostinho, Casa Ricci, in Macau, became the new pilot of the Chinese Mexican repatriation struggle after Ramón Lay Mazo returned to Mexico. The "chaplain of the refugees," as he signed his letters, wrote to Mexican officials beginning in 1960 to thank them for conducting the repatriation and urge them to pressure the governments of Peru and Ecuador to rescue their citizens in China, and he continued his efforts on behalf of refugees in Macau through the 1970s. Over the next decades he was committed to doing good works in southern China and lived in Macau until his death on 26 July 2011, two months before his ninety-eighth birthday.[43]

In 1962 and 1963, Ruiz wrote to Mexican authorities on behalf of Mexican citizens living in Guangdong Province who wished to reunite with their families in Mexico. This group included Federico Cinco Sandoval, Jesús Yink López, Manuela González Viuda de Wong, José Rosalío Wong Martínez, and Kun Kit Kan Wong, who had missed the opportunity to seek documents and repatriation from Bátiz in 1960 because communist officials had refused to grant them permission to leave China. Their plea combined Cold War ideology with Mexican nationalism and paternalistic rhetoric. Until recently, they wrote, their only option had been to remain in China, behind the "iron curtain"; now that they were free, they awaited the assistance of their government and president—their "beacon of light" and the father of all Mexicans—so that they might return to the "land of our dreams, our beloved Mexico." They also noted that many other Chinese Mexicans remained stuck in communist territory, without documents and without freedom. Even though communist officials had begun allowing foreigners to depart, they could enter Macau only if they had passports, and many did not. Furthermore, immigration authorities in Macau required foreigners to deposit one thousand patacas, the local currency, to live in the colony.[44]

These Chinese Mexicans would also take part in the long-standing tradition of maintaining transpacific households, as some men returned with only one child, leaving behind wives and other children to whom they would send money. Mexican-born José Rosalío Wong Martínez returned with his oldest son, Kun Kit Kan Wong, who had been born in China. As the son of a male citizen, the child's Mexican citizenship was undisputed. Cinco Sandoval, Yink López, and González Viuda de Wong all had been born in Mexico, and their names appeared on a list of Mexican citizens residing in communist China that Bátiz had submitted to the Secretaría de Relaciones Exteriores while he was in Hong Kong in 1960. Foreign relations officials soon requested permission to expedite passports for the entire group.[45]

Like Lay Mazo before him, Ruiz drew international organizations into the Chinese Mexican struggle to return to Mexico. The Intergovernment Committee for European Migration, led by Anthony W. Clabon in Geneva, Switzerland, offered its assistance. The committee had organized and helped fund refugee trips on chartered planes first to Europe and then to various countries in the Americas. One plane was scheduled to depart, presumably from Hong Kong, in early 1963, with another slated for the following fall. Ruiz tried to convince Mexican authorities to take advantage of this opportunity to repatriate Mexicans.[46]

The Asociación Hispano-Americana de Nuestra Señora de Guadalupe in Hong Kong also became involved in repatriation after 1960. Members compiled a register of refugees with photographs and forms listing their contacts in Mexico so that Ruiz could send the information to Mexican authorities. These forms provide insight into the lives of Chinese Mexicans in China, painting a picture of people who had lived in extreme poverty and were eager to return to Mexico.[47]

Mexican-born men whose Chinese fathers had died and whose Mexican mothers had died, were still in China, or had already returned to Mexico were among those who sought repatriation during this time. These men had become laborers and married Chinese or Chinese Mexican women in villages in Guangdong Province. Federico Cinco Sandoval, for example, was born in Guamúchil, Sinaloa, in 1918 and had left Mexico around seven years later. He eventually became a worker in Guangdong Province, where he married Matilde Lao, who was born in China in 1918. Their sons, Manuel Cinco Sandoval (age twenty-three by the early 1960s) and Enrique Cinco Sandoval (age ten), and daughters, Alicia Cinco Sandoval (age nineteen) and Chabela Cinco Sandoval (age seventeen), were also born in China.

Federico's brother, Jorge Cinco, and three aunts in Guamúchil served as the family's contacts in Mexico. The photographs of Federico showed what were described as his "oriental features," "formal dress of jacket and tie," and "humble condition." While Federico was in Macau seeking repatriation, his mother, Zenona Sandoval, and his wife and children were in Guangdong Province awaiting news from him.[48]

Ruiz asked Verónica Noquez Lugo (born Beatriz Noquez Lugo in Mexico) and her companions to house and employ two Mexican women who had arrived from mainland China hoping to return to Mexico. Noquez Lugo had settled in Macau in 1966 as a missionary in the religious order Nuestra Señora del Perpetuo Socorro, a group of Mexican sisters who founded a house there and ran a day care center, the Infantario Ave Maria, for seventeen years. The sisters later established the Creche Papa João XXIII, a day school for children.

Zenona Sandoval lived with the sisters and worked at the original day care center. Because she lacked the adequate resources and a Mexican passport, she had been unable to return to Mexico earlier in the decade, when her son, Federico Cinco Sandoval, attempted to repatriate the family. She stayed with the nuns in Macau for about ten years until her other son, Jorge Cinco Sandoval, was finally able to bring her to Mexico. During her time in Macau, Jorge regularly sent her money, and the sisters also paid her for working at the day care center. Noquez Lugo and María del Carmen Lugo Becerrez recalled that Sandoval often lovingly reminisced about her Chinese husband, who had left Guangdong Province for Manila many years earlier. She never saw him again.[49]

Soon after arriving in Hong Kong in the early 1970s, Marta Lei met two middle-aged indigenous Mexican women who were from poor backgrounds and who had many children. Lei met the women in a suite at the former Hilton Hotel, which served as the office and home of the Mexican consul, Ramón Rodríguez Benson, since Mexico did not yet have a consulate. The women told Rodríguez Benson that they had been forced out of mainland China. The consul eventually helped them relocate to the New Territories, Hong Kong, and found them employment opportunities before securing their repatriation to Mexico. Rodríguez Benson and other consuls also helped other Mexicans in the colonies during this time.[50]

After spending most of their lives in China, some Chinese Mexican sons resettled in Mexico during the 1970s and 1980s. Chinese and Mexican father-son bonds played a key role in their transpacific experiences. About twenty years after Cristóbal Chua Wong's parents separated in Hermosillo and he and his mother relocated to Hong Kong, the father asked the mother to bring him his eldest son. Chua Wong's father had remarried and had other children in Hermosillo but became lonely after his second marriage ended in divorce. Cristóbal had spent some of his childhood in mainland China and most of his life in Hong Kong and has never fully understood why his mother agreed to leave Hong Kong for Hermosillo, since she left a good office job only to end up working in a kitchen in Mexico; he speculates that she felt the pressure to be a "good woman"— a faithful and loyal wife, in accordance with prevailing notions in both China and Mexico. In 1970, she and her son, by now in his early twenties, returned to Hermosillo. Father and son at first were like strangers and had trouble relating to one another, but their relationship slowly improved. Recalling the process reminded Chua Wong of an old Chinese adage: Knowing another person too well will doom a relationship; if spouses learn too much about each other, marriages will break apart. Chua Wong and his mother, who eventually naturalized as a Mexican citizen, stayed in Hermosillo even after his father's death in 1993. Chua Wong married a Mexican woman, started a family, and established a well-known Chinese restaurant, Chao's Garden.[51]

Felipe Wong Enríquez returned to Mexico as an adult during the 1980s. His mother and sisters had repatriated after living in Guangdong Province for about a year in the 1930s. Regretful at having left her son with his father in China, Ester Enríquez Andrade and her other children worked for decades for his repatriation but lacked the necessary documentation. Felipe's oldest sister, Antonia Wong Enríquez de López, kept in touch with their father, Felipe Wong Ley, who asked for help in returning to Mexico. By the time she and her family secured her brother's entry, however, her father was too elderly to travel, so the family did not appeal on his behalf. Enríquez Andrade was overjoyed to be reunited with her son after half a century. Although he had come of age in China, Felipe Wong Enríquez integrated into Sonoran society and has since remained in Hermosillo with his Chinese wife and their children. When he first arrived, he worked at Fernando Ma's restaurant, Jo Wah; he later opened his own establishment, Hong Kong.[52]

Like the Chinese Mexicans who repatriated under Cárdenas, those who returned to Mexico in 1960 encountered trouble readjusting to a shifting Mexican society and battled fellow citizens' perceptions of their mixed-race families as foreign. To survive in their new contexts, Chinese Mexicans invoked the strong bonds they had forged during their years abroad with compatriots who were similarly on the fringes of the nation-state.

The expulsion and stages of repatriation guaranteed that Chinese Mexicans would forge strong transpacific ties and cosmopolitan identities. They maintained bonds with friends and relatives who were unable to return to Mexico or chose to live in China, Macau, or Hong Kong. Some carried on the Chinese tradition of the transpacific household after they repatriated. They maintained connections with, sent money to, and tried to bring to Mexico the families they had established in China.

While abroad, Chinese Mexicans had conceived of themselves as Mexicans, as belonging in Mexico. Their nationalism was strategic, fueled by difficult experiences in a Chinese society in flux during war and revolution, and their rhetoric was driven by Cold War ideology and the fear of communism in the West. But their longing for Mexico was also genuine, if romantic and nostalgic. They truly wanted to return. They believed that their lives would be better in the Mexican homeland. Their identification with Mexico was fervent, even though authorities had excluded their families decades earlier and they faced barriers not only as they worked to repatriate but also once they returned. In spite of a history of refusal and contestation, Chinese Mexicans embraced the Mexican homeland. They became Mexican in China. In so doing, they broadened and complicated what it means to be Mexican.

Conclusion

I first traveled to Sonora, where my mother was born and our extended family still resides, when I was six months old. Throughout my childhood, my mother and grandparents took my siblings and me to visit multiple times each year—for weddings, funerals, summer vacation, Semana Santa (Easter Week), and other occasions. Many times we stopped at Jo Wah, Fernando Ma's Chinese restaurant in Hermosillo, the halfway point between Tucson and our destinations of Ciudad Obregón and Navojoa. I remember my grandfather enjoying visits with friends at the restaurant. We also ate at other Chinese restaurants and shopped at Chinese businesses in Obregón and Navojoa. It was always clear to me that the Chinese and Chinese Mexicans were a part of Sonora. They owned numerous restaurants and other businesses and had a general presence in the towns where my relatives lived. I took for granted that they were integral to Sonoran society and never thought much of it.

In graduate school, I came across scholarly literature by Evelyn Hu-DeHart and others on the importance of the Chinese in turn-of-the-twentieth-century Sonora, the rise of campaigns against them during the Mexican Revolution, and their eventual ousting in the 1930s. My lack of knowledge of the anti-Chinese movement in Sonora's past led me to question how the Chinese had become part of the contemporary state.

In 2003 and 2004, I traveled regularly to Sonora as I collected material for my dissertation. The first oral history I did for this project was with Fernando Ma at Jo Wah, and I subsequently talked to many other people. Although some of those with whom I conversed knew different pieces of the history of Chinese Mexicans, few seemed to have a broader sense of their journeys. Nevertheless, particular aspects have survived in the memory of certain communities. In Navojoa, for instance, my relatives relayed their knowledge of persistent speculation about certain wealthy people who probably gained their status with assets local authorities confiscated from the Chinese in the early 1930s. Marta Elia Lau de Salazar broached the same topic in an interview with her niece, Berenice Barreras Ayala, for this project. Local chroniclers in Navojoa, Guaymas, and other towns knew about the importance of Chinese before their mass eviction, as did local archivists and researchers.

But the larger story of Chinese integration in Sonora, the eventual expulsions, the refugees' passage through the United States, their community and identity formation abroad, and ultimately their repatriation is still not widely known. It has permeated neither the education system nor the popular culture. My younger cousins had never heard of the expulsion—nor had I before I went to graduate school. I was drawn to this history partially because I had been unaware of it, even though I grew up traveling across the Arizona-Sonora border with my family and listening to my grandparents' and other older relatives' stories about the past. Once I began asking questions, the story started to unfold.

Toward a Diasporic Mexican History

I first learned of Alfonso Wong Campoy at the Archivo General de la Nación in Mexico City in April 2004, when I found the letter his mother wrote to Adolfo López Mateos just after they repatriated in late 1960. Thanks to my extended family, I soon discovered that he still lived in Navojoa and had a stand at the local *mercado* (central market). After contacting him by phone, I traveled to Navojoa to interview him; one of my uncles suggested that I bring along a copy of Dolores Campoy Wong's letter. During that visit, I first began thinking about what it meant to become Mexican abroad. A few years later, when I saw the Wong Campoy family on an Immigration and Naturalization Service list of "Chinese refugees from Mexico," the story took shape. I have since also met María del Carmen Irma Wong Campoy Maher Conceição and her family, who reside in San Francisco, and been in communication with Antonio René Wong Campoy's family in Florida.

Anti-Chinese hatred in Mexico uprooted the Wong Campoys and other Chinese Mexican families and profoundly disrupted their lives. It caused tremendous suffering. It split some families apart and brought others great tragedy. Alfonso Wong Fang's life was cut short by the heart condition that intensified after he eluded vicious *antichinistas*. In addition to the loss of their husband and father, the Wong Campoys also experienced economic and social turmoil as a consequence of war and revolution in China.

Yet they and other Chinese Mexicans survived in the face of tremendous challenges. Living abroad and conceptualizing and longing for the homeland led to the development of a new national Mexican identity. Mexican mothers of mixed-race children and Chinese Mexican families more generally fought for a place in the nation and conceived of themselves as Mexican. By claiming Mexico, they have broadened and nuanced the definition of Mexicanness. They compel us to rethink Mexican *mestizaje* and the ways Chinese and hybrid Chinese Mexicans have been part of the nation. Chinese men contributed significantly to Mexico's economic growth and modernization. By marrying and forming families and participating in culinary and linguistic fusion, Chinese men and their families have also been a crucial part of the nation's complex cultural fabric.

Despite incredible obstacles, Chinese Mexicans persistently held onto Mexican identities that were both strategic and genuine. Their determination has made this a story of contested national belonging. The history of Chinese Mexicans tells us about the tactics diasporic peoples have employed to claim a place for themselves where they did not automatically fit in. Their experiences of expulsion and the accompanying sense of displacement, loss, and pain as well as the struggle to survive abroad and restore a space for their racially and culturally mixed families in the Mexican nation resonate with a broader story about movement, identity, and humanity.

But not all Chinese Mexicans became Mexican. For diverse reasons, some of these people remained in mainland China, Macau, or Hong Kong. Others eventually became part of Portuguese, American, and other societies. The Wong Campoy siblings exemplify all of these paths. Indeed, the flexibility of identity reverberates in this history. The fact that some Chinese Mexicans remained in China or ultimately settled elsewhere and developed connections to new places is part of a broader and little-known diasporic Mexican history. Chinese men started these families in the northern Mexican borderlands, and Chinese Mexicans took divergent paths after the anti-Chinese movement made it impossible to remain openly in Mexico.

Tracking Transpacific Journeys

In 2007, I traveled to Macau, Hong Kong, and Guangzhou in Guangdong Province to retrace the footsteps of Chinese Mexican families. I reflected on their stories as I walked some of their paths in historic Macau, a place that had been vital in their journey to becoming Mexican. Among other Catholic institutions in the former colony, I visited the Seminario San José, where Roberto M. Fu worked as a porter. I spent time at the Santo Agostinho Casa Ricci Parish, where Father Luis Ruiz worked to help Chinese Mexicans return to Mexico. In Kowloon, Hong Kong, I visited Santa Teresa, the church where members of the Asociación Hispano-Americana de Nuestra Señora de Guadalupe met. I thought about the group's importance to Chinese Mexicans and contemplated their diasporic longing for Mexico as I stood in front of the shrine to the Virgen de Guadalupe. This and other sites had helped bring together Chinese Mexican families expelled by Mexico as well as other Chinese Latin Americans in Portuguese Macau and British Hong Kong. Chinese, Latin, Iberian, and Catholic traditions as well as the cosmopolitan flavor of Macau and Hong Kong had not only helped Chinese Mexicans find spaces as culturally and racially mixed people but also fostered their diasporic Mexican national identity formation.

In Hong Kong, I also visited the Mexican consulate, to which I am indebted for putting me in touch with Nosotras: Asociación de Mujeres de Habla Hispana de Hong Kong (Us: Association of Spanish-Speaking Women of Hong Kong). These women, in turn, gave me a number of contacts—Mexican priests and sisters as well as Chinese Mexicans, Chinese Peruvians, and Latin Americans in Hong Kong and Macau. I spoke far more Spanish than I had ever imagined I would during the trip, and the same has been true for subsequent visits.

Latin American Chinese and Latin Americans in present-day Hong Kong and Macau have created and sustained a vibrant, intricate community. I have been struck by their connections, and I deeply appreciate the warm welcome I have received from so many people. While Chinese, Latin American, Iberian, and Catholic traditions have unified people, so has a broader hybrid sensibility. Every time I travel to the former colonies, I hear echoes of the community that Chinese Mexicans forged in southeastern China during the last century.

Remembering Chinese Mexicans and Claiming a Place in Mexico

As global politics shifted after World War II, Chinese once again began to migrate in greater numbers to diverse areas of Mexico.[1] Today border towns such as Mexicali have large, vibrant, and well-known Chinese enclaves. In contrast, present-day Sonora still has too few Chinese to have separate ethnic enclaves. Rather, they have blended into local society while maintaining Chinese and Chinese Mexican identities.

Sonora and Mexico have begun to pay homage to the importance of Chinese and the hybrid families they formed both in history and contemporary society. Grade-school textbooks in Sonora, for example, have begun to include discussions of the presence of Chinese in the late nineteenth and early twentieth centuries and the events that led to their expulsion.[2] As a sign of the trend toward broader recognition, Mexican writers at the Fundación Para las Letras Mexicanas named borderlands writer and scholar Selfa Chew's poem "Chio Sam," which honors her Chinese grandfather and Chinese Mexican ancestry, as one of the hundred best poems in Mexico in 2005.[3] While there have been other signs that Sonora and Mexico are beginning to recognize Chinese contributions, the state and nation have further to go.

I hope that the story of Chinese Mexicans will one day become a well-known part of Mexico's regional and national cultural fabric. The ideology and discourse of *mestizaje* have overlooked the contributions of the Chinese and Chinese Mexicans. The Mexican Revolution of 1910 brought about a renunciation of foreigners and a notion of the Mexican *mestizo* who grew out of Spanish and indigenous cultural and ethnic intermingling. These ideas have elided the many others who helped forge the Mexican nation. Hybrid and cosmopolitan Chinese Mexican families, their insistence that they were Mexican and belonged in the nation, and their long struggles to negotiate their return from abroad have a lot to teach us about how people on the periphery help define nations and national identities. As Chinese Mexicans navigated their diasporic realities, the difficulties they encountered in mainland China, and their consequent attraction to the foreign colonies, they became cosmopolitan by necessity. But their transnational paths did not preclude them from arguing that they were part of Mexico. Their complex identities and journeys have enriched the Mexican nation.

Chinese Mexicans' place in Mexico is an intervention in the nation's dominant exclusionary discourse. Their history urges us to give a more nuanced account of the Mexican past that widens rather than delimits what it means to be Mexican. A more profound cultural memory of Chinese Mexican journeys not only would complicate notions of Mexican history and *mestizaje* beyond the sole influence of Spanish and indigenous traditions but also would offer lessons about the damage that hatred and exclusion inflict on individuals and families as well as on communities and nations. The story of Chinese Mexicans is most deeply a tale of perseverance in the face of odds and of the persistent drive to belong.

Notes

ABBREVIATIONS

AGES   Archivo General del Estado de Sonora, Hermosillo
AGN   Archivo General de la Nación, Mexico City
AGPJES   Archivo General del Poder Judicial del Estado de Sonora, Hermosillo,
            Sonora
ALMC   Adolfo López Mateos Collection, Archivo General de la Nación,
            Mexico City
File 55771 File 55771, Immigration and Naturalization Service Files, Record Group
            85, National Archives and Records Administration, Washington, D.C.
LCDRC   Lázaro Cárdenas del Río Collection, Archivo General de la Nación,
            Mexico City
PJMA   Papers of José María Arana, Special Collections, University of Arizona
            Library, Tucson
SREAC   Secretaría de Relaciones Exteriores, Archivo de Concentraciones,
            Mexico City
SREAHGE   Secretaría de Relaciones Exteriores, Archivo Histórico Genaro Estrada,
            Mexico City

INTRODUCTION

1. Wong Campoy, interview. All translations from Spanish into English are by the author unless otherwise indicated; the original recordings or copies of the archival documents are available from the author.

2. Knight, "Racism, Revolution, and *Indigenismo*," 71, 86, 102; see also Rénique, "Race, Region, and Nation"; Vasconcelos, *Raza cósmica*; Gamio, *Forjando patria*.

3. Espinoza, *Ejemplo de Sonora*.

4. Regional identification outweighed national affinity, and there were "many Mexicos" in this period. See, for example, Benjamin and McNellie, *Other Mexicos*; Alonso, *Thread of Blood*. On the regional character of Sonora, see Salas, *In the Shadow of the Eagles*. See also Anderson, *Imagined Communities*. Local and regional identities were also stronger than the concept of the nation in China during this time; see Hsu, *Dreaming of Gold*; Chan, *Asian Americans*.

5. On the relationship between national sovereignty and border control and migration laws, see McKeown, *Melancholy Order*; on the Spanish Civil War, see Schuler, *Mexico between Hitler and Roosevelt*.

6. Here I use Lok C. D. Siu's concept of "diasporic citizenship." See Siu, *Memories of a Future Home*; see also Louie, *Chineseness across Borders*; McKeown, "Ritualization of Regulation"; Wang, *China and the Chinese Overseas*; Wang, *Community and Nation*; Gilroy, *Black Atlantic*; Clifford, *Routes*; Lesser, *Searching for Home*; Lesser, *Discontented Diaspora*; Safran, "Diasporas in Modern Societies"; Clifford, "Diasporas."

7. Hsu, *Dreaming of Gold*; see also Hsu, "Unwrapping Orientalist Constraints," 230–53, for a discussion of the ways Chinese drew on homosocial traditions in China during the "bachelor era" of Chinese American history.

8. On the transnational families of Chinese in Mexico, see Robert Chao Romero, *Chinese in Mexico*. On Peru, see Lausent-Herrera, "Mujeres olvidadas." On the United States, see Hsu, *Dreaming of Gold*; Hsu, "Unwrapping Orientalist Constraints," 241–43, 249.

9. Pan, *Encyclopedia*, 77–78; Hsu, *Dreaming of Gold*; Wang, *China and the Chinese Overseas*; Wang, *Community and Nation*; Wang "Sojourning," 1–14; Kuhn, *Chinese among Others*; McKeown, *Chinese Migrant Networks*; Hein, "State Incorporation of Migrants"; see also Bonacich, "Theory."

10. Chan, *Asian Americans*, 5–8; Hsu, *Dreaming of Gold*, 1–5; Pan, *Encyclopedia*, 27–30, 35–37; see also Mei, "Economic Origins." Until 1960, more than half of all Chinese in the United States came from Taishan County. See Hsu, *Dreaming of Gold*, 3, Mei, "Economic Origins," 465.

11. See, for example, Chan, "People of Exceptional Character"; Hill, *Tarnished Gold*; Rohe, "After the Gold Rush"; Ling, *Surviving on the Gold Mountain*; Ettinger, *Imaginary Lines*; see also Owens, *Riches for All*.

12. Saxton, *Indispensable Enemy*; Saxton, *Rise and Fall*.

13. Wunder, "Law and the Chinese," 139.

14. Chan, "Exclusion of Chinese Women"; Salyer, *Laws Harsh as Tigers*; Peffer, *If They Don't Bring*; Chan, *Asian Americans*; Yung, *Unbound Feet*; Luibhéid, *Entry Denied*.

15. See Lee, *At America's Gates*; see also Ngai, *Impossible Subjects*; Robert Chao Romero, *Chinese in Mexico*; Chan, *Entry Denied*; Salyer, *Laws Harsh as Tigers*; Luibhéid, *Entry Denied*; McClain, *In Search of Equality*.

16. Lee, "Orientalisms"; Siu, *Memories of a Future Home*; Rustomji-Kerns, Srikanth, and Strobel, *Encounters*.

17. Scholars have warned against privileging the United States in the history of migration in the Americas. Although we should be mindful of these concerns, as Lee has argued, "we cannot discount the overwhelming role that the United States did play—and continues to play—in the hemisphere, and indeed the world" ("Orientalisms," 250).

18. Lee, *At America's Gates*, 151.

19. Hu-DeHart, "Racism"; Hu-DeHart, "Latin America"; Lee, *At America's Gates*, 157–58; Dennis, "Anti-Chinese Campaigns," 66; see also Mishima, *Destino México*; Kisines, "Migración y legislación."

20. Hu-DeHart, "Racism," 2–4, 13; Lee, *At America's Gates*, 157–58; Dennis, "Anti-Chinese Campaigns," 66; Knight, "Racism, Revolution, and *Indigenismo*," 78–79, 96–97; see also Mishima, *Destino México*; Hu-DeHart, "Latin America"; Kisines, "Migración y legislación."

21. See Ngai, *Impossible Subjects*; Benton-Cohen, *Borderline Americans*; Balderrama

and Rodríguez, *Decade of Betrayal*; Monroy, *Rebirth*; David Gutiérrez, *Walls and Mirrors*; De Genova, *Working the Boundaries*.

22. Robert Chao Romero, *Chinese in Mexico*.

23. Lee, "Orientalisms"; Lara, *Chinos en Sonora*, 51–60; Balderrama and Rodríguez, *Decade of Betrayal*, 202; see also Carreras de Velasco, *Mexicanos*.

24. At least five hundred Chinese Mexican families arrived in China either via the United States or directly from Mexico during the expulsion period. Since they included numerous children, these families numbered at least two thousand people. These are conservative figures based on INS files and Mexican consular and government records. The numbers of Chinese Mexican families and individuals were probably higher. Archival sources suggest that between four hundred and six hundred Mexican women arrived in China with Chinese men. The records consistently point to the numerous children in these families. For example, those included in INS lists had an average of between three and four children per family. Mauricio Fresco, a businessman and honorary Mexican vice consul in Shanghai, reported that Dollar Line records showed that at least six hundred Mexican women and innumerable children arrived in China on the steamship company's ships between 1931 and 1933 alone. The Mexican government later repatriated about four hundred Mexican women and a high but unspecified number of their children in 1937–38. Given the various figures, I have estimated that five hundred families including a minimum of two thousand people arrived in China. See File 55771; File IV-341-13, SREAHGE; Folder 546/3, Box 899, LCDRC; Folder 546.2/1, Box 714, ALMC; File OM-149-5, 1960, SREAC; Pardinas, *Relaciones diplomáticas*, 428–30, 461–65, 466–68, 471, 474, 475–76, 478–79.

CHAPTER 1

1. See, for example, Pan, *Encyclopedia*; Wang, *China and the Chinese Overseas*; Kuhn, *Chinese among Others*; McKeown, *Chinese Migrant Networks*.

2. Wong Campoy, interview.

3. For an overview on Chinese in Latin America, see Hu-DeHart, "Latin America"; Hu-DeHart, "Comunidad china"; Hu-DeHart, "Coolies, Shopkeepers, Pioneers"; Siu, *Memories of a Future Home*; Lausent-Herrera, "Mujeres olvidadas."

4. Wong Campoy, interview; Conceição, interview.

5. See, for example, Radding, *Wandering Peoples*; Ramón E. Ruiz, *People of Sonora*; Salas, *In the Shadow of the Eagles*; Heyman, *Life and Labor*.

6. On the border region and "contact zones," see, for example, Saldívar, *Border Matters*.

7. Salas, *In the Shadow of the Eagles*, 1–16, 17, 22–24, 26, 36, 60–64, 87, 101–2, 110.

8. Robert Chao Romero, *Chinese in Mexico*.

9. See Chan, "Exclusion of Chinese Women"; Peffer, *If They Don't Bring*; McKeown, "Transnational Chinese Families"; Ling, *Surviving on the Gold Mountain*; Ling, "Family and Marriage."

10. When Chinese first migrated to Sonora during the last quarter of the nineteenth century, they were concentrated in Guaymas, a port of entry, and the capital, Hermosillo. They later moved to other areas. See Hu-DeHart, "Coolies, Shopkeepers,

Pioneers," 98–99; see also Hu-DeHart, "Comunidad china"; Hu-DeHart, "Immigrants"; Knight, "Racism, Revolution, and *Indigenismo*," 96–97; Delgado, "In the Age of Exclusion"; Delgado, "At Exclusion's Southern Gate."

11. Robert Chao Romero, *Chinese in Mexico*, 98–129, 141; Salas, *In the Shadow of the Eagles*, 188, 194, 223–29; Hu-DeHart, "Coolies, Shopkeepers, Pioneers"; Hu-DeHart, "Comunidad china"; Hu-DeHart, "Immigrants."

12. Hu-DeHart, "Coolies, Shopkeepers, Pioneers," 98–99; Hu-DeHart, "Comunidad china"; Hu-DeHart, "Immigrants"; Delgado, "In the Age of Exclusion"; Delgado, "At Exclusion's Southern Gate."

13. See Chan, *Asian Americans*; Hsu, *Dreaming of Gold*.

14. Salas, *In the Shadow of the Eagles*, 224–29.

15. Ibid.

16. Pan, *Encyclopedia*, 257; Robert Chao Romero, *Chinese in Mexico*.

17. Hu-DeHart, "Latin America"; Hu-DeHart, "Comunidad china."

18. For example, María de los Angeles Leyva Cervón believes that frugality and economic discipline have set the Chinese apart from Mexicans; saving money for the future is a priority for the Chinese. Her grandfather possessed these qualities, which in time allowed him to regain economic security even though Sonoran officials confiscated his assets during the expulsion period (Leyva Cervón, interview).

19. Lau de Salazar, interview.

20. Juzgado de Guaymas, Ramo Penal, 1921, Vol. 2008, AGPJES.

21. Chinese were certainly not the only victims. A random sampling of court cases in Sonora in the early twentieth century shows that all groups were the victims of assaults, robberies, and other crimes. As the anti-Chinese movement gained power in the 1920s, attacks on Chinese would increase, and they would be targeted during the expulsion period.

22. On gender and cultural norms and the legacy of Spanish colonialism in northern Mexico, see, for example, Alonso, *Thread of Blood*; Martin, *Governance and Society*.

23. Juzgado de Caborca, Ramo Penal, 1921, Vol. 2467, AGPJES.

24. Ibid., 1927, Vol. 517.

25. Juzgado de Alamos, Ramo Penal, 1925–26, Vol. 2192, AGPJES.

26. Cano Ávila, interview.

27. Verdugo Escoboza, interview.

28. María Luisa Salazar Corral Navarro, interview.

29. Chon, interview.

30. Ibid.; Lau de Salazar, interview; see also Leo Sandoval, *Casa de Abelardo*, 25.

31. Juzgado de Hermosillo, Ramo Penal, 1910, Vol. 1091, AGPJES; *El Observador*, 1, 15 January 1927.

32. Juzgado de Hermosillo, Ramo Penal, 1910, Vol. 1091, AGPJES.

33. Juzgado de Nogales, Ramo Penal, 1919, Vol. 2333, AGPJES.

34. Cisneros, *Sucedió en Sonora*, 154–55.

35. Lau de Salazar, interview.

36. See Juzgado de Hermosillo, Ramo Penal, 1910, Vol. 1091, Juzgado de Hermosillo, Ramo Penal, 1920, Vol. 1141, Juzgado de Nogales, Ramo Penal, 1926, Vol. 2372, all in AGPJES.

37. See Rénique, "Race, Region, and Nation," 219–26; Rénique, "Anti-Chinese Racism," 95, 97, 102; Robert Chao Romero, *Chinese in Mexico*; Robert Chao Romero, "'Destierro de los Chinos'"; Schiavone Camacho, "Traversing Boundaries."

38. Juzgado de Magdalena, Ramo Penal, 1924, Vol. 3027, AGPJES.

39. Chan Valenzuela, interview.

40. Supremo Tribunal de Justicia, Ramo Penal, Hermosillo, Sonora, 1932, unnumbered vol., AGPJES.

41. See, for example, Lavrin, *Sexuality and Marriage*; see also Boyer, *Lives of the Bigamists*.

42. Juzgado de Cumpas, Ramo Penal, 1924, Vol. 2723, AGPJES.

43. Ibid. The original quotation reads, "En idilio amoroso aparecen perfectactamente identificados."

44. For a discussion of gender and the modernization of northern Mexico, see Alonso, *Thread of Blood*. On the modernization of Sonora, see Salas, *In the Shadow of the Eagles*.

45. Enríquez de López, interview.

46. Juzgado de Magdalena, Ramo Penal, 1929, Vol. 3036, AGPJES.

47. Ibid.

48. Bliss, *Compromised Positions*, 13, 16; Bay and Bustos, *Historia panorámica*, 382–83, 400.

49. Supremo Tribunal de Justicia, 1931, Vol. 5, AGPJES.

50. Ibid.

51. Lau de Salazar, interview.

52. Ma, interview.

53. Enríquez de López, interview; Chua Wong, interview.

54. Tapia Martens, interview.

55. Ibid.

CHAPTER 2

1. PJMA, 1917 Folder.

2. The anti-Chinese newspaper *El Tráfico* was published in Guaymas between 1889 and 1896 and in Nogales between 1896 and 1905. See Rénique, "Race, Region, and Nation," 232 n. 12.

3. Rénique, "Race, Region, and Nation"; Rénique, "Anti-Chinese Racism"; Hu-DeHart, "Racism"; Robert Chao Romero, *Chinese in Mexico*; Robert Chao Romero, "'Destierro de los Chinos.'"

4. Bliss, *Compromised Positions*, 12; Heyman, *Life and Labor*, 8; Lee, *At America's Gates*, 152, 157–61, 187; see also Rénique, "Anti-Chinese Racism"; Knight, "Racism, Revolution, and *Indigenismo*."

5. Robert Chao Romero, *Chinese in Mexico*, 54.

6. Pan, *Encyclopedia*, 256–58.

7. The original name of the group was Junta Comercial y de Hombres de Negocios de Magdalena. See Rénique, "Región, raza, y nación."

8. Rénique, "Race, Region, and Nation," 219–20.

9. On anti-Chinese campaigns in California, see Saxton, *Indispensable Enemy*; Saxton, *Rise and Fall*.

10. Rénique, "Race, Region, and Nation," 221 n. 36, 233–34.

11. PJMA, 1904–16, 1917, 1918, 1919, and Miscellaneous Material Folders; Rénique, "Race, Region, and Nation"; Rénique, "Anti-Chinese Racism"; Hu-Dehart, "Racism"; Cumberland, "Sonora Chinese"; Jacques, "Anti-Chinese Campaign"; Jacques, "Have Quick"; Dennis, "Anti-Chinese Campaigns"; Lara, "Xenofobia." Llano has argued that the violence against Chinese during the Mexican Revolution alone far outweighed anti-Chinese brutality in the United States over the entire period of intolerance despite the vastly greater number of Chinese in the United States. See Llano, *Entre el río Perla*; see also González Navarro, "Xenofobia y xenofilia"; Knight, "Racism, Revolution, and *Indigenismo*."

12. Rénique, "Race, Region, and Nation," 219–26; Rénique, "Anti-Chinese Racism," 95, 97, 102.

13. Knight, "Racism, Revolution, and *Indigenismo*," 77–83; see also Gamio, *Forjando patria*; Vasconcelos, *Raza cósmica*. Knight shows that *indigenismo* was simply a new formulation of the "Indian problem" that became significant because it arose during the violent phase of the Mexican Revolution (approximately 1910–20); see Knight, "Racism, Revolution, and *Indigenismo*," 77–78, 80, 84–85.

14. Knight, "Racism, Revolution, and *Indigenismo*"; Gamio, *Forjando patria*.

15. Vasconcelos, *Raza cósmica*, 12–15, 76–77, 274, 279; Knight, "Racism, Revolution, and *Indigenismo*," 71, 84–85, 86, 97, 102; see also Rénique, "Anti-Chinese Racism"; Rénique, "Race, Region, and Nation"; Camín, *Frontera nómada*; Gamio, *Forjando patria*; Vasconcelos and Gamio, *Aspects*; see also Rivera, *Fin de la raza cósmica*.

16. Rénique, "Anti-Chinese Racism," 102–4, 114; Rénique, "Race, Region, and Nation," 228–29.

17. Rénique, "Race, Region, and Nation."

18. Calvert, "Institutionalisation," 512: "Aquí vive el presidente. El que manda vive en frente."

19. Rénique, "Anti-Chinese Racism," 102–4, 118; see also Rénique, "Race, Region, and Nation"; Bay and Bustos, *Historia panorámica*.

20. Lee, "Orientalisms," 248.

21. Rénique, "Race, Region, and Nation," 222, 227–28.

22. Hu-Dehart, "Comunidad china"; Hu-DeHart, "Latin America."

23. Vol. 232, Box 114, Vol. 252, Box 124, both in AGES.

24. PJMA, 1919 Folder.

25. Juzgado de Caborca, Ramo Penal, 1921, Vol. 2467, AGPJES. The date of the source, 1921, pertains to a court case that was heard in that year in Caborca, Sonora. At a later date, the transcript of the case was bound in the recycled poster, which evidently was at hand and was used without regard for its message. See also Izquierdo, *Movimiento antichino*, 123.

26. Rénique, "Race, Region, and Nation," 220–21; see also Robert Chao Romero, *Chinese in Mexico*; Robert Chao Romero, "'Destierro de los Chinos.'" Analogous to Chinese men in Sonora vis-à-vis Mexican women, Mexican and black men have been portrayed as threatening to white women. Paul S. Taylor, for example, has shown that growers in

Texas justified segregated schooling to keep Mexican boys away from white girls during the 1920s and early 1930s. See Taylor, *Mexican Labor*; see also Taylor, *American-Mexican Frontier*; Davis, *Women, Race, and Class*; Jordan, *White over Black*.

27. PJMA, Miscellaneous Material Folder.

28. Hu-DeHart, "Racism," 18; Rénique, "Anti-Chinese Racism," 118. See also Espinoza, *Problema chino*; Espinoza, *Ejemplo de Sonora*.

29. Case "Problema Chino," 1927, Vol. 1166, Box 362, AGES. Drawing similar connections among prostitution, government regulation, and exploitation of Mexican women by foreign men, several Mexican prostitutes in Mexico City wrote to President Plutarco Elías Calles in 1927. The women, who referred to themselves as the "daughters of disgrace," told the president that the 1926 Reglamento that regulated prostitution did nothing to benefit Mexicans or Mexico. Calling themselves "nationalists" who were concerned for the good of the nation, they argued that, as a result of the Reglamento, foreign men sexually exploited Mexican women in illegal cabarets. See Bliss, *Compromised Positions*, 2.

30. PJMA, 1904–16 Folder.

31. Case "Problema Chino," 1927, Vol. 1166, Box 362, AGES.

32. Ibid. On Echeverría's Baja California organization, see Rénique, "Anti-Chinese Racism," 124.

33. For a discussion of gendered insults in eighteenth-century Chihuahua, see Martin, *Governance and Society*, 156–58. See also Martin, "Popular Speech and Social Order," 311, 315, 317, 319. See also Ramón Gutiérrez, *When Jesus Came*; Alonso, *Thread of Blood*.

34. Juzgado de Nogales, Ramo Penal, 1926, Vol. 2372, AGPJES. "Hijas de la chingada" is translated literally, as well as crudely, in the text. For a case involving the Manuel Sam Lee Produce Company, see Juzgado de Nogales, Ramo Penal, 1928, Vol. 2381, AGPJES.

35. Juzgado de Magdalena, Ramo Penal, 1927, Vol. 3033, AGPJES.

36. Juzgado de Hermosillo, Ramo Penal, 1929, Vol. 1191, AGPJES.

37. Juzgado de Nogales, Ramo Penal, 1927, Vol. 2379, AGPJES.

38. PJMA, 1917 Folder. See also Espinoza, *Problema chino*; Espinoza, *Ejemplo de Sonora*. Some letters complained that local officials allowed Chinese to smoke opium. The opium poppy, or *amapola* in Spanish, grew very well in the hot and humid areas of southwestern Sonora, including Navojoa. Local historical memory holds that the beautiful white *amapola* blooms could be seen all over Navojoa and nearby communities during the early twentieth century. An old popular song, "Amapola," describes the loveliness of the flowers. After the expulsion of Chinese, Mexicans kept growing *amapola*, and it has become part of the local memory of Chinese (personal communication with Jorge Sosa Salazar and Delfino Robles and family; see also Hernández Salomón, interview).

39. PJMA, 1917 Folder.

40. Robert Chao Romero, *Chinese in Mexico*, 170–71.

41. Juzgado de Magdalena, Ramo Penal, 1917, Vol. 3015, AGPJES.

42. Ibid. López Alvarado had originally accused Alejandro Palomino but later told the court that he had been mistaken; in fact, his brother, Marcos Palomino, had insulted him. López Alvarado continued to defend Chinese during the 1920s and early

1930s. See Espinoza, *Problema chino*; Espinoza, *Ejemplo de Sonora*. López Alvarado also defended Chinese in numerous federal *amparo* (protection) cases against local and state authorities or the state itself. For example, in 1931, López Alvarado represented Félix Cinco y Socios (associates) of Navojoa in a lawsuit against the local *presidente municipal* and the state congress and governor of Sonora for violating their constitutional rights. See Appeal No. 49. Sonora Collection, Amparo Series, PN Subseries, Section 5, J.D., A, 1931, Box/File 2, Casa de la Cultura Jurídica, Suprema Corte de Justicia de la Nación, Hermosillo, Sonora.

43. PJMA, 1918 and Miscellaneous Material Folders; Juzgado de Nogales, Ramo Penal, 1928, Vol. 2381, AGPJES. Bonfiglio had allegedly transported a railcar loaded with tomatoes from Lee's store without paying the import fee or the $1,665 he owed Lee. Lee claimed that the two men had negotiated this price based on the cost of tomatoes in Arizona. The railcar with stolen goods was apparently transported to a buyer in Boston. As part of this case, Lee accused two other men of fraud. Evidently, he never gained redress for his losses. The volume of sales suggests that Lee ran a large, profitable, business and participated in cross-border sales.

44. See Rénique, "Race, Region, and Nation," 220–21; Rénique, "Anti-Chinese Racism," 100.

45. Juzgado de Magdalena, Ramo Penal, 1917, Vol. 3015, AGPJES. Included in the court records of this case is a communication from the state government about the disorder anti-Chinese demonstrations had caused, even though the activists had the right to demonstrate in public. During these early years, the anti-Chinese movement struggled to gain local and state recognition, though, as Rénique has shown, state and national sanction were ultimately forthcoming ("Anti-Chinese Racism"). Regarding the attacks on Chinese in nearby towns, in a separate 1917 case, the court in Magdalena investigated an assault against several Chinese living in a house in San Lorenzo. Manuel Wong, Ramón Chian, Wong Fock, and Wong Qui testified that after hearing dogs bark around midnight, Wong got up to investigate. The attackers then beat and robbed him. The Chinese men were respectively ages forty-five, thirty, thirty-nine, and fifty. Wong, neither the oldest nor the youngest, but nonetheless the head of the group, was the only one attacked. The other men declared in court that they were afraid and remained in their beds when they heard the commotion. Chinese men in Sonora sometimes maintained these kinds of living arrangements. On this phenomenon in nineteenth- and twentieth-century San Francisco, see Shah, *Contagious Divides*, 13, 77–104. Shah demonstrates how anti-Chinese activists there sexualized and racialized Chinese men and accused them of disrupting the normative heterosexual white family through their living patterns. Although some activists in Sonora worried that Chinese inverted gender roles by performing women's domestic roles, the main focus of the anti-Chinese movement in Sonora was on Chinese-Mexican unions and other ties rather than on Chinese men who lived together.

46. Supremo Tribunal de Justicia, Ramo Penal, Hermosillo, Sonora, 1932, unnumbered vol., AGPJES.

47. Ibid. On *amparo* cases, see Pamela del Carmen Corella Romero, "Expulsión." On the Mexican Supreme Court ruling on Law 31, see Rénique, "Anti-Chinese Racism," 113;

on federal disapproval of Laws 27 and 31, see Vol. 232, Box 114, Vol. 25, Box 124, both in AGES. On the Mexican Constitution of 1917, see, for example, Meyer, Sherman, and Deeds, *Course of Mexican History*, 523; Reich, "Recent Research"; see also *Constitution*.

48. *El Intruso*, 24 June 1927.

49. "Ruda Campaña en contra de las Chineras," *El Intruso*, 25 June 1931.

50. Juzgado de Cananea, Ramo Penal, 1929, Vol. 2834, AGPJES.

51. Rénique, "Anti-Chinese Racism," 112–13.

CHAPTER 3

1. Folder 104-CH-1, Box 28, Obregón-Calles Collection, AGN. The AGN organizes collections by presidential administrations; card catalogs describe the contents of folders in each collection.

2. Robert Chao Romero, *Chinese in Mexico*, 56–57.

3. Case "Problema Chino," 1927, Vol. 1166, Box 362, AGES; see also Izquierdo, *Movimiento antichino*, 138; Espinoza, *Ejemplo de Sonora*, 55, 57, 89.

4. Robert Chao Romero, *Chinese in Mexico*, 172–73.

5. During this time, expelled Chinese Mexican families from Sonora also settled in Baja California, especially in the border city Mexicali. Mexicali has continued to house a large, highly visible Chinese population in the neighborhood known as La Chinesca. On Chinese in Baja California and Mexicali in particular, see Marín, "Migración china"; Félix, "Inmigrantes chinos"; Hu-DeHart, "Chinese of Baja California"; Hu-DeHart, "Chinos del norte de México"; Auyón Gerardo, *Dragón en el desierto*.

6. Izquierdo, *Movimiento antichino*, 137–41; Robert Chao Romero, *Chinese in Mexico*.

7. Case "Problema Chino," 1927, Vol. 1166, Box 362, AGES; Robert Chao Romero, *Chinese in Mexico*, 172–74; Izquierdo, *Movimiento antichino*, 138; Espinoza, *Ejemplo de Sonora*, 55, 57, 89, 119–20, 135.

8. Conceição, interview.

9. *Arizona Daily Star*, 5 September 1931; *Nogales Daily Herald*, 25 February 1932; Hu-DeHart, "Comunidad china."

10. Dennis, "Anti-Chinese Campaigns," 69.

11. *Nogales Daily Herald*, 25 February 1932. On the expulsion of Chinese from Mexico, see Hu-DeHart, "Racism"; Hu-DeHart, "Comunidad china"; Robert Chao Romero, *Chinese in Mexico*; Robert Chao Romero, "'Destierro de los Chinos'"; Dennis, "Anti-Chinese Campaigns"; Izquierdo, *Movimiento antichino*; Barkow, "Movimiento antichino," 53–57; Knight, "Racism, Revolution, and *Indigenismo*"; González Navarro, "Xenofobia y xenofilia"; Cumberland, "Sonora Chinese"; Jacques, "Anti-Chinese Campaign"; Schiavone Camacho, "Traversing Boundaries."

12. Hu-DeHart, "Racism"; Dennis, "Anti-Chinese Campaigns."

13. Robert Chao Romero, *Chinese in Mexico*; see also Pamela del Carmen Corella Romero, "Expulsión." Corella Romero is the local chronicler of a small north-central Sonoran town, Ímuris.

14. Bustamante, *Seis expulsiones*.

15. Robert Chao Romero, *Chinese in Mexico*, 68–69; Augustine-Adams, "Making

Mexico," 21–23, 30–31. Augustine-Adams notes that the original data and subsequent changes inconsistently categorized children.

16. File IV-352-28, SREAHGE.

17. Rénique, "Anti-Chinese Racism," 119; Robert Chao Romero, *Chinese in Mexico*, 175.

18. Robert Chao Romero, *Chinese in Mexico*, 195; Izquierdo, *Movimiento antichino*, 150, 161; Rénique, "Race, Region, and Nation," 230; Camín, *Frontera nómada*; Bay, "Conexión Yocupicio."

19. Rénique, "Race, Region, and Nation," 211–13, 219–26; Bay, "Conexión Yocupicio"; Bustamante, *Seis expulsiones*. On the expulsion of Mormons from Sonora and their settlement in southern Arizona, see Benton-Cohen, *Borderline Americans*.

20. Hu-DeHart, "Comunidad china," 210; see also Dennis, "Anti-Chinese Campaigns," 69–70.

21. *San Francisco Chronicle*, 3 July 1932. Mexican authorities corresponded about cross-border ties among Chinese during this time. For example, Manuel Tello, the Mexican consul in Yokohama, Japan, wrote to the Secretaría de Relaciones Exteriores in Mexico City to relay local coverage of this nature in his area. On 21 June 1930, the *Japan Times* reported that Chinese controlled northern Mexico and were financed by Chinese in Los Angeles and San Francisco. According to the article, many Chinese entered Mexico with false documents or documents belonging to others. See File IV-396-13, SREAHGE.

22. Cumberland, "Sonora Chinese," 203–4.

23. Espinoza, *Ejemplo de Sonora*, 140–41, 368–95.

24. María Luisa Salazar Corral Navarro, interview.

25. Verdugo Escoboza, interview.

26. Cano Ávila, interview.

27. Personal communication with Delfino Robles and family; Lau de Salazar, interview; Hernández Salomón, interview.

28. Valdez, interview.

29. Ibid.

30. Wong Campoy, interview; anonymous interviews cited in Dennis, "Anti-Chinese Campaigns," 70–71.

31. Anti-Chinese sentiment was so strong in Sonora during this time that local authorities arrested a visiting diplomatic official because they had assumed that he was a Chinese resident of Sonora. In a similar fashion, officials arrested Gonzalo Rascón's grandfather, who was Japanese, in Navojoa during this time because they believed him to be Chinese. Authorities were about to deport him when he produced documents proving that he was Japanese; they allowed him to remain in Navojoa. Rascón, interview.

32. *Nogales Daily Herald*, 25 February 1932.

33. File 55771.

34. Robert Chao Romero, *Chinese in Mexico*; Pamela del Carmen Corella Romero, "Expulsión." See also Appeal No. 9, Sonora Collection, Amparo Series, PN Subseries, Section 5, J.D., A, 1931, Box/File 1, Casa de la Cultura Jurídica. Suprema Corte de Justicia de la Nación, Hermosillo, Sonora.

35. Rénique, "Anti-Chinese Racism," 123.

36. Aja, interview; Lau de Salazar, interview; Hernández Salomón, interview.

37. Lau de Salazar, interview.

38. Chan Valenzuela, interview; Chan López, interview.

39. Chinese utilized racial passing to live in the United States by disguising themselves as American Indians and Canadian Indians in the north, Mexicans and American Indians in the Southwest, and African Americans in the South. In Mobile, Alabama, for example, a man whom fellow Chinese called Crooked Face was known for his ability to help Chinese pass as African Americans. As Lee has argued, Chinese "learned to use the ways race marked each particular regional landscape to their own advantage." These "racial crossings" point to the complex hybridity of the borderlands (*At America's Gates*, 162).

40. Tapia Martens, interview.

41. Leyva Cervón, interview. Juan Ramírez Cisneros, the local chronicler of Guaymas, corroborated Wong Cervón's story (interview).

42. Chon, interview; Aja, interview.

43. Anonymous interviews cited in Dennis, "Anti-Chinese Campaigns," 70–71.

44. Rénique, "Anti-Chinese Racism," 124.

CHAPTER 4

1. Wong Campoy, interview; Conceição, interview; File 55771. INS records listed the Wong Campoys as a family unit consisting of Alfonso Wong Fang, Dolores C. [Campoy] Wong Fang, and their children, Alfonso Wong, Irma Wong, and Hector Manuel Wong. Even though Alfonso Wong Campoy and his siblings used one of their father's and one of their mother's surnames, U.S. immigration agents recorded only their father's name, imposing on the family the dominant U.S. naming practice.

2. Ngai, *Impossible Subjects*; Lee, *At America's Gates*, 152, 157–61, 187. See also McKeown, "Ritualization of Regulation."

3. File 55771; Criminal Case Files, 1914–47, Box 143, Case 6381, and Box 145, Cases 6461–62, Immigration and Naturalization Service Files, Record Group 21, U.S. District Court, District of Arizona, Tucson Division, National Archives and Records Administration, Pacific Region, Laguna Niguel, California.

4. Balderrama and Rodríguez, *Decade of Betrayal*; Carreras de Velasco, *Mexicanos*.

5. Scholars have critically examined these processes in the United States. According to Nicolosi, the U.S. Expatriation Act of 1907 codified "derivative citizenship"—women's status being derived from the nationality of their husbands. Making women's citizenship and racial status mobile, the 1907 act reveals that the U.S. sex/gender system was highly racialized. Although the official reason for the Expatriation Act was to clarify the citizenship status of Americans living abroad, Nicolosi argues that in fact it gave the state an underhanded means of manipulating immigration and the nation's racial makeup through women. Between 1907 and 1931, many women—some without their knowledge—lost their American citizenship when they married Asian "aliens ineligible for citizenship." Citing a few such cases, Nicolosi shows that this process was worse for Asian American women because naturalization laws meant that they could not regain

their citizenship even if they terminated their marriages. Similarly, Yung demonstrates that many American-born Chinese women who married foreign-born men lost the rights to own property, vote, travel abroad freely, and pass on their citizenship to their children born outside the United States. For Nicolosi, the Expatriation Act was closely tied to dominant desires for racial purity, especially as states increasingly passed antimiscegenation laws during this time. The Cable Act of 1922 began to alter the 1907 act, but not until the passage of the Cable Amendment of 1931 was the 1922 act repealed and the 1907 stipulations removed. See Nicolosi, "'We Do Not Want'"; Yung, *Unbound Feet*, 168–69; see also Cott, "Marriage and Women's Citizenship"; Ngai, *Impossible Subjects*.

6. On the construction of the categories of "legal" and "illegal" immigrants and Chinese exclusion, see Ngai, *Impossible Subjects*.

7. Lee, *At America's Gates*; Ngai, *Impossible Subjects*; Ettinger, *Imaginary Lines*.

8. McKeown, *Melancholy Order*, 295, 320, 327, 350.

9. File III-1729-17, SREAHGE. See also Izquierdo, *Movimiento antichino*, 142–43. On the Arizona-Sonora border in general, see Salas, *In the Shadow of the Eagles*; Martínez, *U.S.-Mexico Borderlands*.

10. Box 1 of 1, U.S. District Court (Arizona) Final Mittimus Records, 1930–32, Arizona Historical Society, Tucson. See also Dennis, "Anti-Chinese Campaigns," 69–70.

11. *Nogales Daily Herald*, 25 February 1932.

12. File 55771. INS records set apart members of Chinese Mexican families by case numbers and naming patterns. Although Mexican women's names were absent from the first and second lists, the Third Supplemental List and every register thereafter included the names of Mexican women and Chinese Mexican children along with Chinese men. The records often listed Mexican women with two surnames, one Spanish and one Chinese, at times separated by "de" (of or belonging to), signifying that the woman was married to the person whose surname followed that of her family. The INS often listed children with both parents' surnames. Each family/group traveling together was assigned a file number, helping to clarify the composition of Chinese Mexican families. Records indicate the dates of departure to San Francisco, names, and file numbers of families who were deported during this time.

13. For a comprehensive history of the facility, see Lee and Yung, *Angel Island*.

14. Dirección General del Gobierno, Box 10, Folder 5, 2.360 (29) 8109, AGN.

15. Yong Chen, *Chinese San Francisco*; Lai, *Becoming Chinese American*.

16. Dirección General del Gobierno, Box 10, Folder 5, 2.360 (29) 8109, AGN.

17. Ibid.; Lai, *History Reclaimed*, 69–74.

18. File 55771.

19. Ibid.

20. Ibid.

21. Ibid.

22. Enríquez de López, interview; File 55771.

23. File 55771.

24. Ibid.

25. Ibid.

26. Ibid.

27. Lo's name appeared on a list of people the agency deported on 29 August, 11 Sep-

tember, or 26 September. See File 55771. On 31 March 1933, Edward J. Shaughnessy, the assistant commissioner general, wrote to the district director in El Paso regarding the wives and children who traveled with Chinese men. He requested that information on all members of a particular family be placed in one file so that a single case number could be assigned. He noted that the recent documentation had been inconsistent on this matter. Subsequent records kept better track of family units.

28. File 55771.

29. Ibid.

30. Ibid.

31. Ibid.; Folder 546.2/1, Box 714, ALMC. INS records and Ramón Lay Mazo's letters included the identical names for the children, without discrepancy, except for Lay Mazo's spelling of "Bentura" and the INS listing "Ventura." In this case, the children apparently used only their father's surname.

32. File 55771; Loyola, *Chinos-mexicanos cautivos*; Luis Spota, "24 Horas," in *Novedades*, 24 March 1961, cited in Loyola.

33. File 55771; Villalba Yee, website. The INS listed the members of the family as Chee Tun [Antonio Yee Sr.], Cruz Arredondo de Chee, Jacinto Chee, Alfonso "Poncho" Chee, and Antonio Chee [Jr.]. The discrepancy in surnames may be an error in INS records, or "Chee" may have become "Yee" in Mexico, as Chinese migrants in Latin America often modified their names.

34. File 55771; Loyola, *Chinos-mexicanos cautivos*; Folders 546.2/1, 546.2/12, Box 714, ALMC.

35. Files III-121-39, IV-341-13, SREAHGE; Pardinas, *Relaciones diplomáticas*, 475–76, 477.

36. File 55771. Dennis has written that the United States cooperated with the Sonoran government by allowing Chinese to travel through its terrain en route to China ("Anti-Chinese Campaigns," 69–70). INS communications, however, suggest that the situation was more complicated and that U.S. officials believed that Sonora and Mexico were taking advantage of their neighbor to the north.

37. File 55771; Immigration and Naturalization Service Files, Record Group 21, U.S. District Court, District of Arizona, Tucson Division, National Archives and Records Administration, Pacific Region, Laguna Niguel, California.

38. File 55771.

39. Ibid.

40. Ibid.

41. Ibid.

42. Ibid.

43. Ibid.

44. Ibid.

45. Ibid.

46. Case "Problema Chino," 1927, Vol. 1166, Box 362, AGES.

47. File 55771; File 17-W-3, 55855/380, Box 506, Immigration and Naturalization Service Files, Record Group 85, National Archives and Records Administration, Washington, D.C.

48. File 55771.

49. Ibid.; *El Continental*, 25 July 1933. See also Estrada, "Mexinese."

50. On the effects of the expulsion on U.S.-Mexican relations, see Dennis, "Anti-Chinese Campaigns"; Anahí Parra Sandoval, "Expulsados chinos"; see also Espinoza, *Ejemplo de Sonora*, 106, 114–15, 133, 151–60.

51. File III-121-39, SREAHGE.

52. Ibid.

53. Ibid., Files IV-396-24, III-396-27.

CHAPTER 5

1. Files IV-341-13, IV-550-9, SREAHGE.

2. Ibid., File IV-341-13. Consular communications about Mexican women in China during this time also appear in Pardinas, *Relaciones diplomáticas*, 428–30, 461–65, 466–68, 471, 474, 475–76, 478–79.

3. Augustine-Adams, "Making Mexico."

4. Files IV-396-37, IV-396-41, SREAHGE.

5. Ibid., Files IV-341-13, IV-419-63.

6. Ibid., File IV-341-13.

7. Pardinas, *Relaciones diplomáticas*, 428–29, 463, 467, 474, 475, 479, 480.

8. Villalba Yee, website. See also File 55771.

9. Tran, "Sex and Equality."

10. For legal and social practices and changes in marriage in twentieth-century China, see Tran, "Sex and Equality"; Tran, "Concubinage"; see also Hsu, "Unwrapping Orientalist Constraints"; Mann, "Male Bond"; McIsaac, "'Righteous Fraternities'"; for bigamy in colonial Mexico, see Boyer, *Lives of the Bigamists*; see also Alonso, *Thread of Blood*. Under China's nineteenth-century gender system, which carried over into the first part of the twentieth century, families privileged male heirs, who would continue the lineage. Chinese families arranged marriages, and young wives were subordinate to their husbands' families. It was possible, however, for Chinese women to gain power through increased status later in life as mothers and mothers-in-law, a key similarity with gender norms in Mexico. See Pascoe, "Gender Systems," 632–34; McKeown, "Transnational Chinese Families." Marriage customs in Mexico and China were parallel in key ways. Robert Chao Romero has shown that some Mexican women who married successful Chinese merchants in Mexico assumed a status comparable to that of native Chinese wives (*Chinese in Mexico*, 73–76).

11. Pan, *Encyclopedia*, 77; Robert Chao Romero, *Chinese in Mexico*, 66, 68–69, 74.

12. Enríquez de López, interview.

13. File IV-341-13, SREAHGE. De Lasala's background is unclear in the record. Writing in Spanish, she may have been Latin American or Spanish. Presumably, she offered her mother's help because she spoke Spanish, too. Her surname suggests that her husband was Latin American or Spanish, perhaps working in China as a merchant, businessman, or official. But he may have been Chinese, since men adopted Spanish surnames in Latin America.

14. Ibid., IV-550-9.

15. Ibid., III-121-39, IV-341-13; Pardinas, *Relaciones diplomáticas*, 475–76, 477;

Izquierdo, *Movimiento antichino*, 159. The Mexican saying is translated figuratively as "paid the price" (literally as "paid for the broken plates").

16. File IV-341-13, SREAHGE.

17. See, for example, Hsu, *Dreaming of Home*; Hsu, "Unwrapping Orientalist Constraints"; Robert Chao Romero, *Chinese in Mexico*.

18. Files IV-341-13, IV-550-9, SREAHGE.

19. Ibid.

20. Ibid.

21. *El Paso Herald Post*, 26 December 1933; Lai, *History Reclaimed*, 69–74.

22. Files IV-341-13, IV-550-9, SREAHGE.

23. Ibid.

24. Ibid.

25. Ibid., File IV-341-13.

26. Lausent-Herrera has found that Macau also drew Peruvian women who had formed ties with Chinese men during the nineteenth century; see "Mujeres olvidadas."

27. File IV-352-28, SREAHGE.

28. Wong Campoy, interview; Conceição, interview.

29. File IV-420-11, SREAHGE.

30. Ibid., File III-1143-9; Dirección General del Gobierno, 2.360 (29) 8152, Folder 23, Box 11, AGN.

31. Files IV-341-13, IV-550-9, SREAHGE.

32. Ibid.

33. Ibid.

34. Ibid.

35. Dirección General del Gobierno, 2.360 (29) 8152, Folder 23, Box 11, AGN.

36. Files III-121-39, IV-341-13, SREAHGE; Pardinas, *Relaciones diplomáticas*, 475–76, 477.

37. Gaona, *¿Legitimación revolucionaria del poder en México?*, 75–77, 81–84; Camín and Meyer, *A la sombra*, 156–57, 179–82; Morgan, "United States Press Coverage," 2, 21, 341–58, 419–555. See also Bantjes, *As If Jesus Walked on Earth*, xii, xvi, 125–28, 221.

38. Files III-121-39, IV-341-13, SREAHGE; Pardinas, *Relaciones diplomáticas*, 475–76, 477.

39. *Excélsior*, 1 March 1933: ". . . salvar los intereses morales de México en posibles casos semejantes del futuro."

40. Ibid., 19 April 1933.

41. *El Continental*, 25 July 1933.

42. Files III-121-39, IV-341-13, SREAHGE; Pardinas, *Relaciones diplomáticas*, 475–76, 477; Rénique, "Anti-Chinese Racism."

43. Files III-121-39, IV-341-13, SREAHGE; Pardinas, *Relaciones diplomáticas*, 475–76, 477.

CHAPTER 6

1. See Ngai, *Impossible Subjects*; Powell, *Mexico and the Spanish Civil War*; Falcoff and Pike, *Spanish Civil War*.

2. Leonard, *Making Ethnic Choices*.

3. Enríquez de López, interview.

4. This translation is Allman's.

5. Files IV-341-13, IV-550-9, SREAHGE. In 1931, Tello complained to the Secretaría de Relaciones Exteriores that Allman did not appear to take seriously his position as honorary Mexican consul since he never informed Tello of matters of interest; only Mauricio Fresco alerted Tello of important issues concerning Mexico, which Tello in turn reported to the Secretaría de Relaciones Exteriores.

6. Ibid.

7. A few women or their families in Mexico had the ability to finance their return. Many others who lacked the resources necessary to travel to Mexico were unable to leave China during this time. Fresco suggested that fund-raisers in their home states might help some of the women return home; it is unclear whether such benefits occurred.

8. File IV-341-13, SREAHGE; Folder 546/3, Box 899, LCDRC; on the National Committee on Repatriation, see Sánchez, *Becoming Mexican American*, 219.

9. Files IV-341-13, IV-550-9, SREAHGE; Folder 546/3, Box 899, LCDRC.

10. Files IV-341-13, IV-550-9, SREAHGE.

11. Ibid.

12. Ch'i, *Nationalist China at War*, 27, 40; Li, "Origins of the War," 3–5; *Excélsior*, 1 March 1933.

13. Gaona, *¿Legitimación revolucionaria del poder en México?*, 75–77, 81–84; Camín and Meyer, *A la sombra*, 156–57, 179–82; Balderrama and Rodríguez, *Decade of Betrayal*, 135; Powell, *Mexico and the Spanish Civil War*. The Sino-Japanese War, which started in the summer of 1937, was the most important factor in Cárdenas's decision to repatriate Mexicans in China; see Schuler, *Mexico between Hitler and Roosevelt*, 57, 94; Powell, *Mexico and the Spanish Civil War*; Gaona, *¿Legitimación revolucionaria del poder en México?*, 75–77, 81–84; Camín and Meyer, *A la sombra*, 156–57, 179–82; Morgan, "United States Press Coverage of Mexico," 2, 21, 341–58, 419–555; see also Bantjes, *As If Jesus Walked on Earth*.

14. Demonstrating his affinity for the politics of inclusion, Cárdenas renamed the Partido Nacional Revolucionario the Partido Revolucionario Institucional and incorporated entire industrial unions, peasant associations, and small business organizations into various "sectors" of the party during his presidency. See He, *From Revolution to Reform*, 44–45.

15. Schuler, *Mexico between Hitler and Roosevelt*, 54, 94. The First Sino-Japanese War took place in 1894–95. The Second Sino-Japanese War lasted from 1937 to 1945. On the latter conflict, see Ch'i, *Nationalist China at War*, 27, 40, 42–43; Li, "Origins of the War," 3–5; Izquierdo, *Movimiento antichino*, 129–30, 161–62.

16. *Excélsior*, 21 October 1937.

17. *El Universal*, 7 January 1937.

18. Duarte letter, Museo de la Universidad de Sonora, Hermosillo, Sonora. For Duarte's appeal to Mexican authorities for her return in 1936, see Folder 549.5/40, Box 925, LCDRC.

19. *Excélsior*, 10, 29 March 1937; *El Universal*, 10 March 1937.

20. File 55771; Villalba Yee website. See also Asian Wind Forum, website.

21. Folder 546.2/1, Box 714, ALMC.

22. Wong Campoy, interview; Conceição, interview.

23. Folder 546.2/1, Box 714, ALMC.

24. Folder 549.5/40, Box 925, Folder 549.5/135, Box 926, LCDRC.

25. Ibid.

26. Folders 549.5/112, 549.5/129, Box 926, LCDRC. Despite the limitations of the repatriation, visions of women, gender, and sexuality in the nation began to change under Cárdenas. Although it caused significant controversy, the Cárdenas administration adopted a platform that included teaching sexual education in public schools. With the support of Cárdenas, women gained the right to vote in several states. Furthermore, according to Meyer, Sherman, and Deeds, "In 1900 a woman in Mexico City would not have dreamed of carrying a placard of protest in a parade. By the time Cárdenas left office such activities were commonplace" (*Course of Mexican History*, 590–91). For a discussion of gender and the Cárdenas administration, see Becker, *Setting the Virgin on Fire*.

27. Luis Ruiz, interview. On the repatriations of Peruvian women and children, see Lausent-Herrera, "Mujeres olvidadas," 304–8.

28. Folder 546/3, Box 899, LCDRC.

29. Folder 549.5/40, Box 925, LCDRC.

30. In August 1932, the *San Francisco Chronicle* reported that cholera and floods had led to high death tolls in Guangdong Province. See *San Francisco Chronicle*, 1, 2 August 1932; Hu, *China*, 19; *Excélsior*, 21 October 1937. Worries about disease in the United States became racialized and tied with Chinese and Mexican immigration. As Nayan Shah has shown, in the late nineteenth and early twentieth centuries, common negative views of Chinese became subsumed into medical discourse, which infiltrated the popular imagination. Anti-Chinese activists cast Chinese as both racial and health contaminants. Shah argues that race allowed public health agencies to become powerful during this time. See Shah, *Contagious Divides*. Alexandra Minna Stern has demonstrated that Mexicans also became racialized through fears of disease in the United States. During the Mexican Revolution, reports of disease in Mexico and increased concerns about the nation's health caused U.S. immigration and public health agencies to step up requirements, including medical examination and disinfection processes, for the entry of Mexicans. As Stern argues, these changes were tied to U.S. visions of Mexico as barbarous. See Alexandra Minna Stern, "Buildings, Boundaries, and Blood," 41, 45–49, 50–52, 63–64, 68. See also Alexandra Minna Stern, *Eugenic Nation*.

31. File III-352-19, SREAHGE; Folder 546/3, Box 899, LCDRC. See also Bantjes, *As If Jesus Walked on Earth*, 102, 170.

32. Folder 111/3779, Box 47, Folder 546/3, Box 899, LCDRC.

CHAPTER 7

1. File OM-149-5, 1960, SREAC.

2. Communist intolerance of religious affiliation may have also pushed Chinese Mexicans to Macau after 1949. See Gu, "Revitalizing Chinese Society," 72–73.

3. Cremer, *Macau*, 1, 103, 115, 119–20; Shipp, *Macau, China*, 78.

4. Cremer, *Macau*; Shipp, *Macau, China*; Ch'i, *Nationalist China at War*, 27, 40, 42–43; Li, "Origins of the War," 3–5.

5. Gunn, *Encountering Macau*, 153–55. Macau remained a Portuguese colony until 1976, when it became a Chinese territory under Portuguese administration. It shifted completely to China's sovereign control at the end of 1999. Cremer, *Macau*, 1; Shipp, *Macau, China*, 81; Boyle, *China and Japan at War*, 54; Shen, "Food Production and Distribution," 168.

6. Wong Campoy, interview.

7. On cosmopolitanism, see, for example, Shelby, "Cosmopolitanism, Blackness, and Utopia"; Lott, "New Cosmopolitanism."

8. Conceição, interview.

9. Wong Campoy, interview; Conceição, interview.

10. Wong Campoy, interview.

11. On Peruvian women in Macau in the late nineteenth and early twentieth centuries, see Lausent-Herrera, "Mujeres olvidadas."

12. Leonard, *Making Ethnic Choices*, 99.

13. Folders 546.2/1, 546.2/12, Box 714, ALMC; Anaya, interview.

14. Loyola, *Chinos-mexicanos cautivos*, 52–53.

15. Folders 546.2/1, 546.2/12, Box 714, ALMC; Anaya, interview.

16. See, for example, Brading, *Mexican Phoenix*.

17. Wong Campoy, interview.

18. File OM-149-5, 1960, SREAC; Folder 546.2/1, Box 714, ALMC; *Excélsior*, 17 November 1960.

19. Although the formation of the People's Republic of China in 1949 marked the beginning of a new period, Macau maintained a relatively unmolested sovereignty. This was true even though Portugal did not establish diplomatic relations with Beijing until 1979, while Great Britain did so in 1950. During the Korean War, Macau was known as a smuggling point for petroleum, war materials, and munitions into China. In 1952, China attempted to pressure Lisbon to end cross-border smuggling. In July of that year sentries at the Macau Barrier Gate moved a guard post into the mainland, and gunfire erupted at the boundary, with casualties on both sides. After the "border incident," China cut off food supplies and exports into Macau for almost a month. See Gunn, *Encountering Macau*, 153–55; Chan and Lo, *Historical Dictionary*, 268.

20. File IV-352-28, SREAHGE; File OM-149-5, 1960, SREAC. China was in profound economic, social, political, and cultural transformation during most of the twentieth century. The changing dynamics of Macau, Hong Kong, and Guangdong Province during the Sino-Japanese War, World War II, the Communist Revolution, and the Cold War created complex boundaries for Chinese Mexicans to negotiate. According to Chen Jian, Chinese communist leader Mao Zedong utilized "anti-foreign-imperialist propaganda . . . to mobilize the Chinese masses" in the 1940s. Many Chinese probably viewed Mexicans and Chinese Mexicans as foreigners during this time (*Mao's China and the Cold War*, 13).

21. File OM-149-5, 1960, SREAC.

22. Loyola, *Chinos-mexicanos cautivos*, 40–44.

23. File OM-149-5, 1960, SREAC; Folder 546.2/1, Box 714, ALMC.

24. The S.S. *Fat Shan* capsized and sank in 1971 as Typhoon Rose assailed Hong Kong; only four of the ninety people aboard survived (S.S. *Fat Shan*, website).

25. File OM-149-5, 1960, SREAC; Folder 546.2/1, Box 714, ALMC.

26. Ramón Lay Mazo referred to León Sosa Mazo as his nephew. It is common in Mexico to consider the children of first cousins as nephews and nieces. Many Chinese Mexicans upheld informal Mexican social and familial practices such as these in China.

27. Chiang Kai-shek had come to power in China during the late 1920s. Franklin D. Roosevelt's administration had supported Chiang unilaterally during the period of Sino-Japanese conflict in the late 1930s and early 1940s. Subsequent U.S. administrations would also support Chiang, against whose Nationalist forces Communists struggled during the Chinese Civil War (1945–49). In 1949, the Communists defeated the Nationalists, who fled to Taiwan. The Chinese Communist Party and the Nationalist Party remained in constant conflict across the Taiwan Strait, as the Communists wanted to include Taiwan in the new Chinese communist state. See Camilleri, *Chinese Foreign Policy*, 7–8, 12, 31–34, 41, 197; Chen Jian, *Mao's China and the Cold War*, 17, 165; Boyle, *China and Japan at War*, 9–10, 20–21.

28. File OM-149-5, 1960, SREAC; Folder 546.2/1, Box 714, ALMC.

29. File OM-149-5, 1960, SREAC; Folder 546.2/1, Box 714, ALMC.

30. File OM-149-5, 1960, SREAC.

31. Folder 546.2/1, Box 714, ALMC; File OM-149-5, 1960, SREAC.

32. Chen Jian, *Mao's China and the Cold War*, 41.

33. Folder 546.2/1, Box 714, ALMC; File OM-149-5, 1960, SREAC; Sergio Chin-Ley to author, 12–15, 18 August 2011, 2, 6 September 2011.

34. File OM-149-5, 1960.

35. Folder 546.2/1, Box 714, ALMC; File OM-149-5, 1960, SREAC; Gunn, *Encountering Macau*, 153–55.

36. Folder 546.2/1, Box 714, ALMC.

37. Ibid.; File 55771.

38. Folder 546.2/1, Box 714, ALMC.

39. Ibid.

40. In the 1930s, China was concerned about its image in the world and urged Chinese men to contain their wives' negative views. Japan also assumed responsibility and expressed concern for the Japanese diaspora during the nineteenth and twentieth centuries. See, for example, Ichioka, *Issei*; Hirabayashi, *New Worlds, New Lives*. On the construction of the nation-state in relation to migration and border control, see McKeown, *Melancholy Order*.

41. On conservative organizations and the rise of reactionary movements in Mexico, see Montfort, *Estampas de nacionalismo*; Von Mentz, Montfort, and Radkau, *Fascismo y antifascismo*.

42. Folder 546.2/1, Box 714, ALMC; File OM-149-5, 1960, SREAC.

43. Folder 546.2/1, Box 714, ALMC; File OM-149-5, 1960, SREAC.

44. Folder 546.2/1, Box 714, ALMC; File OM-149-5, 1960, SREAC.

45. Folder 546.2/1, Box 714, ALMC; File OM-149-5, 1960, SREAC.

46. Rodrigues, interview; Folder 546.2/1, Box 714, ALMC; File OM-149-5, 1960, SREAC.

47. Folder 546.2/1, Box 714, ALMC; File OM-149-5, 1960, SREAC.

48. File OM-149-5, 1960, SREAC. My sources have indicated people's strong affiliation with Mexico, even among those who waited more than two decades to repatriate. The Chinese Mexican community in Macau stayed focused on repatriation and cultivated a profound love for Mexico. But others might have lost faith in the nation over the years. Some of those who traveled to China during the expulsion may have remained in Guangdong Province or other areas. Over time, they and their descendants perhaps lost their sense of Mexicanness. Nevertheless, preliminary evidence suggests that descendants of some Chinese Mexicans who have remained in certain villages in Guangdong Province have retained an awareness of being Mexican and speak a version of Spanish.

CHAPTER 8

1. Wong Campoy, interview; Folder 546.2/1, Box 714, ALMC.

2. It was in this period that the categories "First," "Second," and "Third World" were formulated. On these categories, see Coronil, "Beyond Occidentalism."

3. See, for example, Ngai, *Impossible Subjects*.

4. Gaona, *¿Legitimación revolucionaria del poder en México?*, 95–96. See also Camín and Meyer, *A la sombra*, 187–235; Meyer, Sherman, and Deeds, *Course of Mexican History*, 622–26.

5. Chua Wong, interview. Before meeting Wong, I had heard about him and his restaurant from many people I met at archives and universities in the capital. Fernando Ma also mentioned Wong's father. According to Ma, Antonio Chua Wong was "100 percent Mexican" but learned Cantonese from his adoptive parents when he was young (Ma, interview).

6. Ma, interview.

7. "Chinese Transits along the Mexican Border," File 17-W-3, 56077/450, box 506, Immigration and Naturalization Service Files, Record Group 85, National Archives and Records Administration, Washington, D.C.

8. Folder 546.2/1, Box 714, ALMC.

9. Gaona, *¿Legitimación revolucionaria del poder en México?*, 75–77, 81–84; Camín and Meyer, *A la sombra*, 98–99, 102, 187–235; Yáñez, *Proyección universal de México*; Yáñez, *Misión económica, política, y social*; Faust and Franke, "Attempts at Diversification."

10. *Macau*, 187, 296.

11. Faust and Franke, "Attempts at Diversification"; Yáñez, *Proyección universal de México*, 8; Yañez, *Misión económica, política, y social*; Gaona, *¿Legitimación revolucionaria del poder en México?*, 98; Meyer, Sherman, and Deeds, *Course of Mexican History*, 627–37; Camilleri, *Chinese Foreign Policy*, 10, 55, 62–63, 72–73, 79, 86–88; Chen Jian, *Mao's China and the Cold War*, 337 n. 36, 343 n. 35; see also Wang, *China and the World*.

12. Meyer, Sherman, and Deeds, *Course of Mexican History*, 627–37.

13. File OM-149-5, 1960, SREAC.

14. Folder 546.2/12, Box 714, ALMC.

15. Schiavone Camacho, "Traversing Boundaries," 63–111; see also Juán Ramón Gutiérrez, "José María Arana," 2–3. Echeverría's Campaña Nacionalista continued to exist well after the expulsion of Chinese in the early 1930s, celebrating its thirtieth anniversary in 1955. A banner commemorating the event is housed at the Museo de la Universidad de Sonora in Hermosillo. Leo Sandoval showed me the banner and discussed what it represented (Sandoval, interview; see also Leo Sandoval, *Casa de Abelardo*).

16. See Lee and Yung, *Angel Island*.

17. When I gave a paper on this topic in Hermosillo, numerous persons in the audience laughed at the suggestion that Chinese Mexicans could have been resettled on Tiburón because of the island's limited resources and historic lack of good land. See Schiavone Camacho, "'Aunque vayamos a escarbar camotes amargos a la sierra.'" On La Isla del Tiburón, see Salas, *In the Shadow of the Eagles*, 61.

18. Folder 546.2/12, Box 714, ALMC.

19. Files OM-149-1, 1960, OM-149-5, 1960, SREAC; Folder 546.2/1, Box 714, ALMC.

20. Folder 546.2/1, Box 714, ALMC.

21. Wong Campoy, interview.

22. Loyola noted that 267 people repatriated in 1960 and 70 more remained in communist China, hoping to repatriate. Monica Cinco Basurto's father, Jorge Cinco, remembered that there were 365 repatriates in total. See Loyola, *Chinos-mexicanos cautivos*, 63; Basurto, "China in Mexico," 17.

23. "De Hong Kong vuelven mexicanos en avión," *Excélsior*, 8 November 1960; "Repatriación de chinomexicanos," *Excélsior*, 16 November 1960; "Más repatriados de China, regresaron," *Excélsior*, 17 November 1960.

24. Folder 546.2/12, Box 714, ALMC; Wong Campoy, interview.

25. Loyola, *Chinos-mexicanos cautivos*, 54–55, citing Luis Spota, "24 Hours," *Novedades*, 24 March 1961; Anaya, interview; File 55771.

26. Paul Tsang to author, 11, 12 November, 4–6 December 2010.

27. Wong Campoy, interview; Conceição, interview; Folder 546.2/1, Box 714, ALMC.

28. Wong Campoy, interview; Conceição, interview.

29. Basurto vividly described the feeling of being between cultures ("China in Mexico").

30. Wong Campoy, interview.

31. Wong Campoy, interview; File 55771; Folder 546.2/1, Box 714, ALMC.

32. Wong Campoy, interview; Conceição, interview.

33. *Excélsior*, 8, 16, 17 November 1960; Loyola, *Chinos-mexicanos cautivos*, 11, 25; Wong Campoy, interview; Conceição, interview; Sergio Chin-Ley to author, 12–15, 18 August 2011, 2, 6 September 2011.

34. Loyola, *Chinos-mexicanos cautivos*, 3.

35. Ibid., 5, 34.

36. Ibid., 16–19, 45.

37. Ibid., 47–48.

38. Ibid., 37, 45.

39. Ibid., 4, 6, 51.

40. Ibid., 7–15.

41. Ibid., 60–63.

42. Loyola, *Chinos-mexicanos cautivos*, 54–55, citing Luis Spota, "24 Hours," *Novedades*, 24 March 1961; Anaya, interview.

43. Folders 546.2/1, 546.2/12, Box 714, ALMC; Luis Ruiz, interview; Verónica Noquez Lugo, interview.

44. Folders 546.2/1, 546.2/12, Box 714, ALMC.

45. Ibid.

46. Ibid.

47. Ibid. The Archivo General de la Nación in Mexico City later added documentation about the photographs accompanying the forms, with descriptions that in some cases listed the names and ages as well as notes about the phenotype and style of dress of the people pictured.

48. Ibid. Loyola's account disagreed with the records of the Latin American Association of Hong Kong and Verónica Noquez Lugo's account. According to Loyola, Zenona Sandoval and her son, Jorge Cinco Sandoval, had returned to their place of origin, Guamuchil, Sinaloa, by 1961. Loyola noted that her husband and other children had been killed under the communist regime, but she and her son escaped after spending a long time in jail. See Loyola, *Chinos-mexicanos cautivos*, 32. See also Chen Jian, *Mao's China and the Cold War*, 82–83; Camilleri, *Chinese Foreign Policy*, 78, 85, 93–94, 109, 114, 116, 252; Tang, *Cultural Revolution*.

Among the other cases described in the Asociación's forms were those of Angel Ley and José Rosalío Wong Martínez. Ley was born in Guamuchil, Sinaloa, in 1933, and had left Mexico as a small child. His wife, Margarita Ley, was born in Zhongshan, Guangdong Province, in 1939. Their sons, Angel Manuel Ley (age three) and Juan Ley (age one), and daughter, Josefina Ley (age four), were also born in Zhongshan. The father had "slight oriental features" and the family wore traditional Chinese dress. Wong Martínez was born in Mazatlán, Sinaloa, in 1920. He had been a laborer in China and married Kan Sit Chan, who was born in Zhongshan in 1931. Their sons, Kun Kit Kan Wong (age ten) and Mey Kit Kan Wong (an infant), and daughters Ley Bei Kan Wong (age five) and Ley Muy Kan Wong (age two), were also born in Zhongshan. José Rosalío Wong Martínez's unmarried brother, Juan Francisco Wong Martínez, born in Mazatlán in 1924, also lived in China.

49. Verónica Noquez Lugo, interview; María del Carmen Lugo, interview. Contrary to Loyola's account, Zenona Sandoval's husband and their other sons died in Manila during the Japanese invasion of the Philippines. See Basurto, "China in Mexico," 16.

50. Verónica Noquez Lugo, interview; María del Carmen Lugo, interview; Anaya, interview; Lei, interview.

51. Chua Wong, interview.

52. Enríquez de López, interview; Ma, interview.

CONCLUSION

1. See, for example, Pan, *Encyclopedia*.

2. For example, in one 2003 third-grade state textbook, the "Reorganización de

Sonora" (The Reorganization of Sonora) section follows segments on the revolutionary and postrevolutionary periods and contains information on the Chinese in Sonora. It states:

In those years [late 1920s–early 1930s], the Chinese population, which had arrived in our state during the Porfiriato, dedicated itself to mining, business, and agriculture and with time some accumulated large fortunes; for some wealthy Sonorans it was difficult to compete with Chinese businesses and this is why they began to pressure the Chinese.

Francisco Serrano's government pressured the Chinese through arbitrary measures such as high taxes, exaggerated sanitary sanctions, the sale of only one type of product in their businesses, prohibition of marriages between Chinese men and Mexican women, and others, until Governor Rodolfo Elías Calles . . . decreed the expulsion of the Chinese population in 1931.

[Por esos años [late 1920s–early 1930s], la población china que había llegado a nuestra entidad durante el Porfiriato, se dedicaba a la minería, el comercio y la agricultura, y con el tiempo algunos acumularon grandes fortunas; para algunos sonorenses adinerados era difícil competir con los negocios de los chinos, por eso comenzaron a presionarlos.

Durante el gobierno de Francisco Serrano, se presionó a los chinos con medidas arbitrarias, tales como altos impuestos, medidas sanitarias exageradas, venta de un solo tipo de producto en sus negocios, prohibición de matrimonios entre chinos y mexicanas y otras más, hasta que en 1931, siendo gobernador Rodolfo Elías Calles . . . se decretó la salida de la población china de Sonora.] (*Sonora*, 147–48).

3. Chew, "Chio Sam," in *Azogue en la raíz*, 77–78. After being selected as one of the top poems, "Chio Sam" appeared in Hernández, *Mejores poemas mexicanos*, 13.

Bibliography

UNPUBLISHED MATERIALS

Manuscript Sources

Hermosillo, Sonora
  Archivo General del Estado de Sonora
    1927. Box 362. Vol. 1166. Case "Problema Chino"
  Archivo General del Poder Judicial del Estado de Sonora
    Juzgado de Alamos. Ramo Penal, 1925–26
    Juzgado de Arizpe. Ramo Penal, 1923
    Juzgado de Caborca. Ramo Penal, 1921
    Juzgado de Cananea. Ramo Penal, 1928
    Juzgado de Cumpas. Ramo Penal, 1924, 1929
    Juzgado de Guaymas. Ramo Penal, 1921, 1929
    Juzgado de Hermosillo. Ramo Penal, 1910, 1920, 1924, 1929
    Juzgado de Magdalena. Ramo Penal, 1913, 1917, 1924, 1927, 1929
    Juzgado de Navojoa. Ramo Penal, 1923
    Juzgado de Nogales. Ramo Penal, 1910, 1914, 1919, 1922, 1926, 1927, 1928
    Juzgado de Sahuaripa. Ramo Penal, 1922–25
    Juzgado de Urcs. Ramo Penal, 1912, 1916, 1922
    Supremo Tribunal de Justicia, Hermosillo. Ramo Penal, 1927, 1932
  Casa de la Cultura Jurídica. Suprema Corte de Justicia de la Nación
    Appeal No. 9. Sonora Collection, Amparo Series, PN Subseries, Section 5
    Appeal No. 49. Sonora Collection, Amparo Series, PN Subseries, Section 5
  Departamento de la Estadística Nacional
    Censo General de Habitantes, 30 November 1921, State of Sonora
Laguna Niguel, California
  National Archives and Records Administration, Pacific Region
    Immigration and Naturalization Service Files, Record Group 21, U.S. District
      Court, District of Arizona, Tucson Division, Criminal Case Files, 1914–47
Mexico City
  Archivo General de la Nación
    Dirección General del Gobierno
    Adolfo López Mateos Collection
    Lázaro Cárdenas del Río Collection
    Obregón-Calles Collection

Secretaría de Relaciones Exteriores. Archivo de Concentraciones
    File OM-149-1, 1960
    File OM-149-5, 1960
Secretaría de Relaciones Exteriores. Archivo Histórico Genaro Estrada
    File III-121-39
    File III-352-19
    File III-396-27
    File III-1143-9
    File III-1729-17
    File IV-211-2
    File IV-341-13
    File IV-343-16
    File IV-352-28
    File IV-396-13
    File IV-396-24
    File IV-396-37
    File IV-396-41
    File IV-419-63
    File IV-420-11
    File IV-550-9
Tucson, Arizona
    Arizona Historical Society
        U.S. District Court (Arizona) Final Mittimus Records, 1930–32
    University of Arizona, Special Collections
        Papers of José María Arana
Washington, D.C.
    National Archives and Records Administration
        Immigration and Naturalization Service Files, Record Group 85

Oral History Interviews
All interviews by author, unless otherwise noted.

Aja, Carlos Lucero. 10 August 2004, Hermosillo, Sonora. Digital recording.
Anaya, José Serafín. 10 August 2007, Kowloon, Hong Kong, China. Digital recording.
Cano Ávila, Gastón. 8 October 2004, Hermosillo, Sonora. Digital recording.
Chan López, Guillermo. 9 August 2004, Hermosillo, Sonora. Digital recording.
Chan Valenzuela, Luis. 11 October 2004, Hermosillo, Sonora. Digital recording.
Chua Wong, Cristóbal. 7 October 2004, Hermosillo, Sonora. Digital recording.
Cisneros, Juan Ramírez. 26 June 2004, Guaymas, Sonora. Digital recording.
Conceição, María del Carmen Irma Wong Campoy Maher. 15 August 2010, San Francisco. Digital recording.
Enríquez de López, Antonia Wong. 8 October 2004, Hermosillo, Sonora. Digital recording.
Fonseca Chon, Ignacio. 27 February 2004, Hermosillo, Sonora. Digital recording.
Gil, Bertha Lourdes Amador. 8 December 2003, Oakland, California. Digital recording.

Hernández Salomón, Manuel. 31 July 2004, Navojoa, Sonora. Digital recording.

Lau de Salazar, Marta Elia. Interview by Berenice Barreras Ayala, 19 August 2004, Bacobampo, Sonora. Tape recording.

Lei, Marta. Phone interview, 1, 11 August 2007, Hong Kong, China.

Leyva Cervón, María de Los Angeles. 26 June 2004, Guaymas, Sonora. Digital recording.

Lugo, María del Carmen. 4 August 2007, Macau, China. Digital recording.

Lugo, Verónica Noquez. 4 August 2007, Macau, China. Digital recording.

Ma, Fernando. 13 November 2003, Hermosillo, Sonora. Digital recording.

Navarro, María Luisa Salazar Corral. 15 November 2003, Navojoa, Sonora. Digital recording.

Rascón, Gonzalo. 31 July 2004, Navojoa, Sonora. Digital recording.

Rodrigues, Lancelot Miguel. 4 August 2010, Macau, China. Digital recording.

Ruiz, Luis. 5, 14 July 2010, Macau, China. Digital recordings.

Sandoval, Leo. 14, 17 November 2003, Hermosillo, Sonora. Digital recordings.

Tapia Martens, José de Jesus. 27 February 2004, Hermosillo, Sonora. Digital recording.

Valdez, Luisa María. 12 January 2004, Nogales, Arizona. Digital recording.

Verdugo Escoboza, Jesús. 7 October 2004, Hermosillo, Sonora. Digital recording.

Wong Campoy, Alfonso. 10 October 2004, Navojoa, Sonora. Digital recording.

Websites

Asian Wind Forum. http://www.asiawind.com/forums/read.php?f=4&i=290&t=290. Accessed 12 December 2009.

S.S. *Fat Shan*. http://www.casttv.com/video/bzs4wb1/fat-shan-ferry-sinking-1971-video. Accessed 21 July 2010.

Villalba Yee, Conchita. http://thecity.sfsu.edu/~galeria/cycles.html. Accessed 23 September 2003.

Dissertations, Theses, and Papers

Barkow, Patricia Irma Figueroa. "El movimiento antichino en Mexico de 1916–1935: Un caso de 'racismo económico.'" Master's thesis, Universidad Nacional Autónoma de Mexico, 1976.

Bay, Ignacio Almada. "La conexión Yocupicio: soberania estatal, tradición civico-liberal y resistencia al reemplazo de las lealtades en Sonora, 1913–1939." Ph.D. diss., Colegio de México, 1993.

Castillo-Muñoz, Verónica. "Divided Communities: Agrarian Struggles, Transnational Migration, and Families in Northern Mexico, 1910–1952." Ph.D. diss., University of California, Irvine, 2009.

Chang, Jason Oliver. "Outsider Crossings in the Chinese Diaspora: Race, Class, and Nation in the U.S.-Mexico Borderlands, 1902–1952." Ph.D. diss., University of California, Berkeley, 2010.

Chew, Selfa A. "The Removal of Japanese and Japanese Mexicans from the United

States/Mexico Borderlands during World War II." Ph.D. diss., University of Texas at El Paso, 2010.

Delgado, Grace Peña. "In the Age of Exclusion: Race, Religion, and Chinese Identity in the Making of the Arizona-Sonora Borderlands, 1863–1943." Ph.D. diss., University of California, Los Angeles, 2000.

Estrada, José Sebastian. "Mexinese: Cultural Diffusion in the Mexican-American Borderlands, 1880–1950." Paper presented at the Frances G. Harper Student History Conference, El Paso, Texas, 7 May 2011.

Jacques, Leo Michael Dambourges. "The Anti-Chinese Campaign in Sonora, Mexico, 1900–1931." Ph.D. diss., University of Arizona, 1974.

Kisines, Claudia Rocío Rivera. "Migración y legislación en México, 1863–1910." Unpublished paper. N.d.

Llano, Juan Mauricio Magín Puig. "La matanza de chinos, en 1911: historia de un incidente internacional." Master's thesis, Universidad Nacional Autónoma de México, 1986.

Morgan, Hugh. "The United States Press Coverage of Mexico during the Presidency of Lázaro Cárdenas, 1934–1940." Ph.D. diss., Southern Illinois University, 1984.

Ortoll, Servando. "¿Enemigos indispensables? Chinos y japoneses en Sonora y Arizona, durante los años treinta." Unpublished paper. N.d.

Rénique, Gerardo. "Región, raza, y nación en el antichinismo sonorense: cultura regional y mestizaje en el México posrevolucionario." Unpublished paper. N.d.

Romero, Pamela del Carmen Corella. "La expulsión de Agustín Chang: nacionalismo excluyente durante la revolución." Master's thesis, El Colegio de Sonora, 2008.

Romero, Robert Chao. "The Dragon in Big Lusong: Chinese Immigration and Settlement in Mexico, 1882–1940." Ph.D. diss., University of California, Los Angeles, 2003.

Romero Sotelo, María Eugenia and María Elena Ota Mishima. *Destino México: un estudio de las migraciones asiáticas a México, siglos XIX y XX*. Mexico City: El Colegio de México, 1997.

Sandoval, Anahí Parra. "Expulsados chinos en Sonora: un caso de etnofobia en el México de los años treinta." Paper presented at the Simposio de Antropología e Historia de la Universidad de Sonora, Hermosillo, 25 February 2005.

Schiavone Camacho, Julia María. "'Aunque vayamos a escarbar camotes amargos a la sierra, queremos México': nacionalismo mexicano en China, 1930–1960, y la repatriación de la década de 1960," paper presented at the Simposio de Historia y Antropología de Sonora: Treinta años escribiendo la historia del noroeste de México, Hermosillo, Sonora, 23–26 February 2005.

———. "Traversing Boundaries: Chinese, Mexicans, and Chinese Mexicans in the Formation of Gender, Race, and Nation in the Twentieth-Century U.S.-Mexican Borderlands." Ph.D. diss., University of Texas at El Paso, 2006.

Tran, Lisa. "Concubinage under Modern Chinese Law." Ph.D. diss., University of California, Los Angeles, 2005.

Books

Alonso, Ana María. *Thread of Blood: Colonialism, Revolution, and Gender on Mexico's Northern Frontier*. Tucson: University of Arizona Press, 1995.

Anderson, Benedict. *Imagined Communities: Reflections on the Origins and Spread of Nationalism*. New York: Verso, 1983.

Auyón Gerardo, Eduardo. *El dragón en el desierto: los pioneros chinos en Mexicali*. Mexicali: Instituto de Cultura de Baja California, 1991.

Balderrama, Francisco E. *In Defense of la Raza: The Los Angeles Mexican Consulate, 1929–1936*. Tucson: University of Arizona Press, 1982.

Balderrama, Francisco E., and Raymond Rodríguez. *Decade of Betrayal: Mexican Repatriation in the 1930s*. Albuquerque: University of New Mexico Press, 1995.

Bantjes, Adrian A. *As If Jesus Walked on Earth: Cardenismo, Sonora, and the Mexican Revolution*. Wilmington, Del.: Scholarly Resources, 1998.

Bay, Ignacio Almada. *Diccionario de historia, geografía, y biografía Sonorenses*. Hermosillo: Gobierno del Estado de Sonora, 1983.

Bay, Ignacio Almada, and José Marcos Medina Bustos. *Historia panorámica del Congreso del Estado de Sonora, 1825–2000*. Mexico City: Cal y arena, 2001.

Becker, Marjorie. *Setting the Virgin on Fire: Lázaro Cárdenas, Michoacán Peasants, and the Redemption of the Mexican Revolution*. Berkeley: University of California Press, 1995.

Benjamin, Thomas, and William McNellie, eds. *Other Mexicos: Essays of Regional Mexican History, 1876–1911*. Albuquerque: University of New Mexico Press, 1984.

Benton-Cohen, Kathcrine. *Borderline Americans: Racial Division and Labor War in the Arizona Borderlands*. Cambridge: Harvard University Press, 2009.

Bliss, Katherine Elaine. *Compromised Positions: Prostitution, Public Health, and Gender Politics in Revolutionary Mexico City*. University Park: Pennsylvania State University Press, 2001.

Boyer, Richard. *Lives of the Bigamists: Marriage, Family, and Community in Colonial Mexico*. Albuquerque: University of New Mexico Press, 1995.

Boyle, John Hunter. *China and Japan at War, 1937–1945: The Politics of Collaboration*. Stanford: Stanford University Press, 1972.

Brading, D. A. *Mexican Phoenix: Our Lady of Guadalupe, Image, and Tradition, 1531–2000*. Cambridge: Cambridge University Press, 2003.

Bustamante, Aarón Grageda. *Seis expulsiones y un adiós: despojos y exclusiones en Sonora*. Mexico City: Plaza y Valdez, 2004.

Camilleri, Joseph. *Chinese Foreign Policy: The Maoist Era and Its Aftermath*. Seattle: University of Washington Press, 1980.

Camín, Hector Aguilar. *La frontera nómada: Sonora y la Revolución Mexicana*. Mexico City: Siglo XXI, 1977.

Camín, Héctor Aguilar, and Lorenzo Meyer. *In the Shadow of the Mexican Revolution: Contemporary Mexican History, 1910–1989*. Translated by Luis Alberto Fierro. Austin: University of Texas Press, 1993.

————. *A la sombra de la Revolución Mexicana: un ensayo de historia contemporánea de México, 1910–1089.* Mexico City: Cal y arena, 1989.

Carreras de Velasco, Mercedes. *Los Mexicanos que devolvió la crisis, 1929–1932.* Mexico City: Secretaría de Relaciones Exteriores, 1974.

Chan, Ming K., and Shui-hing Lo. *Historical Dictionary of the Hong Kong SAR and the Macao SAR.* Lanham, Md.: Scarecrow, 2006.

Chan, Sucheng. *Asian Americans: An Interpretive History.* Boston: Twayne, 1991.

————, ed. *Entry Denied: Exclusion and the Chinese Community in America, 1882–1943.* Philadelphia: Temple University Press, 1991.

Chen, Jian. *Mao's China and the Cold War.* Chapel Hill: University of North Carolina Press, 2001.

Chen, Yong. *Chinese San Francisco, 1850–1943: A Trans-Pacific Community.* Stanford: Stanford University Press, 2000.

Chew, Selfa A. *Azogue en la raíz.* Mexico City: Artes Impresas, 2005.

Ch'i, Hsi-Sheng. *Nationalist China at War: Military Defeats and Political Collapse, 1937–1945.* Ann Arbor: University of Michigan Press, 1982.

Cisneros, Juan Ramírez. *Sucedió en Sonora.* 2nd ed. Guaymas: Talleres de Imagen Digital del Noroeste, 2004.

Clifford, James. *Routes: Travel and Translation in the Late Twentieth Century.* Cambridge: Harvard University Press, 1997.

Constitution of the United States of Mexico: Signed January 31, 1917, and Promulgated February 5, 1917. N.p., 1926.

Cremer, R. D., ed. *Macau: City of Commerce and Culture.* Hong Kong: UEA Press, 1987.

Daniels, Roger, ed. *Not Like Us: Immigrants and Minorities in America, 1890–1924.* Chicago: Dee, 1997.

Davis, Angela Y. *Women, Race, and Class.* New York: Random House, 1981.

De Genova, Nicholas. *Working the Boundaries: Race, Space, and "Illegality" in Mexican Chicago.* Durham: Duke University Press, 2005.

De León, Arnoldo. *Racial Frontiers: Africans, Chinese, and Mexicans in Western America, 1848–1890.* Albuquerque: University of New Mexico Press, 2002.

Eng, David. *Racial Castration: Managing Masculinity in Asian America.* Durham: Duke University Press, 2001.

Espinoza, José Angel. *El ejemplo de Sonora.* Mexico City: n.p., 1932.

————. *El problema chino en Sonora.* Mexico City: n.p., 1931.

Ettinger, Patrick. *Imaginary Lines: Border Enforcement and the Origins of Undocumented Immigration, 1882–1930.* Austin: University of Texas Press, 2009.

Falcoff, Mark, and Frederick B. Pike, eds. *The Spanish Civil War, 1936–1939: American Hemispheric Perspectives.* Lincoln: University of Nebraska Press, 1982.

Gamio, Manuel. *Forjando patria: nacionalismo.* Mexico City: Librería de Porrúa Hermanos, 1916.

Gaona, Enrique Suárez. *¿Legitimación revolucionaria del poder en México?: Los presidentes, 1910–1982.* Mexico City: Siglo Veintiuno, 1987.

Gilroy, Paul. *The Black Atlantic.* Chicago: University of Chicago Press, 1993.

Gluck, Sherna Berger, and Daphne Patai, eds. *Women's Words: The Feminist Practice of Oral History.* New York: Routledge, 1991.

González Félix, Maricela. *El proceso de aculturación de la población de origen chino en la ciudad de Mexicali.* Cuadernos de ciencias sociales, ser. 4, 7. Mexicali: 1988.

Gunn, Geoffrey C. *Encountering Macao: A Portuguese City-State on the Periphery of China, 1557–1999.* Boulder, Colo.: Westview, 1996.

Gutiérrez, David. *Walls and Mirrors: Mexican Americans, Mexican Immigrants, and the Politics of Ethnicity.* Berkeley: University of California Press, 1995.

Gutiérrez, Ramón. *When Jesus Came the Corn Mothers Went Away: Marriage, Sexuality, and Power in New Mexico, 1500–1846.* Stanford: Stanford University Press, 1991.

Hall, Linda B., and Don M. Coerver. *Revolution on the Border: The United States and Mexico, 1910–1920.* Albuquerque: University of New Mexico Press, 1988.

He, Li. *From Revolution to Reform: A Comparative Study of China and Mexico.* Lanham, Md.: University Press of America, 2004.

Hernández, Francisco, ed. *Los mejores poemas mexicanos.* Mexico City: Joaquín Mortiz/Fundación Para las Letras Mexicanas, 2005.

Heyman, Josiah M. *Life and Labor on the Border: Working People of Northeastern Sonora, Mexico, 1886–1986.* Tucson: University of Arizona Press, 1991.

Hill, Winifred Storrs. *Tarnished Gold: Prejudice during the California Gold Rush.* San Francisco: International Scholars, 1996.

Hirabayashi, Lane Ryo. *New Worlds, New Lives: Globalization and People of Japanese Descent in the Americas and from Latin America in Japan.* Stanford: Stanford University Press, 2002.

Hsu, Madeline Yuan-yin. *Dreaming of Gold, Dreaming of Home: Transnationalism and Migration between the United States and South China, 1882–1943.* Stanford: Stanford University Press, 2000.

Hu, Chang-tu. *China: Its People, Its Society, Its Culture.* New Haven, Conn.: HRAF, 1960.

Ichioka, Yuji. *The Issei: The World of the First Generation of Japanese Immigrants, 1885–1924.* New York: Free Press, 1988.

Izquierdo, José Jorge Gómez. *El movimiento antichino en México (1871–1934): problemas del racismo y del nacionalismo durante la Revolución Mexicana.* Mexico City: Instituto Nacional de Antropología e Historia, 1991.

Jordan, Winthrop. *White over Black: American Attitudes toward the Negro, 1550–1812.* Chapel Hill: University of North Carolina Press, 1968.

Knight, Alan. *The Mexican Revolution.* Vol. 2. Cambridge: Cambridge University Press, 1986.

Kuhn, A. *Chinese among Others: Emigration in Modern Times.* Lanham, Md.: Rowman and Littlefield, 2008.

Lai, H. Mark. *Becoming Chinese American: A History of Communities and Institutions.* Walnut Creek, Calif.: AltaMira, 2004.

———. *A History Reclaimed: An Annotated Bibliography of Chinese Language Materials on the Chinese of America.* Los Angeles: Resource Development and Publications, Asian American Studies Center, University of California, 1986.

Lai, H. Mark, Genny Lim, and Judy Yung. *Island: Poetry and History of Chinese Immigrants on Angel Island, 1910–1940.* Seattle: University of Washington Press, 1980.

Lara, José Luis Trueba. *Los chinos en Sonora: una historia olvidada*. Hermosillo: Universidad de Sonora, 1990.

Lavrin, Asunción, ed. *Sexuality and Marriage in Colonial Latin America*. Lincoln: University of Nebraska Press, 1989.

Lee, Erika. *At America's Gates: Chinese Immigration during the Exclusion Era, 1882–1993*. Chapel Hill: University of North Carolina Press, 2003.

Lee, Erika, and Judy Yung. *Angel Island: Immigrant Gateway to America*. Oxford: Oxford University Press, 2010.

Leonard, Karen Isaksen. *Making Ethnic Choices: California's Punjabi Mexican Americans*. Philadelphia: Temple University Press, 1992.

Lesser, Jeffrey. *A Discontented Diaspora: Japanese Brazilians and the Meanings of Ethnic Militancy*. Durham: Duke University Press, 2007.

———. *Negotiating National Identity: Immigrants, Minorities, and the Struggle for Ethnicity in Brazil*. Durham: Duke University Press, 1999.

———. *Searching for Home Abroad: Japanese-Brazilians and Transnationalism*. Durham: Duke University Press, 2003.

Ling, Huping. *Surviving on the Gold Mountain: A History of Chinese American Women and Their Lives*. Albany: State University of New York Press, 1998.

Llano, Juan Mauricio Magín Puig. *Entre el río Perla y el Nazas: la China decimonónica y sus braceros emigrantes, la colonia china de Torreón y la matanza de 1911*. Mexico City: Consejo Nacional para la Cultura y las Artes, 1993.

López, Rick A. *Crafting Mexico: Intellectuals, Artisans, and the State after the Revolution*. Durham: Duke University Press, 2010.

Louie, Andrea. *Chineseness across Borders*. Durham: Duke University Press, 2004.

Lowe, Lisa. *Immigrant Acts: On Asian American Cultural Politics*. Durham: Duke University Press, 1996.

Loyola, Alberto Antonio. *Chinos-mexicanos cautivos del comunismo: su repatriación fue una gran proeza*. Mexico City: n.p., 1961.

Luibhéid, Eithne. *Entry Denied: Controlling Sexuality at the Border*. Minneapolis: University of Minnesota Press, 2002.

Macau: Puente entre China y América Latina. Macau: MAPEAL and IIM, 2006.

Martin, Cheryl English. *Governance and Society in Colonial Mexico: Chihuahua in the Eighteenth Century*. Stanford: Stanford University Press, 1996.

Martínez, Oscar J., ed. *U.S.-Mexico Borderlands: Historical and Contemporary Perspectives*. Wilmington, Del.: Scholarly Resources, 1996.

McClain, Charles J. *In Search of Equality: The Chinese Struggle against Discrimination in Nineteenth-Century America*. Berkeley: University of California Press, 1994.

McKeown, Adam. *Chinese Migrant Networks and Cultural Change: Peru, Chicago, Hawaii, 1900–1936*. Chicago: University of Chicago Press, 2001.

———. *Melancholy Order: Asian Migration and the Globalization of Borders*. New York: Columbia University Press, 2008.

Meyer, Michael C., William L. Sherman, and Susan M. Deeds. *The Course of Mexican History*. 8th ed. New York: Oxford University Press, 2007.

Mishima, María Elena Ota, ed. *Destino México: un estudio de las migraciones asiáticas a México, siglos XIX y XX*. Mexico City: El Colegio de México, 1997.

Monroy, Douglas. *Rebirth: Mexican Los Angeles from the Great Migration to the Great Depression*. University of California Press, 1999.

Montfort, Ricardo Pérez. *Estampas de nacionalismo popular mexicano: diez ensayos sobre cultura popular y nacionalismo*. Mexico City: CIESAS, 1994.

Ngai, Mae M. *Impossible Subjects: Illegal Aliens and the Making of Modern America*. Princeton: Princeton University Press, 2004.

Owens, Kenneth N. *Riches for All: The California Gold Rush and the World*. Lincoln: University of Nebraska Press, 2002.

Pan, Lynn, ed. *Encyclopedia of the Chinese Overseas*. Cambridge: Harvard University Press, 1999.

Pardinas, Felipe. *Relaciones diplomáticas entre China y México, 1898–1948*, caja 1. Mexico City: Secretaría de Relaciones Exteriores, 1982.

Peffer, George Anthony. *If They Don't Bring Their Women Here: Chinese Female Immigration before Exclusion*. Urbana: University of Illinois Press, 1999.

Powell, Thomas G. *Mexico and the Spanish Civil War*. Albuquerque: University of New Mexico Press, 1981.

Radding, Cynthia. *Wandering Peoples: Colonialism, Ethnic Spaces, and Ecological Frontiers in Northwestern Mexico, 1700–1850*. Durham: Duke University Press, 1997.

Rivera, José Antonio Aguilar. *El fin de la raza cósmica: consideraciones sobre el esplendor y decadencia del liberalismo en México*. Mexico City: Océano, 2001.

Romero, Robert Chao. *The Chinese in Mexico, 1882–1940*. Tucson: University of Arizona Press, 2010.

Ruiz, Ramón E. *The People of Sonora and Yankee Capitalists*. Tucson: University of Arizona Press, 1988.

Rustomji-Kerns, Roshni, Rajini Srikanth, and Leny Mendoza Strobel, eds. *Encounters: People of Asian Descent in the Americas*. Lanham, Md.: Rowman and Littlefield, 1999.

Salas, Miguel Tinker. *In the Shadow of the Eagles: Sonora and the Transformation of the Border during the Porfiriato*. Berkeley: University of California Press, 1997.

Saldívar, José David. *Border Matters: Remapping American Cultural Studies*. Berkeley: University of California Press, 1997.

Salyer, Lucy. *Laws Harsh as Tigers: Chinese Immigrants and the Shaping of Modern Immigration Law*. Chapel Hill: University of North Carolina Press, 1995.

Sánchez, George. *Becoming Mexican American: Ethnicity, Culture, and Identity in Chicano Los Angeles, 1900–1945*. New York: Oxford University Press, 1993.

Sandoval, Leo. *La Casa de Abelardo*. Hermosillo: Artes Gráficas y Editoriales Yescas, 1990.

Saxton, Alexander. *The Indispensable Enemy: Labor and the Anti-Chinese Movement in California*. Berkeley: University of California Press, 1971.

———. *The Rise and Fall of the White Republic: Class Politics and Mass Culture in Nineteenth-Century America*. London: Verso, 1990.

Schuler, Friedrich E. *Mexico between Hitler and Roosevelt: Mexican Foreign Relations in the Age of Lázaro Cárdenas, 1934–1940*. Albuquerque: University of New Mexico Press, 1998.

Scott, James C. *Dominance and the Arts of Resistance: Hidden Transcripts*. New Haven: Yale University Press, 1990.

Segal, Uma A. *A Framework for Immigration: Asians in the United States*. New York: Columbia University Press, 2002.

Shah, Nayan. *Contagious Divides: Epidemics and Race in San Francisco's Chinatown*. Berkeley: University of California Press, 2001.

Shipp, Steve. *Macau, China: A Political History of the Portuguese Colony's Transition to Chinese Rule*. Jefferson, N.C.: McFarland, 1997.

Sih, Paul K. T., ed. *Nationalist China during the Sino-Japanese War, 1937–1945*. Hicksville, N.Y.: Exposition-University, 1977.

Simpson, Leslie Byrd. *Many Mexicos*. New York: Putnam, 1941.

Siu, Lok C. D. *Memories of a Future Home: Diasporic Citizenship of Chinese in Panama*. Stanford: Stanford University Press, 2005.

Sonora: historia y geografía tercer grado. Mexico City: Comisión Nacional de Libros de Texto Gratuitos, 2003.

Spickard, Paul, ed. *Race and Immigration in the United States: New Histories*. New York: Routledge, 2012.

Stern, Alexandra Minna. *Eugenic Nation: Faults and Frontiers of Better Breeding in Modern America*. University of California Press, 2005.

Stern, Steve J. *The Secret History of Gender: Women, Men, and Power in Late Colonial Mexico*. Chapel Hill: University of North Carolina Press, 1995.

Tang, Tsou. *The Cultural Revolution and Post-Mao Reforms: A Historical Perspective*. Chicago: University of Chicago Press, 1986.

Taylor, Paul S. *An American-Mexican Frontier, Nueces County, Texas*. 1934; New York: Russell and Russell, 1971.

———. *Mexican Labor in the United States*. 3 vols. Berkeley: University of California Press, 1928–34.

Takaki, Ronald. *Strangers from a Different Shore: A History of Asian Americans*. New York: Little, Brown, 1998.

Trouillot, Michel-Rolph. *Silencing the Past: Power and the Production of History*. Boston: Beacon, 1995.

Truett, Samuel, and Elliott Young, eds. *Continental Crossroads: Remapping U.S.-Mexico Borderlands History*. Durham: Duke University Press, 2004.

Vasconcelos, José. *La raza cósmica, mission de la raza iberoamericana*. Paris: Agencia Mundial de Librería, 1925.

Vasconcelos, José, and Manuel Gamio. *Aspects of Mexican Civilization*. Chicago: University of Chicago Press, 1926.

Von Mentz, Brígida, Ricardo Pérez Montfort, and Verena Radkau, eds. *Fascismo y antifascismo en américa Latina y México (apuntes históricos)*. Mexico City: SEP Cultura, Centro de Investigaciones y Estudios Superiores en Antropología Social, 1984.

Wang, Gungwu. *China and the Chinese Overseas*. Singapore: Times Academic Press, 1991.

———. *China and the World since 1949*. New York: St. Martin's, 1977.

―――. *Community and Nation: Essays on Southeast Asia and the Chinese*. Singapore: Heineman, 1981.

Wong, K. Scott. *Americans First: Chinese Americans and the Second World War*. Cambridge: Harvard University Press, 2005.

Yáñez, Agustín. *Misión económica, política, y social en el Oriente: una gira de trabajo y buena voluntad en favor de la amistad y la solidaridad por la India, el Japon, Indonesia y Filipinas, con base en los principios de la democracia, de la cultura y de la paz/ALM; con una breve introducción de Antonio Luna Arroyo, Documentos para la historia de un gobierno, no. 92*. Mexico City: Editorial "La Justicia," 1962.

―――. *Proyección universal de México: crónica del viaje realizado por el Presidente de México, ALM, a India, Japón, Indonesia, y Filipinas, el año 1962*. Mexico City: n.p., 1963.

Yu, Henry. *Thinking Orientals: Migration, Contact, and Exoticism in Modern America*. New York: Oxford University Press, 2001.

Yung, Judy. *Unbound Feet: A Social History of Chinese Women in San Francisco*. Berkeley: University of California Press, 1995.

Articles and Essays

Augustine-Adams, Kif. "Making Mexico: Legal Nationality, Chinese Race, and the 1930 Population Census." *Law and History Review* 27 (2009). http://ssrn.com/abstract=1033061. Accessed 1 June 2009.

Basurto, Monica Cinco. "China in Mexico: Yesterday's Encounter and Today's Discovery." In *Encounters: People of Asian Descent in the Americas*, edited by Roshni Rustomji-Kerns, Rajini Srikanth, and Leny Mendoza Strobel, 13–18. Lanham, Md.: Rowman and Littlefield, 1999.

Bonacich, Edna. "A Theory of Middleman Minorities." *American Sociological Review* 38 (1973): 583–94.

Calvert, Peter. "The Institutionalisation of the Mexican Revolution." *Journal of Inter-American Studies* 11 (1969): 503–17.

Camín, Hector Aguilar. "The Relevant Tradition: Sonoran Leaders in the Revolution." In *Caudillo and Peasant in the Mexican Revolution*, edited by D. A. Brading, 92–123. New York: Cambridge University Press, 1980.

Chan, Sucheng. "The Exclusion of Chinese Women, 1870–1943." *Chinese America: History and Perspectives* (1994): 75–125.

―――. "A People of Exceptional Character: Ethnic Diversity, Nativism, and Racism in the California Gold Rush." *California History* 79 (2000): 44–85.

Clifford, James. "Diasporas." *Cultural Anthropology* 9 (1984): 302–38.

Coronil, Fernando. "Beyond Occidentalism: Toward Nonimperial Geohistorical Categories." *Cultural Anthropology* 11 (1996): 21–49.

Cott, Nancy F. "Marriage and Women's Citizenship in the United States, 1830–1934." *American Historical Review* 103 (1998): 1440–74.

Cumberland, Charles C. "The Sonora Chinese and the Mexican Revolution." *Hispanic American Historical Review* 40 (1960): 191–211.

Daniels, Roger. "Westerners from the East: Oriental Immigrants Reappraised." *Pacific Historical Review* 35 (1966): 373–83.

Delgado, Grace Peña. "At Exclusion's Southern Gate: Changing Categories of Race and Class among Chinese Fronterizos." In *Continental Crossroads: Remapping U.S.-Mexico Borderlands History*, edited by Samuel Truett and Elliott Young, 183–207. Durham: Duke University Press, 2004.

———. "Of Kith and Kin: Land, Leases, and *Guanxi* in Tucson's Chinese and Mexican Communities, 1880s–1920s." *Journal of Arizona History* 46 (2005): 33–54.

Dennis, Philip A. "The Anti-Chinese Campaigns in Sonora, Mexico." *Ethnohistory* 26 (1979): 65–80.

Faust, Jörg, and Uwe Franke. "Attempts at Diversification: Mexico and Pacific Asia." *Pacific Review* 15 (2002): 299–324.

González Félix, Maricela. "Los inmigrantes chinos y la hacienda pública del Distrito Norte de la Baja California, 1910–1920." In *China en las Californias*, edited by Centro Cultural Tijuana. Tijuana: Consejo Nacional para la Cultura y las Artes, 2002.

González Navarro, Moisés. "Xenofobia y xenofilia en la Revolución Mexicana." In *México: el capitalismo nacionalista*, edited by Moisés González Navarro, 569–614. Guadalajara: Universidad de Guadalajara, 2003.

Gu, Xin. "Revitalizing Chinese Society: Institutional Transformation and Social Change." In *China: Two Decades of Reform and Change*, edited by Wang Gungwu and John Wong, 67–100. Singapore: Singapore University Press, 1999.

Gutiérrez, Juán Ramón. "José María Arana y el comercio chino de Magdalena." *Historia de Sonora* 91 (1994): 2–3.

Hein, Jeremy. "State Incorporation of Migrants and the Reproduction of a Middleman Minority among Indochinese Refugees." *Sociological Quarterly* 29 (1988): 463–78.

Hsu, Madeline Yuan-yin. "Unwrapping Orientalist Constraints: Restoring Homosocial Normativity to Chinese American History." *Amerasia* 29 (2003): 230–53.

Hu-DeHart, Evelyn. "The Chinese of Baja California, 1910–1934." In *Baja California and the North Mexican Frontier*. Proceedings of the Pacific Coast Council on Latin American Studies, vol. 12. San Diego: San Diego State University Press, 1985–86.

———. "Los chinos del norte de México, 1875–1930: la formación de una pequeña burguesía regional." In *China en las Californias*, edited by Centro Cultural Tijuana. Tijuana: Consejo Nacional para la Cultura y las Artes, 2002.

———. "La comunidad china en el desarrollo de Sonora." In *Historia general de Sonora*, vol. 4, *Sonora moderno, 1880–1929*, edited by Cynthia Radding de Murrieta, 195–211. Hermosillo: Gobierno del Estado de Sonora, 1985.

———. "Coolies, Shopkeepers, Pioneers: The Chinese of Mexico and Peru (1849–1930)." *Amerasia* 15 (1989): 91–116.

———. "Immigrants to a Developing Society: The Chinese in Northern Mexico, 1875–1932." *Journal of Arizona History* 21 (1980): 275–312.

———. "Latin America in Asia-Pacific Perspective." In *What Is in a Rim?: Critical Perspectives on the Pacific Region Idea*, 2nd ed., edited by Arif Dirlik, 251–82. Lanham, Md.: Rowman and Littlefield, 1998.

———. "Racism and Anti-Chinese Persecution in Sonora, Mexico, 1876–1932." *Amerasia* 9 (1982): 1–28.

Jacques, Leo Michael Dambourges. "Have Quick More Money Than Mandarins: The Chinese in Sonora." *Journal of Arizona History* 17 (1976): 201–18.

Knight, Alan. "Racism, Revolution, and *Indigenismo*: Mexico, 1910–1940." In *The Idea of Race in Latin America, 1870–1940*, edited by Richard Graham, 71–113. Austin: University of Texas Press, 1990.

Lara, José Luis Trueba. "La xenofobia en la legislación sonorense: el caso de los chinos." In *Memoria del XIII Simposio de Historia y Antropología de Sonora*, edited by Departamento de Historia y Antropología, 341–73. Hermosillo: Universidad de Sonora, 1989.

Lausent-Herrera, Isabelle. "Mujeres olvidadas: esposas, concubinas, e hijas de los inmigrantes chinos en el Perú republicano." In *Mujeres, familias, y sociedad en la historia de América Latina, siglos XVIII–XXI*, edited by Scarlett O'Phelan Godoy and Margarita Zegarra Florez, 287–312. Lima: PUCP, 2006.

Lee, Erika. "Orientalisms in the Americas: A Hemispheric Approach to Asian American History." *Journal of Asian American Studies* 8 (2005): 235–56.

Li, Yun-han. "The Origins of the War: Background of the Lukouchiao Incident, July 7, 1937." In *Nationalist China during the Sino-Japanese War, 1937–1945*, edited by Paul K. T. Sih, 3–32. Hicksville, N.Y.: Exposition-University, 1977.

Lim, Julian. "Chinos and Paisanos: Chinese Mexican Relations in the Borderlands." *Pacific Historical Review* 79, no. 1 (2010): 50–85.

Lin, George C. S. "Hong Kong and the Globalisation of the Chinese Diaspora: A Geographical Perspective." *Asia Pacific Viewpoint* 43 (2002): 63–91.

Ling, Huping. "Family and Marriage of Late-Nineteenth and Early-Twentieth Century Chinese Immigrant Women." *Journal of American Ethnic History* 19 (2000): 43–63.

López, Kathleen. "The Revitalization of Havana's Chinatown: Invoking Chinese Cuban History." *Journal of Chinese Overseas* 5 (2009): 177–200.

Lott, Eric. "The New Cosmopolitanism" (review essay). *Transition* 72 (1996): 108–35.

Lowe, Lisa. "The International within the National: American Studies and Asian American Critique." *Cultural Critique* 40 (1998): 29–47.

Mann, Susan. "The Male Bond in Chinese History and Culture." *American Historical Review* 105 (2000): 1600–1614.

Martin, Cheryl English. "Popular Speech and Social Order in Northern Mexico, 1650–1830." *Comparative Studies in Society and History* 32 (1990): 305–24.

McIsaac, Lee. "'Righteous Fraternities' and Honorable Men: Sworn Brotherhood in Wartime Chongqing." *American Historical Review* 105 (2000): 1641–55.

McKeown, Adam. "Ritualization of Regulation: The Enforcement of Chinese Exclusion in the United States and China." *American Historical Review* 108 (2003): 377–403.

———. "Transnational Chinese Families and Chinese Exclusion." *Journal of American Ethnic History* 18 (1999): 73–110.

Mei, June. "Economic Origins of Emigration: Guangdong to California, 1850–1882." *Modern China* 5 (1979): 463–501.

Murray, Alice Yang. "Oral History Research, Theory, and Asian American Studies." *Amerasia Journal* 26 (2000): 105–18.

Nicolosi, Ann Marie. "'We Do Not Want Our Girls to Marry Foreigners': Gender, Race, and American Citizenship." *National Women's Studies Association Journal* 13 (2001): 1–21.

Pascoe, Peggy. "Gender Systems in Conflict: The Marriages of Mission-Educated Chinese American Women, 1874–1939." *Journal of Social History* 22 (1989): 631–52.

Portelli, Alessandro. "What Makes Oral History Different?" In *The Oral History Reader*, edited by Robert Perks and Alistair Thomson, 32–42. New York: Routledge, 1998.

Quintana, Isabella Seong-Leong. "'Shaken as by an Earthquake': Chinese Americans, Segregation, and Displacement in Los Angeles, 1870–1938. *Gum Saan Journal* 32 (2010). http://www.chinatownremembered.com/index.php?option=com_content&view=article&id=79&Itemid=113. Accessed 31 May 2011.

Reich, Peter L. "Recent Research on the Legal History of Modern Mexico." *Mexican Studies/Estudios Mexicanos* 23 (2007): 181–93.

Rénique, Gerardo. "Anti-Chinese Racism, Nationalism, and State Formation in Post-Revolutionary Mexico, 1920s-1930s." *Political Power and Social Theory* 14 (2001): 89–137.

———. "Race, Region, and Nation: Sonora's Anti-Chinese Racism and Mexico's Postrevolutionary Nationalism, 1920s–1930s." In *Race and Nation in Modern Latin America*, edited by Nancy P. Appelbaum, Anne S. Macpherson, and Karin Alejandra Rosemblatt, 211–36. Chapel Hill: University of North Carolina Press, 2003.

Rohe, Randall E. "After the Gold Rush: Chinese Mining in the Far West, 1850–1890." *Montana* 32 (1982): 2–19.

Romero, Robert Chao. "'El destierro de los Chinos': Popular Perspectives on Chinese-Mexican Intermarriage in the Early Twentieth Century." *Aztlan: A Journal of Chicano Studies* 32 (2007): 113–44.

Safran, William. "Diasporas in Modern Societies: Myths of Homeland and Return." *Diasporas* 1 (1991): 83–99.

Schiavone Camacho, Julia María. "Crossing Boundaries, Claiming a Homeland: The Mexican Chinese Transpacific Journey to Becoming Mexican, 1930s–1960s." *Pacific Historical Review* 78 (2009): 545–77.

Shelby, Tommie. "Cosmopolitanism, Blackness, and Utopia: A Conversation with Paul Gilroy." *Transition* 98 (2008): 116–35.

Shen, Tsung-han. "Food Production and Distribution for Civilian and Military Needs in Wartime China, 1937–1945." In *Nationalist China during the Sino-Japanese War, 1937–1945*, edited by Paul K. T. Sih, 167–93. Hicksville, N.Y.: Exposition-University, 1977.

Stern, Alexandra Minna. "Buildings, Boundaries, and Blood: Medicalization and Nation-Building on the U.S.-Mexican Border, 1910–1930." *Hispanic American Historical Review* 79 (1999): 41–81.

Tran, Lisa. "Sex and Equality in Republican China: The Debate over the Adultery Law." *Modern China* 35 (2009): 191–223.

Wang, Gungwu. "Sojourning: The Chinese Experience in Southeast Asia." In *Sojourners and Settlers: Histories of Southeast Asia and the Chinese*, edited by Anthony Reid, 1–14. Honolulu: University of Hawai'i Press, 1996.

Wilmsen, Carl. "For the Record: Editing and the Production of Meaning in Oral History." *Oral History Review* 28 (2001): 65–85.

Wong, K. Scott. "The Transformation of Culture: Three Chinese Views of America." *American Quarterly* 48 (1996): 201–32.

Wunder, John R. "Law and the Chinese on the Southwest Frontier, 1850s–1902." *Western Legal History* 2 (1989): 139–58.

Newspapers

Arizona Daily Star (Tucson)

El Continental (El Paso, Texas)

El Paso Herald Post

Excélsior (Mexico City)

El Intruso (Cananea, Sonora)

Japan Times (Yokohama)

El Nacionalista (Cananea)

Nogales (Arizona) Daily Herald

Novedades (Mexico City)

El Observador (Hermosillo, Sonora)

San Francisco Chronicle

El Universal (Mexico City)

Index